W9-ATK-262

PRESENTING

Young Adult
Science Fiction

Twayne's United States Authors Series
Young Adult Authors

Patricia J. Campbell, General Editor

TUSAS 709

PRESENTING

Young Adult Science Fiction

Suzanne Elizabeth Reid

Twayne Publishers
An Imprint of Simon & Schuster Macmillan
New York

Prentice Hall International
London Mexico City New Delhi Singapore Sydney Toronto

Twayne's United States Authors Series No. 709

Presenting Young Adult Science Fiction
Suzanne Elizabeth Reid

Twayne Publishers
An Imprint of Simon & Schuster Macmillan
1633 Broadway
New York, NY 10019

Library of Congress Cataloging-in-Publication Data

Reid, Suzanne Elizabeth.
    Presenting young adult science fiction / Suzanne Elizabeth Reid.
        p.   cm. — (Twayne's United States authors series. Young
    adult authors)
        Includes bibliographical references (p.   ) and index.
        ISBN 0-8057-1653-X (alk. paper)
        1. Science fiction, American—History and criticism.   2. Young
    adult fiction, American—History and criticism.   I. Title.
    II. Series.
    PS374.S35R43   1998
    813'.08762099283—dc21   98-35178
                                                                                                CIP

This paper meets the requirements of ANSI/NISO Z3948-1992 (Permanence of Paper).

10 9 8 7 6 5 4 3

Printed in the United States of America

In honor of my husband, Robin Reid,
and my children, Jennifer Bradlee Reid
and Tristan Lanier Reid—
for all the good time we share together.

Contents

Foreword

The advent of Twayne's Young Adult Authors Series in 1985 was a response to the growing stature and value of adolescent literature and the lack of serious critical evaluation of the new genre. The first volume of the series was heralded as marking the coming-of-age of young adult fiction.

The aim of the series is twofold. First, it enables young readers to research the work of their favorite authors and to see them as real people. Each volume is written in a lively, readable style and attempts to present in an attractive, accessible format a vivid portrait of the author as a person.

Second, the series provides teachers and librarians with insights and background material for promoting and teaching young adult novels. Each of the biocritical studies is a serious literary analysis of one author's work (or one subgenre within young adult literature), with attention to plot structure, theme, character, setting, and imagery. In addition, many of the series writers delve deeper into the creative writing process by tracking down early drafts or unpublished manuscripts by their subject authors, consulting with their editors or other mentors, and examining influences from literature, film, or social movements.

Many of the authors contributing to the series are among the leading scholars and critics of adolescent literature. Some are even novelists for young adults themselves. Most of the studies are based on extensive interviews with the subject author, and each includes an exhaustive study of his or her work. Although the general format is the same, the individual volumes are uniquely shaped by their subjects, and each brings a different perspective to the classroom.

The goal of the series is to produce a succinct but comprehensive study of the life and art of every leading writer for young adults to trace how that art has been accepted by readers and critics, and to evaluate its place in the developing field of adolescent literature. And—perhaps most important—the series is intended to inspire a reading and rereading of this quality fiction that speaks so directly to young people about their life experiences.

Patricia J. Campbell,
General Editor

Preface

It would be easy to drown in this vast sea of tantalizing ideas and images that we call science fiction—to swim out too far or dive too deep to return gracefully to the surface. Tantalizing because as readers we are invited to join in designing the future, to escape the sometimes painful present, complicated by emotional and cultural attachments and yearnings that pull us away from the elegance of simple logic. Perhaps it is the combination of freedom and security that the imaginative use of logic offers that attracts many of us to science and science fiction; perhaps it is its illusive neatness. At a time when the field is expanding so rapidly, I have tried to keep my head above water to retain a sense of direction and perspective while diving deeper in spots to get a sense of what lies below the surface. As a result, I have omitted many works, many writers, and much information; this is an introductory swim. Readers who want more information about science fiction should explore further the many wonderful references available. My indebtedness to the extensive research of John Clute and Peter Nicholls is obvious. I particularly enjoyed their flashes of wit and thoughtful insights in *The Encyclopedia of Science Fiction,* although I did not always agree with their assessments.

The focus of this book is science fiction for young readers. It is not a separate genre, though some excellent works are written and marketed specifically for young readers. Generally, the protagonists are exploring their own development as individuals, but this is a subject that can take a whole lifetime. This is fiction that can be appreciated by readers with mature minds and young hearts, who like to explore new ideas and speculate about which directions people in the present could take to ensure a better future.

Thank you again, Patty Campbell, for offering me the opportunity to take on this ambitious project. I am also indebted to Janice Antczyk for the use of her selection of authors, and the insights of her book cited in the bibliography. My son, Tristan Reid, an inveterate reader of science fiction and a special fan of Orson Scott Card, researched and wrote the first draft of the third chapter. My husband, Robin Reid, an avid tinkerer with words, edited out my "Freudian slips" and got the notes right. My daughter, Jenny, insightful and intelligent about life as a whole, was especially sweet when it mattered. Thank you.

I am also grateful to the staff of the Kelly Library at Emory & Henry College, who help make research fun.

1. Introduction and History

Science fiction: traditionally readers claim to either love it or loathe it; either they avoid it like poison or they devour favorite works and authors like chocolate addicts gulping down fudge truffles. Young science fiction readers tend to be intellectual—interested and articulate about ideas, technology, or science but not always top students in school, although most eventually attend college. More than most readers, science fiction buffs tend to be enthusiasts, joining clubs, subscribing to fanzines, attending conferences, and even composing their own music ("filk songs," perhaps named after a misprint on a widely distributed sheet of music). Science fiction readers form an in crowd with its own esoterica and jargon, some of which has been collected into books such as Roberta Rogow's *Futurespeak: A Fan's Guide to the Language of Science Fiction* (1991). As with Rogow and other fans, science fiction becomes a way of life, another world separate from that mundane place called reality. Rogow's book includes lists of the many organizations, conferences, contests, publications, and rules that abound for the world of science fiction.

Defining the Genre

In a more conventional dictionary of literary terms, science fiction is "a popular modern branch of prose fiction that explores the probable consequences of some improbable or impossible transformation of the basic conditions of human (or intelligent nonhuman) existence."[1] Many scholars categorize science fiction as a type of fantasy, but others differentiate between the kind of magical intervention and animal characters of imaginative fantasy, which are scientifically impossible, and science fiction, which only seems unlikely at the present time. "Science fiction deals with improbable possibilities, fantasy with plausible impossibilities," summarizes author Miriam Allen deFord.[2] Definitions published in another collection of science fiction lore, *The SF Book of Lists* (1983), focus more on given realities of the marketplace and of sf writers. Critics Clute and Nicholls simply acknowledge that "science fiction is a label applied to a publishing category, and its application is subject to the whims of editors and publishers." Author Frederik Pohl comments disarmingly on the nature of educated instinct: "It is that thing that people who understand science fiction point to, when they point to something and say 'That's science fiction!' "[3]

The "science" part of this genre of fiction points to its proliferation of inventions that depend on "logical extrapolation" of changes from current reality,[4] though often set in the future or on places other than Earth. It is connected to our current understanding of how our world works.

Describing the Genre

The themes of science fiction focus on changes that might become possible in the future. These works describe either the dangerous results of tinkering with the natural world, or the wonderful solutions to global problems made possible by human—or superhuman—intervention through technology. In his thoughtful introduction to *Science Fiction: The Future* (1983), critic Dick Allen describes the various types of science fiction that spring from its basic premise: "What if?"[5] Many of the earlier works focus on technological inventions that now, a century later, have been realized or at least seem more probable in the foreseeable future: television, submarines, spaceships, space travel, and time travel. Like scientists designing an experiment, writers of science fiction select which elements will remain constant and which variables to introduce. "Science is made up of many things that appear obvious after they are explained," notes Frank Herbert (Rotsler, 119), and science fiction offers an opportunity to propose explanations to the general public without the onus of laboratory proof. In this sense, science fiction allows nonscientists to participate in the hypothesizing stage of scientific discovery, unfettered by the doubting caution that institutional science instills. Of course, science fiction is also entertaining, and like other entertainers, science fiction writers have discovered popular ideas and icons that work so well that they have become clichés, some described in *The SF Book of Lists:* "The tentacled aliens prey on Earth's fairest daughters; . . . With a fibre-wrenching jerk, the mighty ship burst into hyperspace; . . . the awesomely omniscient Brain dwarfed any mere human intellect; and . . . those danged radiation-spawned Mutants can read your mind!" (Jakubowski, 73–74). Many of these motifs, exploiting a central fascination with science's mysterious and dangerous power, hark back to Mary Shelley's *Frankenstein:* "There are secrets of the Universe with which Man should not meddle!" and "With terrible irony, the monster had destroyed its own creator!" (Jakubowski, 73).

In more recent works, technologically enhanced humans or humanlike aliens or robots use their amazing physical and mental powers to perform feats that either endanger or save the world. These "characters" include cyborgs, supermen, ESPers, androids, robots, mutants, and clones. Either they live on other planets or alternate worlds, or they may have invaded Earth or even arisen from a part of our world previously unexplored. New discoveries about the possibility of life on Mars and the advances in cloning and enhancing individual mammals emphasize the relevance of thinking about how we could adjust to different kinds of beings in our midst.

Topics and Themes

Setting up a new world or describing an alien society provides a natural context in which to address social problems and pose solutions. A common topic in science fiction is the devastating effect of overpopulation and the concomitant scarcity of food and drinkable water; another is the centralization of economic and military power by beings with superior technological knowledge or devices. These fictional worlds act as metaphors to help us imagine how humanity might react in the real world to centralized power, virtualized reality, or the waning supply of material resources. Increasingly, readers can imagine these frightening realities within their own lifetimes. Unfortunately, humanity is more often depicted as the ultimate destructive force, one that is anything but humane.

James Gunn identifies three philosophic stances endemic to science fiction:

1. An assumption that the future will be qualitatively different from past or present human life because of technological innovation;
2. An open imagination about the nature of the universe and the place of humans in it;
3. A view of humans not as a race or a tribe but as a species.[6]

These criteria address questions about time, space, and the role of humanity on a very large scale. Already, a popular television advertisement notes that through the Internet, widely different cultures can communicate with each other free of the traditional cultural barriers of race, religion, age, gender, nationality, economic status, or educational level; in this way humanity can communicate in ways that are qualitatively different from those of the past. Through this revolutionary technology the English language has become the medium of worldwide communication. Use of the Internet and other instantaneous methods of communication, which disregard the boundaries of physical geography and sociopolitical differences, has defined new images of humanity and its place in the world. As communication across geographical, political, and linguistic borders increases, along with awareness about the place and effect of humans in environmental chains, we will become less concerned about the traditional racial, national, and cultural differences that separate us than about our mutual survival as a species. Our global situation, along with the daily patterns of our lives, is bringing us into closer alliance with the generic concerns of science fiction. It has become an increasingly relevant genre.

Allen notes that although sf has accurately predicted many technological and sociological events, its value is more in the "acts of contemplation, meditation, and extrapolation giving rise to such predictions" (Allen, 8). "What science fiction does is train its readers to look for the future," declares critic John Clute,[7] defending the genre from the frequent criticism that some of its past predictions have not proved true. Science fiction readers practice critical intelligence as they unfold the implications of a qualitative change from the actual present. Sf encourages readers to think about the large issues often confined to religious discussions, and thus could be of great worth to those young people who will be the designers of our future, especially as our daily lives become increasingly and inextricably involved with sophisticated technology. Will we survive the twenty-first century? How? And to what ultimate end?

Some sf writers strive to impress on us the probable results of continuing to live as we do, unless we mend our ways: "I don't try to predict the future; I try to prevent it," writes Ray Bradbury (quoted in Rotsler, 125). Often sf writers try to invent alternate futures. Of course, not all sf writers take themselves so seriously as to consider themselves soothsayers about the direction of our future. More common is a brand of subtle irony that saves the wisest of writers from the pomposity of the deeply earnest. Most sf writers strike a pose of sophistication, using understatement, dry satire, and that tough world-weary tone of the intellectual cynic, a tone that challenges naive enthusiasms, narrow visions, or faith in anything simple.

Beginnings of Science Fiction

The roots of science fiction as a literary genre can be traced back at least as far as the Syrian-Greek writer Lucian (ca. 120–180), who wrote about a trip to the moon and a space war, but science fiction proper was not formulated until the Industrial Revolution made the public aware of the power of technology to bring about drastic changes in lifestyles. Other important precedents for this genre include Mary Wollstonecraft Shelley's *Frankenstein* (1818) and Jules Verne's *Journey to the Centre of the Earth* (1863, trans. 1870) and *Twenty Thousand Leagues Under the Sea* (1872, trans. 1873 and 1991). Mary Shelley began to write her story of Dr. Frankenstein after a catastrophic period of love affairs, dying infants, suicides, and troubled relationships with her brilliant father and her famous husband, the English Romantic poet Percy Bysshe Shelley. Her grippingly horrific story of the scientist's creation of a lonely, ugly monster has an "essential science fiction core . . . a fascinating experiment that goes wrong."[8] Still praised for its metaphorical depth and the emotional effectiveness of its style, *Frankenstein* is prophetic, a novel about a "scientist" even before the term was born, a fantasy centered around a rationally conceived alternative future. In this complex novel, Shelley poses very pertinent questions about the morality of trying to reproduce human beings. Who will give these new beings a home, and how responsible are scientists for the beings they create? How will these artificial creatures fit into our society, which is already overcrowded with individuals who feel unloved and superfluous? To a profound degree Shelley's work was the philosophic progenitor of many serious science fictions. She could well be called the "mother of science fiction" for formulating such a seminal archetype of the potentially monstrous impact of scientific technology on human nature. In writing *Frankenstein* she recognized a primal issue that prefigured the themes of countless stories and novels written since that time.

Many other early fantasies and utopias have been defined as "science fiction in retrospect" (Bleiler, 5) because the genre was not adequately conceived and connected with the impact of science and technology until the early twentieth century. If we have to name a "father of science fiction," it would be the man who first self-consciously invented and promoted this new type of literature, though his work was only a simple prototype of what followed. Jules Verne (1828–1905), a playwright and novelist from the French seaport of Nantes, became entranced with the science fiction elements in the stories of Edgar Allan Poe and expanded them in his own writing. Because his works never edge beyond known science (Clute and Nicholls, 1276) and do not explore the future, many consider them precursors to science fiction rather than early examples of it. Yet the detailed descriptions in his voyage narratives, whether of traveling around the world in a balloon, cruising 20,000 leagues under the sea, or exploring a volcano shaft to the center of the earth, still provide fascinating stimuli for the scientific imagination. Verne's habit of using multiple protagonists to provide various viewpoints (an ordinary person, a scientist, an athletic extrovert) is still evident in much science fiction. Optimistic and enthusiastic at the beginning of his career about the impact of science, Verne's attitude soured as the twentieth century approached; yet the adjective "Vernian" is still applied to sf writers who insist on scientific accuracy and who focus on the plausibility of the machinery they introduce.

Recent scholarship indicates many more science fiction prototypes than were previously acknowledged; Bleiler lists 618 sf works between 1863 and 1895. Along with Tom Clareson, Darko Suvin, and other recent researchers, he shows that the sf tradition was much more popular and more richly developed than early surveys suggested. The 1880s were a seedbed for the tradition that the famous H. G. Wells refined.

H. G. Wells is often recognized as the first writer of modern science fiction because he introduced many themes familiar to our modern sense of the genre. In contrast to Verne's stress on plausible mechanical technology, Wells focuses on radical speculation, on capturing the reader's imagination. He is also a superb writer of polished, intelligent prose, which is unusual in later sf. Wells's attempts to venture beyond the known and the probable were noted, rather scornfully, by Verne himself, who wryly observed, "I make use of physics. He invents" (Gunn, 324).

In H. G. Wells's most famous work, *The Time Machine* (1895), a nameless character merely identified as "the Time Traveler" invents a machine that propels him into distant future landscapes and cultures, providing him with an amazingly intimate yet detached perspective from which he watches the earth waste away. Like many other moralistic writers after him who invented social cultures, Wells contrasted a physically weaker but more refined and effeminate people, the Eloi, with a muscular worker race lacking intellectual awareness, the Morlocks. Within the next two years he published a monster story loosely patterned on *Frankenstein* (*The Island of Doctor Moreau*, 1896) and *The Invisible Man* (1897), which explores the curse of invisibility. In 1898 *The War of the Worlds*, which caused panic among radio listeners when it was broadcast by Orson Welles in 1938, introduced the concept of aliens invading the earth. The volume, variety, and popularity of H. G. Wells's work not only brought him critical respect but also gave credence to the genre of "scientific romance," an early name for these new kinds of novels.

The Age of Science Fiction Magazines

The term science fiction wasn't used by the general public until the 1930s, shortly after Hugo Gernsback became the editor of *Amazing Stories*, the first magazine devoted solely to science fiction. Gernsback's original definition was "scientifiction," which he used in his editorial in the first issue of *Amazing Stories* (April 1926), but the term "science fiction" is what stuck in the consciousness of the public. It came into popular usage in America in the 1930s after John W. Campbell publicized it as editor of *Astounding Science-Fiction*.

Readers, reviewers, and fans of this genre formed a subculture, attracted to these sensational tales as a way of critiquing limitations and failures of the present technology and as an exciting way of "extrapolating" new lives from scientific hypotheses. A spate of magazines fed this new interest, as did radio "space operas." Modeled on the newly popular soap operas, these were action-figure adventures in space, often with an obligatory but rather stereotypical romantic twist. They were scorned by critics such as Wilson Tucker, who in 1941 coined the phrase space opera to ridicule the newly emerging genre and to decry the "hacky grinding, stinking, outworn spaceship yarn" (Clute and Nicholls, 1138). But these programs were adored by young listeners, who often reveled in the genre's cultural underdog status. The blend of interplanetary conflict and romance typical of this type of story is evident in the long-running *Star Trek* TV series as well as in novels by Poul Anderson and Samuel Delany, and in comic parodies like Harry Harrison's *Bill, the Galactic Hero* (1965) and Douglas Adams's hilarious spoofs in the *Hitchhiker's Guide to the Galaxy* series. Many popular video games continue this tradition of fast-paced, do-or-die plots, so perfect for a quick emotional fix and a cheap escape from mundane reality.

Beyond the Magazine

From the 1930s until the 1960s, most science fiction appeared in magazines. This helped to define it as a short story genre, limited in theme by size and bound by conventional morality. However, the popularity of these interstellar war stories extended beyond this golden age of magazine science fiction to Ace Books, which published more of this genre than any other company from the early 1950s until 1987. Other publishers, including Ballantine, Bantam, Signet, and Pyramid, began to compete. Their acceptance of book-length fictions meant that authors could create whole worlds, indulging their imaginations in detail and developing universes and characters that lasted through extensive series. Fantasy became more popular as authors had more room and more license to stretch the boundaries of conventional morality and logic.

The phrase "sci fi," pronounced "sky fi" or "si fi," was introduced by Forrest J. Ackerman, a writer fond of wordplay, during the 1950s when the term "hi-fi" (for high-fidelity recordings) was popular. However, for aficionados, "sf," pronounced "esseff" and often printed in lowercase letters, is the preferred term. Sci fi, generally the most common term used by nonreaders, the media, and the public, is scorned by insiders, who use it only to denote hackwork. In 1978 critic Susan Wood popularized the pronunciation "skiffy," which, because it sounds cuter than the scornful "sci fi," has been generally welcomed by critics, authors, and readers who consider themselves experts: "Skiffy is colourful, sometimes entertaining, junk sf: Star Wars is skiffy," notes the eminent insider critic Nicholls (Clute and Nicholls, 1079).

The surge of science fiction books published in the 1950s, paralleling the American public's demand for a more sophisticated technology and accelerated scientific research, developed the depth and range of the genre, which began its slow rise to a level of intellectual respectability. Among others, Robert Heinlein popularized the term "speculative fiction" to focus attention on the concept of predicting the future from present hypotheses and to emphasize usefulness to society in connecting scientifically authorized data with imagined possibilities.

One of the many attempts to describe the history of science fiction depicts it in the image of a tree, with its "sturdy and powerful roots [the nineteenth-century 'fathers and mother'], one strong stem [the American magazine period ca. 1920–1950], and after that, such a branching and leafing and flowering as has seldom been seen in any form of art or literature."[9] This proliferation of themes and formats is what fascinates many traditional readers of the genre and what attracts an increasing number of new readers and greater respect from literary critics and commentators.

Since the 1960s the writing style of published science fiction has changed from the wooden, "tell-it-like-it-is" plot-centered earlier stories to a range of moods and literary techniques. The advent of more women writers in the 1970s may have encouraged the increasing replacement of stereotypical characterizations with subtler, fuller relationships between developed personalities. In the 1980s cyberpunk added a spark of sophistication to the genre with its emphasis on a strobelight rhythm, high-tech imagery, and sardonic dialogue, though the jaded aesthetics and brutal violence of this subgenre are not welcomed by readers concerned with its effect on public morality.

Since most readers of sf begin reading the genre during their adolescent years, it is difficult to delineate those works written specifically for young people. Publishers, however, have helped in this regard by producing books developed for young adults, works with adolescent protagonists and plots centered on coming-of-age themes. Space adventures traditionally star a young male who uses his physical strength, courageous nature, and logical intelligence to overcome the superior forces of older enemies with evil intentions. Other works feature highly cerebral heroes or heroines whose interactions and conversations are motivated more by difficult moral values the author wishes to teach than by entertainment and excitement. Some recent works for young people include an emphasis on tolerance of cultural, racial, and gender differences, on preservation of the natural environment of Earth, and on avoidance of war and destruction. Currently, science fiction for young people seems to be developing in two directions. Some works focus on horror and fantasy, titillating young imaginations with electrically paced action and gory images of monstrous creations and disgusting vistas. Others threaten futures dominated by totalitarian forces. As the twentieth century looms to a close, the question "What's next?" is raised in fiction with an increasing sense of urgency. Are our young people doomed, or does an age of excitement and unimaginable opportunity gleam on the horizon?

Historical Stages

Historians of science fiction often trace its stages by the increasingly sophisticated media in which this genre has prospered. In the sense articulated by Marshall McCluhan in the 1960s that "the medium is the message," this historical viewpoint is particularly relevant for a genre whose themes center on the development of science and technology, especially the science of communication. Lester del Rey's Five Ages of Science Fiction from his *World of Science Fiction, 1926–1976* (1980) prove useful as a historical summary that correlates with other similar charts:

1. The Age of Wonder, 1926–1937: This period is dominated by pulp magazines featuring science fiction, the

start of fandom, and the reign of editor Hugo Gernsback. Science fiction is considered lowbrow entertainment by the critical public.

2. The Golden Age, 1938–1949: John W. Campbell is editor of a magazine empire that fosters new writers like Asimov, Heinlein, and other masters. The Atomic Age heightens interest in those fictions that seem to have prophesied fact. The first World SF Convention brings fans together to hear the star writers speak, and the public begins to listen, though not often with approval.

3. The Age of Acceptance, 1950–1961: Paperbacks begin to replace magazines as the main vehicle of publication; authors indulge themselves with more intricate tales and more far-fetched themes. The public begins to gain respect for the ideas presented in science fiction if not for the literary style.

4. The Age of Rebellion, 1962–1973: The rise of anthologies introduces new authors with different styles and outrageous ideas to the reading audience. Schools begin to offer courses in science fiction, and attendance at the World SF Conference surpasses 2,000. Intellectuals begin to note the sophistication of some writers and their improvement in style.

5. The Fifth Age, 1974–present: Science fiction enjoys a surge of popularity, permeating television, films, video games, and even mainstream fiction, raising questions about the boundaries between genres and, in the case of virtual reality, between fiction and life. Science fiction is no longer marginalized. Mainstream writers of adult fiction influenced by sf include Thomas Pynchon, Kurt Vonnegut, Doris Lessing, Italo Calvino, Dean Koontz, and Robin Cook. Although not designated as sf writers by critics or publishers, these and other authors recognize the all-encompassing impact of modern science and technology on human habits of thinking, and their writing reflects the imaginative freedom demonstrated in fantasy and science fiction. They realize the limits of

character-driven fiction of manners that describes events only in comparison to the cultural norms of the past. The genre of science fiction, with its emphasis on events and plots that move the narrative forward, encourages readers to engage in futurist speculations, either by painting disastrous consequences of technological or environmental events or by suggesting utopian possibilities. The imminent end of the millennium and the lack of new frontiers on Earth challenge sf thinkers to explore beyond the known regions of the galaxy and beyond the usual dilemmas of human behavior. Even the prestigious literary critic Harold Bloom has admitted in print to preferring speculative fiction for pleasure reading. One of his predecessors as a leader of literati, T. S. Eliot, reported a preference for mysteries, puzzling knots of logic that could be untied and solved. At this end of the century, open-ended exploration of a possible future seems more relevant and even more necessary than examining patterns of the past. While Eliot decried the breakup of orderly tradition, Bloom urges readers to create new questions.

The Literary Status of Science Fiction

Science fiction has also become respectable in educational arenas. The first college course on science fiction was taught in 1953 by Sam Moskowitz at City College of New York; the next two decades saw a proliferation of such courses, which peaked in popularity in the seventies. Since then, their number has declined, but only because the masterpieces of science fiction are now included in general survey courses of literature. Once considered a fringe genre of American literature, important works of science fiction are now part of the mainstream.

As sf gained recognition as a genuine field of literature, several annual awards for excellence were established. The Hugo Award was named for Hugo Gernsback (1884–1967). Beginning in 1953, this award has been presented at the World SF Convention (nick-named Worldcon) to artists nominated and selected by fans who have registered for the conference. The Hugo is both highly valued and denigrated because it is awarded by hard-core fans who care enough to lobby and vote for their favorites, regardless of critical acclaim. The first award went to Alfred Bester for *The Demolished Man* (1953), a hard-edged novel centering on the effects of ESP on a murderer and the system that catches him. The Nebula Award was established in 1965 by professional members of the Science Fiction Writers of America (since renamed Science Fiction and Fantasy Writers of America); its first recipient was Frank Herbert for *Dune* (1965), which also won the Hugo. The few novels so honored with double recognition include Ursula Le Guin's *The Left Hand of Darkness* (1969) and Larry Niven's *Ringworld* (1970). Other important honors bear the names of other revered members of the science fiction pantheon: the John W. Campbell Award, the Arthur C. Clarke Award, the Theodore Sturgeon Award, and the Philip K. Dick Award.

Science fiction's apparent increase in respectability is not pleasing to all of its proponents. Some fans prefer their former status as outsiders, too cool to be mainstream. In their scholarly *Encyclopedia of Science Fiction,* Clute and Nicholls note that some insiders fear that the academic study of sf will domesticate it: "A common catchphrase among sf fans is 'Kick sf out of the classroom and back to the gutter where it belongs' " (1065). Yet the chatty tone and witty asides of Clute and Nicholls, long-term readers who write the kinds of resources that are used in classrooms, should disarm all but the grumpiest devotees. Their light-hearted style is typical of much of the recent scholarship about science fiction that embodies the ironic intelligence of its most renowned writers. Like other genres that began as popular culture, science fiction has outgrown some of the scruffiness of its beginnings, especially as a burgeoning market allows publishers to be more selective. Critical attention and a more sophisticated audience have encouraged writers to refine their styles, sharpen their wits, thicken their plots, and flesh out their characters. As our lives become more entwined with technological inventions and the pace of change quickens, these "thought experiments," as Le Guin calls them, and adventures into futures not so impossible may engender ideas necessary for the survival of humanity.

No wonder there is an increased demand for excellence among sf aficionados and a wider tolerance for the stylistic quirks indigenous to this genre. Readers and critics have come to realize the limits of character-driven fiction, unless the characters are engaged by the complexities, the rapid pace of change, and the limitless speculative possibilities of modern life. Science fiction has become as much a seedbed for thinking about reality as an escape into fantasy, a relevant field of study for intellectuals as much as a titillating pleasure for the young and the restless. Like other genres previously scorned, science fiction has developed its own standards of excellence. A high degree of verisimilitude demands a sophisticated knowledge of many technological devices and an ability to explain inventions with plausible logic; characters must be realistically motivated and the writing must be witty, quick-moving, and interesting. Critics of science fiction demand intelligence and innovation to meet the challenges of a future that may well move beyond our Earth and depend on superseding our present cultural divisions.

2. The Classical Masters

"Science Fiction writers do have their blind spots despite the fact that we're all geniuses, we're all marvelous people, and some of us can spell," declared Isaac Asimov of himself and his sf colleagues (Rotsler, 102). His allusion to the close-knit world of science fiction, where writers feel as if they belong to a club of like-minded intelligentsia, underlines a problem with the subject of this chapter. Any attempt to identify the "classics" of science fiction, much less to rank them in any order, results in a long, long rope of names, many intertwined inextricably in networks of influence, friendship, and rivalry. The masters (and mistresses) of science fiction are more allied than writers of other genres because of the initially small size of their readership and the limited number of publishers who would receive their work. The leading figures of the canon who defined and developed science fiction as a genre certainly include the authors Isaac Asimov, Ray Bradbury, Arthur C. Clarke, Lester del Rey, Robert Heinlein, Frank Herbert, Ursula K. Le Guin, Ben Bova, and Robert Silverberg. Many talented writers, however, got their start because a more experienced mentor spent the time and energy to include them in this great web of personalities and ideas.

The Mentor

Chief among these mentors is the editor of the most popular and influential magazine, *Astounding Science Fiction* (later, *Analog*), which ushered in sf's golden age. John W. Campbell Jr. began as a popular author, publishing his first story in 1930. He soon became a superb composer of the formulaic space operas that sold so well to magazines during this formative period of science fiction. He used a format similar to the episodic adventures of knights in shining armor but set his stories in a mythical future with rocket ships and lasers instead of the steeds and lances of a mythical past. After a few years Campbell became bored with the repetitive plots and began to write stories that raised more philosophic questions, using pseudonyms such as Don A. Stuart, Karl Van Kampen, and Arthur McCann so as not to confuse his readers. Collected in *Who Goes There?* and *Cloak of Aesir,* these varied stories set the stage, and to some degree the standard, for the "masters"—Heinlein, van Vogt, del Rey, and Asimov—whom he helped along when in 1937 he became editor of *Astounding Science-Fiction,* the newly prominent magazine that replaced Gernsback's first efforts and that developed into the highly respected *Analog* in 1960. As editor he generated many ideas for stories, which he shared with other writers while helping them polish their own. His effect is summed up by Searles's accolade: "Campbell accomplished something allowed few men: he remade, single handedly and single mindedly, the entire field of . . . science fiction" (Searles et al., 34).

Mr. Science Fiction

During the 1940s, the writer who appeared most often in Campbell's *Astounding Science Fiction* was Robert A. Heinlein (1907–1988). Known as "Mr. Science Fiction" for his prolific output during the magazine's golden age of the 1940s and 1950s, he was also renowned for charting a fictional human future. Published in *Astounding Science Fiction* in 1941, his history began the "day after tomorrow" and continued into the twenty-second century, thrilling readers of the pre–World War II era with the promise of science and technology and the strength of American sensibilities. After returning from military service in World War II, he introduced sf to many young readers through junior novels published by Scribner's, beginning with *Rocket Ship Galileo* (1947).

Some of his best young adult novels include *Citizen of the Galaxy* (1957), in which Thorby develops from a slave on Jubbul into the ruler of a galaxy of cultures; *Have Space Suit—Will Travel* (1958); and *Starship Troopers* (1959), which depicts in violent detail a militaristic future. His most popular novel, *Stranger in a Strange Land* (1961), attracted unwanted attention as the partial inspiration for Charles Manson's murder of actress Sharon Tate in the late 1960s. In the book, Valentine Michael Smith, human but reared and educated on Mars, shares the art of "grokking," opening himself to another's spirit to the extent that physical being becomes subordinate, even unnecessary, to comprehending another's mind and feelings. The counterculture of the 1970s adopted Heinlein's novel concept of grokking and his deeply satis-fying image of communal families living in "nests" as metaphors for the kinds of love that transcend conventional social bound-aries. The sweepingly satiric critique of modern American culture as a "strange land" matched the rebellious mood of many young readers, and the coming-of-age story of a hero whose life paral-leled the familiar story of the Christian gospel, along with a heightened discovery of sexuality, mirrored their vision of them-selves. Heinlein's endlessly inventive and mystically suggestive story made this provocative work the defining classic of a genera-tion.

Heinlein's themes epitomize the thrusting energy of science fic-tion plots of the first half of this century. He writes plainly and clearly, preaching the right to rebel for independence and explain-ing in extensive detail the technology of his inventions. His works are satisfying to many readers who look to this genre for military order and chauvinistic inspiration. In *Methuselah's Children* (1958) Lazarus Long rebels against living forever, yet reappears in his memoirs, *Time Enough for Love* (1973), to have an Oedipal relationship with his mother. Independence is important to Hein-lein, justifying even revolution, as in *The Moon Is a Harsh Mis-tress* (1966), the story of human colonies on the moon. But then revolution is how our own nation began. The danger, however, of elevating the individual will is self-righteousness. Heinlein's increasingly harsh conservatism and chauvinistic views have drawn much criticism in recent years, but the depth and extent of his influence on the genre have never been questioned. Like many old masters, he may have outlived the era he helped define; science fiction has since taken a direction away from the ethic of national self-reliance and the belief in the efficacy of self-discipline that are the centers of Heinlein's work. At the end, Heinlein's autobiographical work *Grumbles from the Grave* (1989) reveals a man disappointed in the political directions of the future he had hoped to help design.

The Good Doctor

Another of John W. Campbell's protégés was Isaac Asimov (1920–1992), nicknamed "the good doctor" in science fiction circles because of his expertise in an amazingly wide range of subjects. This insatiably curious writer was born in Russia, but his family emigrated to New York City when he was three, so he is considered American. Magazines in his father's candy store introduced him to science fiction, which he started writing at quite a young age: his first story was published in 1939. During World War II, after earning a master's degree in chemistry, he worked with Robert Heinlein, who is considered the father of science fiction only because he preceded Asimov. Critic John Clute compares the two masters in detailed if not flattering terms:

> Hyperactive, intense, amiable, and prolific, [Asimov] *sounded* like SF. But Heinlein, a more powerful and cunning writer, came just before him and was a born father figure: suave, personable, austere, demanding, and charismatic. Asimov was never suave. Instead, he played the younger brother: a brash, boastful, workaholic geek, ruthless (but inept) with women, self-assertive (but strangely self-defeating) as a publicist of his own miracles of productivity.[1]

After earning a Ph.D., Asimov taught biochemistry at Boston University for nine years before leaving to write full-time. Asimov's science fiction is classical in style, with plots and characters combining equally the elements of "hard" and "soft" sciences, balanced by clear rationality to modulate the passionate tone. While Heinlein's writing was smoother stylistically, Asimov's prolific output made him just as influential; at his death in 1992 more than 500 of his books had been published. Asimov's best stylistic achievement is the short story "Nightfall" (1941), based on one of Campbell's ideas and continually voted "the best short story of all time" (Clute and Nicholls, 56). It describes the reaction of humans who see stars shine only once every 2,000 years, and who go mad when they suddenly realize how inconsequential their own world is.

Asimov is also famous for his three laws of robotics. First published in "Liar" (1941) as part of his Robot series, these principles were also partially credited to Campbell. They were offered to the public in an effort to thwart the fearful, horrific image of these artificial humans and, implicitly, to suggest the intrinsic goodness of science and technology in general:

1. A robot may not cause injury to a human being,
2. A robot must obey orders unless doing so would cause injury to humans,
3. A robot must protect its own existence unless doing so breaks the first two laws.

Asimov stayed faithful to these laws in robot novels written over a span of fifty years. In these novels, Detective Lije Baley and his robot sidekick, R. Daneel Olivaw, solve problems caused by overpopulation and serve humanity in the best way they can. Based on the Czech word for statute labor, *robota,* the term robot originally referred to artificial human beings but was soon applied to machines designed to perform a specific task. The word robot was introduced in Karl Capek's play *R.U.R.* (1921, trans. 1923). Robot philosophy occurs in Stanislaw Lem's *The Cyberiad* (coll. 1965; trans. 1974). Robot religion and mythology are described in Robert Young's "Robot Son" (1959) and most notably in Robert Silverberg's "Good News from the Vatican," in which a robot pope is elected. In Philip K. Dick's stories, humans and androids are so closely allied that they can scarcely be distinguished. Asimov's robots were at first mere auxiliaries to human intelligence; in his later work he tried to deal with the ramifications of artificial intelligence that would make robots capable of independent action.

Asimov's other major science fiction work is the Foundation series (1941–1953), collected in *The Foundation Trilogy* in 1963. Winner of the 1965 Hugo Award for Best All-Time Series, it describes the work of Hari Seldon, who has founded the imaginary science of psychohistory and sets up two foundations to help ease the transition of power and cultural values between two galactic empires. Threatened by the barbarity of a Dark Age, particularly as personified by the antihero Mule, these foundations strive to re-civilize humankind. Asimov's background in history and sociology provides fascinating allusions that enrich the novel's texture.

Asimov wrote 400 columns for *The Magazine of Fantasy and Science Fiction* from 1958 to 1991 and was awarded a special Hugo in 1963 for "adding science to science fiction." His many works, often written in collaboration with his wife, Janet Jeppson Asimov, range from novel-length treatises on chemical elements and books on math to historical fictions and a commentary on the Bible. Highly readable, most are full of informational details described almost chattily in contexts familiar to most young readers. In the 1980s Asimov returned to science fiction, combining the Robot and Foundation series in novels that include *The Robots of Dawn* (1983), *Robots and Empire* (1985), and *Foundation's Edge* (1982), also a Hugo winner. These were less successful than his previous work, but Asimov was still recognized as a dominant voice in the sf field for the preceding fifty years.

A Brief Catalog of Other Masters

Although Campbell, Heinlein, and Asimov were unquestionably the giants of science fiction in the first half of the century, the talents of many other stars contributed to the development of this new field. Only a few are mentioned here.

Like most of the traditional masters, Fritz Leiber (1910–1992) practiced his craft in the magazines of the 1930s, but even then his superb writing style set him apart. Son of the actor Fritz Leiber and an actor himself, he learned to use language to manipulate the emotions, particularly those aroused by horror. Winner of a Hugo Award, *The Big Time* (Ace, 1961) describes an intergalactic war between snakes and spiders that takes place in a time warp. The collection *The Mind Spider* (Ace, 1961) relates further episodes of this war. Other disasters occur in *The Wanderer* (Ballantine, 1964) when another planet moves into an orbit close to Earth, disturbing its equilibrium. Called "the ultimate motorcycle epic" (Searles, 105), this comic novel features action and surprise. *Conjure Wife* (Twayne, 1953), a cross between rational science and gothic horror that won the Radcliffe Award, deals with college faculty wives who seem to be playing with witchcraft on campus, but whose magic is ultimately explained in logical terms. Leiber's sophisticated wit is evident in his Gray Mouser series, which was introduced in 1939 and continued into the 1960s, as the rakish Mouser and his sidekick, Fafhrd, dash stylishly through their fantastic adventures. Winner of many awards, this prolific writer is still enjoyed by modern readers. He also contributed to the field as editor of *Science Digest.*

Another popularizer of science fiction was Arthur C. Clarke (1913?–), a master of the philosophical humanism typical of the English tradition and one of the few British writers of sf to achieve popularity in the United States. His novels, with their well-rounded characters and lack of obvious villains, contrast with the morally polarized American novels of his era. His clear descriptions and logical imagination make his work a good starting place for science fiction novices. Clarke, who held degrees in physics and mathematics, writes optimistically about technology and science, which is unusual in the field.

Clarke's first novel, *Against the Fall of Night,* published in 1948 in the magazine *Startling Stories,* is especially suitable for younger readers. It was later published in an expanded version, *The City and the Stars* (1956), which describes in detail two human cultures, one a model of technological convenience and the other more humane. His imaginative worlds are memorable: the underwater prairies of *The Deep Range* (1954, 1957), where dolphins keep herds of whales in line; the generous humanity of *Imperial Earth: A Fantasy of Love and Discord* (1976); and many short stories that challenge our cultural assumptions. These works and many of his nonfiction articles draw on his love of skin diving, especially in the environs of Sri Lanka, where he has lived since 1956.

Clarke has become one of the most famous sf writers in the world. *Childhood's End* (1953), in which technologically superior overlords from outer space force earthlings to evolve morally at a faster pace, was a campus favorite during the sixties. Its "finale . . . can only be described as Wagnerian" (Searles, 41). Clarke's real fame arrived with the success of *2001: A Space Odyssey* (1968), the film and later novelization based on his short story "The Sentinel" (1951) about the discovery of a more advanced alien race that might well be the ancient precursors to our present humanity. Among his later works, *Rendezvous with Rama* (1973) received many awards, most likely in recognition of Clarke's long-term achievements rather than for that particular book. After developing a debilitating nerve disease in the mid-1980s, Clarke worked mostly in collaboration with other writers. However, by 1990 he was writing solo again: *The Ghost from the Grand Banks* (1990), about an attempt in the future to raise the *Titanic,* includes sophisticated references to mathematics and complex technical speculation. In 1996, he wrote another best-seller, *3001, The Final Odyssey,* in which a hero of *2001, A Space Odyssey* returns to life just in time to save us all. Clarke also returned to the public eye as the host of a television show about scientific oddities.

Lester del Rey (1915–) is also known as Ramon Felipe Rey y de los Verdes, John Alvarez, Marion Henry, Philip James, Charles Satterfield, and Edson McCann. As del Rey, this man is important not so much as an author of adult novels but as a major figure in the business of science fiction. He worked as an editor, anthologizer, reviewer, and historian as well as a writer of sf until his retirement in 1991. His Moon series, including *Attack from Atlantis* (1953) and *Mission to the Moon* (1956), consists of typical del Rey sf adventure stories, a bit dated but still fun to race through and full of vivid, sensual descriptions. *Nerves* (1948) foresees public concern about nuclear power plants. *Pstalemate* (1971) describes how ESP could drive a person mad. *The Eleventh Commandment* (1962), like so many other novels of the last forty years, portrays an overpopulated world, yet del Rey draws a conclusion that surprises even jaded readers. Books like *Marooned on Mars* (1952) and *Rocket Jockey* (1952) were written for the juvenile market and introduced many young readers to the genre. Rey's fourth wife, Judy-Lynn (Benjamin) del Rey, was an editor who markedly increased the audience for sf books before her death in 1986; the Del Rey imprint of Ballantine Books is named after her. In 1990 del Rey received the Nebula Grand Master Award for his lifetime achievement in the field of science fiction. And yes, Lester del Rey also wrote the popular children's series about that mischievous monkey Curious George.

Other writers contributed a great deal to both defining the genre as well as establishing a wider, more respectable audience of readers. One such writer is recognized by most readers who pay attention during high school English class, where literature anthologies almost always include one of his stories. Ray Bradbury (1920–   ) is familiar even to many people who never read science fiction, yet sf aficionados are reluctant to include him in the field because many of his stories challenge the ethical conventions of science fiction: they tend to question the benefits of science and technology, and they turn to the past rather than face forward to the future.

Born in 1920, Bradbury grew up in the Midwest and then moved to Los Angeles, where at age nineteen he began publishing a fanzine, *Futuria Fantasia*. He also published his first story that year. *The Martian Chronicles* (1950; TV miniseries, 1980) is a collection of linked stories that describe the loneliness of colonists on Mars; these stories deal more with past and present human emotions than with any future possibility. His only novel, *Fahrenheit 451* (1951), which dramatically described a book-burning society, engaged America's political imagination during a time of paranoid fear of Communism instigated by Senator Joe McCarthy's investigations in 1949. Many editions of the novel were published, one even bound in asbestos (Searles, 25), and in 1966 François Truffaut made the story into a highly acclaimed movie, recently remade in an updated version. In 1989 his contributions won Bradbury the Nebula Grandmaster Award for lifetime achievement.

Ironically, much of Bradbury's work cannot be classified as hard-core sf. Because his imagery is softer and his tone more sentimental than most science fiction work, many of his more than 300 stories have appeared regularly in mainstream literary magazines and anthologies. His prolific output and gentle mood led the reading public to accept his work at a time when few were claiming to read science fiction. Bradbury's tremendous popularity and his growing reputation as a major literary talent have helped erase critics' disdain of the field of sf.

Two authors who wrote prolifically during the middle decades of the century and served science fiction faithfully need to be mentioned here. Frederick Pohl (1919–) began his first writing career in the 1930s, penning several novels with C. M. Kornbluth and publishing widely under a large number of pseudonyms, including Paul Flehr, Scott Mariner, Dirk Wylie, Edson McCann, and Charles Satterfield (the last two pseudonyms were shared with Lester del Rey). Pohl's energetic intelligence led him to become a central figure in the sf world, editing magazines, acting as a literary agent, networking at conferences, and publishing anthologies. Young readers of the 1950s delighted in the satirical edge of the novels he cowrote with Kornbluth: *The Space Merchants* (Ballantine, 1953) and *Wolfbane* (Ballantine, 1959). His later works, written individually, have garnered more critical respect. *Gateway* (St. Martin's, 1977) depicts the glorious challenge of space travel; *JEM: The Making of a Utopia* (St. Martin's, 1979) is self-descriptive; *Chernobyl* (Bantam, 1987) adds a twist to the nuclear accident in Russia; and *Outnumbering the Dead* (Legend, 1990) portrays a land of immortality through the eyes of an outsider. Frederik Pohl has grown into his star status over a long and eventful career.

Poul Anderson (1926–) is admired for the consistently high literary quality of his dark, rich romantic visions. A master at inventing military tactics, he creates thrilling battles. *Tau Zero*

(Doubleday, 1970), one of his best books, takes the reader beyond the universe and succeeds in making real "the psychic shock of relativity and the physical ambience of a starship" (Searles, 7). *After Doomsday* describes the search for survivors in space after the Earth has blown up. Innovative though not philosophical, Anderson has created two particularly memorable characters: the supremely greedy capitalist Nicholas van Rijn, a merchant with a Falstaffian frame and appetite, dominates the *Psychotechnic* series, and secret agent Flandry stars in the *Dominic Flandry* books. These works complement each other to form a loosely woven futurist chronicle titled *The Technic History*. A more recent work, *Harvest of the Stars* (Tor, 1993), takes a critical look at the destruction of Earth's environment and the possibilities of finding other homes.

Frank Herbert (1920–1986), a writer of sociological sf from the state of Washington, created one of the undisputed masterpieces of the genre, the massive *Dune* (Chilton, 1965). The plot, loosely based on the life of Mohammed, traces the development of Paul Atrides from a weak young individual to a politically powerful master of a universe with the moral strength to recognize and resist the corruption of power. Herbert's carefully detailed descriptions of Dune's culture and ecology have earned this work the highest praise and attracted even nonreaders of sf to this completely comprehensive creation. After *Dune* came three sequels: *Dune Messiah* (Putnam, 1969), *Children of Dune* (Berkley, 1976), and *Heretics of Dune* (Gollanz, 1984). In these and several other novels Herbert portrays the complexity of environmental change, a particularly relevant concern for today's readers. In *The Green Brain* (Ace, 1966) the destruction of insect pests brings about natural disaster; *The Eyes of Heisenberg* (Berkley, 1966) exposes the dangers of a carefully planned and genetically controlled society, the kind many of us dream about in this messy, chaotic world. *Hellstrom's Hive* (Doubleday, 1973) also describes a carefully engineered society in the insect world. Herbert's relentless challenge to his readers to consider the environmental effects of our present habits makes him something of a missionary, one who has attracted many followers.

Ben Bova (1932–), known primarily as an editor of technical science fiction, writes stories that reflect his interest in predicting the foreseeable future. *Multiple Man* (1976) presupposes that the President of the United States has been cloned, and three doubles have been murdered; is the "real" man in the White House? *Millennium* (1976) is set on the moon in 2000, as the Russian and American militaries rebel against war, a story now a bit dated. After the death of John Campbell in 1971, Bova became the editor of *Astounding Science Fiction* and brought a younger man's vision to the magazine, including more updated stories and anthologizing of outstanding stories in *Analog Annual*. His influence was rewarded with the Hugo for best editor each year from 1973 to 1977. From 1978 to 1982 he edited *OMNI*, a highly successful magazine of popular science that included a large selection of sf in its slick monthly issues. Bova's works indicate a belief that in order to survive, the human race will need to explore other planets, particularly Mars.

Robert Silverberg (1934–) is also known as Calvin M. Knox, David Osborne, and more than a dozen other pseudonyms, some of which represent solo efforts (T. D. Bethlen, Dan Malcolm, Eric Malcolm) and others collaborative works (Robert Randall, Ralph Burke, Alexander Blade, S. M. Tenneshaw). Since publishing his first book, *Revolt on Alpha* (1955), at the age of 19, Silverberg has written and published hundreds of works, making him one of the most prolific writers in history. His first science fiction space operas were written for the magazine market, which began to dry up by 1960. In the early sixties he wrote profusely but unremarkably, except for his nonfiction. In 1967 his novels became more intense and artistically creative. They include *Thorns* (1967); *Hawksbill Station* (1968); *A Time of Changes* (1971), which won a Nebula Award; *The Book of Skulls* (1971); and the shorter *Nightwings* (1969), which won a Hugo. His short stories are more critically acclaimed, and his influence in the field is compounded by his editing of several journals and many anthologies.

Philip K. (for Kindred) Dick (1928–1982) is one of sf's most philosophically challenging as well as diabolically playful writers. He poses questions few others think to ask and then offers clever, mostly surreal answers. What if the government were controlled by leaders whose directions were driven more by chance than by plan, and these leaders and most of their followers were corrupt as well, as in *Solar Lottery* (1955)? What if the Axis powers had won World War II, as in *The Man in the High Castle* (1962), Dick's most widely known novel? What would happen if the Earth's population decreased and mechanical substitutes were used to supplement biological life-forms, as in *Do Androids Dream of Electric Sheep* (1968)? That novel was made accessible to the general public by Ridley Scott's classic film *Blade Runner* (1982), which encouraged a resurgence of interest in Dick's life and work. Born in California, Dick set most of his novels there, in a "Los Angeles bleached into surreal perspectives and populated by driven hordes of Americans who have found that the Pacific Ocean marks the end of their travels in search of paradise" (Clute and Nicholls, 163). A consummate pessimist, Dick persistently portrays a society ruled by wrongheaded leaders—a reality as shifty as sand and a future as corrupt, tawdry, and bleak as the cyberpunk worlds that followed, yet infinitely more complex. Although his writing is often confusing to read, Dick is receiving increasing critical notice for the sympathetic humaneness of his characters and the profound inventiveness of his plots. Two of his later novels address particularly complex questions about reality in a depleted world. In *Ubik* (Doubleday, 1969) a group of society's leaders is mechanically resurrected from accidental death, yet they continue to rule over humanity—or do they? *A Maze of Death* (Doubleday, 1970) questions the nature of human belief in a supreme being. Sadly, the author's last years and books marked a descent into paranoia and apparent madness that manifested itself in religious writing that few can or want to comprehend. His last major work, *VALIS* (Bantam, 1981), probes into his own psyche with a mocking tone too sharp for most readers, who cringe at his disturbingly realistic portrayal of the future. Even after his death, however, his work has found a growing audience. Dick is a favorite of at least one other intellectual with a sense of whimsy—Ursula K. Le Guin.

Ursula K. Le Guin (1929–   ), classy, graceful, and intellectually adventurous, is both highly respected and greatly beloved within and outside the science fiction community for the lucid complexity of her ideas and the poetry of her imagery. Her first three novels, *Rocannon's World* (1966), *Planet of Exile* (1966), and *City of Illusions* (1967), establish her central themes of interracial societies and cooperative government and also introduce the ansible, which solves the problem of communication when people travel faster than light. Her first sf masterpiece, *The Left Hand of Darkness* (1969), perennially popular with young adult readers, features an androgynous society on the Gethenian planet Winter; the hero, Genly Ai, tries to overcome his prejudices and the Gethenian aversions to his own sexuality as he learns to understand both himself and this alien culture. In *The Lathe of Heaven* (1971) Le Guin uses the image of dreams that change reality to explore the effect of absolute power. *The Word for World Is Forest* (1985) is a terrifying picture of how colonialism by westerners destroyed the fragile land and gentle culture of Vietnam. Le Guin's second science fiction masterpiece, *The Dispossessed* (1974), cleverly compares Urras, a capitalist society, and Anarres, a cooperative anarchy. Her Earthsea series (coll. 1979) is more fantasy than sf, yet she makes "her magic obey such rigorous laws that it may be seen as a kind of imaginary science" (Clute and Nicholls, 215); she is less concerned with humanity's technical prowess than with its metaphysical and moral choices. Her more recent works experiment with language, reality, and cultural prejudices in the best tradition of science fiction and fantasy. *Always Coming Home* (1985) is an anthropological and media experiment in which Le Guin invents a culture of the future, including its music on an accompanying tape and its language in a glossary. Provocative and poetic, Le Guin is a constant surprise to her readers.

Masters of Juvenile Science Fiction

Le Guin is an author who writes as easily for young readers as for adults, a feat she admits is not as easy as people think. Such science fiction must satisfy the deep sense of logic inherent in young thinkers while providing a rapid pace of action, believable characters, and an imaginative conclusion. Literature for children of all ages must be authentic and wise as well as entertaining. Few young readers will tolerate boredom or undeserved pomposity. Many select their own favorite works from the literature they happen to see or hear about from fellow readers regardless of its designated age range.

Jules Verne's books, over sixty published between 1863 and 1920, were marketed to young boys, as was the Great Marvel series (1906–1935), authored by a writers' stable collectively named Roy Rockwood. The themes of this early fiction, which assumed an exclusively male audience, include the Lost World, a war of the future, and the invention of drastically different technology. Most of the literature written for young people contains a large quantity of fantasy: C. S. Lewis's Narnia series uses time travel and parallel worlds, as does Lucy Boston's Green Knowe series. Major authors of science fiction who also published for young people include Robert A. Heinlein, Isaac Asimov, and Ursula K. Le Guin.

Andre Norton (1912–   ), born Alice Mary Norton and also known as Andrew North, began her career writing historical novels marketed to young people but moved into science fiction for young adults with "The People of the Crater" in 1947, under the pseudonym Andrew North. Some of her early novels feature American Indian characters, which widened her appeal among many young readers. In *The Beast Master* (Harcourt Brace, 1959), Hosteen Storm, a young Navajo, must leave the war-ravaged Earth to live in an alien world, a journey that harks back to the settlement of North America by Europeans. In *The Sioux Spaceman* (Ace, 1960) Kade Whitehawk's gift for understanding animals helps save Earth from destruction by an alien culture. *Star Man's Son 2250 A.D.* (1952) portrays the peaceful coexistence of several diverse cultures, one based on scientific expertise, one focused on craft work, and another following the Plains Indians' way of life. This subject was also explored by Le Guin in *Always Coming Home.* Norton's sf series, which often focuses on the growth of young people into wise adults, includes *Central Control* (1953–1955), *Astra* or *Company of Pax* (1954–1957), *Dane Thor-*

son or *Solar Queen* (1955–1969), and *Star Ka'at* (1976–1981), the latter written with Dorothy Madlee specifically for young people. Her young protagonists are often telepathic, especially with animals, whom she treats with affection and respect.

Like other writers affected by the women's movement that began in the 1960s, Norton included strong female characters in her later books. *Judgment on Janus* (Harcourt, Brace and World, 1963) and *Victory on Janus* (Harcourt, Brace and World, 1966) feature a young woman who becomes an alien trapped in a forest-like environment. Ziantha, a female mindreader, is the main protagonist of *Forerunner Foray* (Viking, 1973). Norton's feminism, however, never becomes more radical than portraying women as victims of a patriarchal culture. In the 1960s Norton turned toward fantasy with the Witch World sequence, which takes place on the planet Estcarp, where women rule and good will dominates. Norton's books number over 100; they incorporate information from her readings in anthropology, natural history, archaeology, and psychology. Her popular stories have introduced science fantasy to many young people. Many adults also read her work, especially those books with no age reference on their covers. Quite popular in recent years has been *Golden Trillium* (Bantam, 1993), which describes the Kingdom of Ruwenda, conceived in collaboration with Julian May and Marion Zimmer Bradley, two other women writers of science fiction and fantasy, as part of the Trillium saga. Like *Flight of Vengeance* (cowritten with P. M. Griffin, Tor, 1992) these later works are more intricate, with numerous adventures and richer characterizations. Norton's romantic visions and clean sense of ethics color the exciting adventures she writes with a hopefulness that shines bright against the murkier works of other contemporary writers.

Novelist and playwright Madeleine L'Engle (1918–   ), who sometimes uses her married name, Madeleine L'Engle Camp, also worked as an actress in her twenties. Her first sf novel, *A Wrinkle in Time* (1962), won the 1963 Newbery Medal and the hearts and attention of generations of young readers. L'Engle describes the time travel in her novel as "tesselation," based on a sophisticated theory of physics, but the warmth and nobility of her characters what inspire first-time readers of science fiction to seek more of her works. The story of Meg Murray and her family continues in *A Swiftly Tilting Planet* (1978), *Many Waters* (1986), and *An Acceptable Time* (1989), in which love and personal connection overcome tremendous odds of evil. The Canon Tallis series includes *The Arm of the Starfish* (1965) and *The Young Unicorns* (1968), two international mysteries centering on scientific experimentation, so close to actual current research as to be barely recognizable as science fiction.

Robert O'Brien, aka Robert Lesly Carroll Conly (1922–73), is unusual among sf authors in that he made his reputation as a writer of juvenile literature. *The Silver Crown* (1968) centers around a robotic power that causes a king to kidnap a young girl. *Mrs. Frisby and the Rats of NIMH* (1971), a quaintly told story about laboratory rats that develop superintelligence and finally escape their prison, won a Newbery Medal. *Z for Zachariah* (1975) focuses on two humans who survive the holocaust but cannot manage to live together peaceably, although their cooperation seems necessary to endure the aftermath. The young female protagonist decides that survival is not worth being raped by the other survivor, an unpleasantly aggressive man. The book is disturbing in its sour image of mistrust, even in times of ultimate danger, but it is often cited as a classic science fiction novel for young people.

Monica Hughes (1925–   ) was born in the United Kingdom but lived in Egypt, Scotland, and Southern Rhodesia before settling in Canada at the age of 27 in 1952. Since then she has won awards for her young adult literature, including the Canadian Council Children's Literature Prize in 1982 and 1983. Her works often focus on young protagonists who must struggle to survive and the ultimate personal costs of those efforts. *Crisis on Conshelf Ten* (1975) describes an undersea threat, and *Earthdark* (1977) takes place on the moon. The Isis trilogy, including *The Keeper of the Isis Light* (1980), *The Guardian of Isis* (1981), and *The Isis Pedlar* (1982) is the heartrending story of an orphaned adolescent with only a robot as a companion; for years she yearns for the friendship she imagines possible with other living beings. When humans arrive, she discovers that her reptilian body is repulsive to them, and that they will be unable to survive as a race without her help. The Arc One sequence includes *Devil on My Back* (1984), *The Dream Catcher* (1986), *Sandwriter* (1985), and *The Promise* (1989). In *Invitation to the Game* (1990) a government of the near future exports problem teenagers to an unknown destination, supposedly to quell their complaints about their present environment and get them out of the way. This scenario, similar to the ColSec series by Douglas Hill, might seem justifiable to high school teachers on difficult days, but Hughes describes its chillingly cruel effects on her young protagonists.

An author who does not write specifically for young people but whose works are often very popular with them is Harlan Ellison (1934–   ). His hopeful view of humankind is encouraging; he expects individuals to make a difference on the side of good, even in a world full of evil craziness. A popular example is "A Boy and His Dog," a story (also made into a film) that seems to be the normal mild saga for young people until its shocking end. This prolific writer of sf short stories—collected in *Ellison Wonderland; Deathbird Stories; I Have No Mouth, and I Must Scream; Alone Against Tomorrow;* and *The Beast That Shouted Love at the Heart of the World,* among others—has earned seven Hugo and two Nebula awards, more than anyone else to date. He is best known for his anthologies. *Dangerous Visions* (Doubleday, 1967) and its sequel, *Again, Dangerous Visions* (Doubleday, 1972), are critically acclaimed for their daring suppositions about what is possible to question. Ellison's satire is biting, and his style is dramatic and histrionic, fun to read and easy to understand. He writes trendy stories; his frequent pose of despair for life misspent and for love lost matches current popular country music. His references to traditional classical and Jewish mythology link his work to the conventional roots of Americana. Ellison is as well known as a personality as he is for his writing. He thrives on publicity and will feed his appetite for notoriety by writing in public places like bookstores, pronouncing his views to hordes of listeners. In science fiction circles, "Harlan stories" abound. Though critics and intellectuals tend to scorn his obvious plots and blatant characters, many readers appreciate the easy clarity of his style. His work has inspired many readers to explore other works of science fiction. Booksellers concur that Ellison is a best-seller among young people.

In *House of Stairs* (Dutton, 1974), William Sleator III (1945–   ) paints a chilling picture of a behavior-modification experiment in which adolescents are treated like guinea pigs at the point in their lives when they are the most socially vulnerable, a scenario that also appears in works by Douglas Hill, Orson Scott Card, and H. M. Hoover. Like most of Sleator's later works, this early book focuses on the inability of current Western society to reward individual initiative. *Interstellar Pig* (Dutton, 1984), his most successful book and one that is closer to pure fantasy than the others, captures the fascination of many young people with computer games. It pits a sixteen-year-old boy trying to enjoy a summer at the beach without upsetting his parents against a group of wily, sharp-witted aliens who systematically set out to destroy his peaceful home. Part of this book's popularity can be attributed to its wry, humorous edge. While *Singularity* (1985) is not scientific, the novel's portrayal of the changing relationship between twin brothers, where the younger, weaker twin begins to mature much faster than his older sibling, seems plausible if one accepts the possibility of slips in time. *The Boy Who Reversed Himself* (Dutton, 1986) also explores personal changes through a force independent of time or space. *The Duplicate* (Dutton, 1988) deals with the feeling of being cloned, and *Strange Attractors* (Dutton, 1989) explores the impact of time travel. *The Spirit House* (1991) is an exploration of the Thai sense of reality that accepts spirits as logical and plausible. In all his writing, Sleator focuses more on behavioral sciences than on experimental technology or social sciences, more on character analysis than on setting or plot. He carefully traces the human effects of a scientific phenomenon rather than detailing how or why it might work. This makes his stories more accessible to readers who don't traditionally read science fiction and attractive to mystery lovers who like the unraveling of his plots.

Like the "old masters" of adult science fiction, writers of science fiction for young people attract followers of all ages who hear about their work, read some, and then choose their special allegiances. More than general readers, the science fiction public tends to become deeply attached to particular authors, often getting hooked on a series. They are attracted by the worlds these writers create, their thematic emphasis, their unique style, or all these qualities.

Since the mid-1970s most science fiction works marketed for young people have been moralistic, aiming to persuade their readers to become antiracist, antinuclear, antinationalist, and antipollution. Popular themes in these books are postholocaust scenarios, rebellion against totalitarian societies, universal harmony, and cultural open-mindedness, often exemplified by contact between humans and aliens. Often the conflicts of these books pit gifted, innocent children against power-hungry adults, or ecologists against technocrats. In short, writers and publishers of science fiction seem to be missionaries bent on saving the citizens of the future from continuing the dangerous sins of the present that threaten human life on Earth as we know it. Science fiction as mere entertainment is evolving into literature with a cautionary burden. The most skillful masters of the genre, however, mix their warnings and predictions into the kinds of stories that invigorate the wit and spirit as they nourish the mind with moral imperatives.

3. A New Master: Orson Scott Card

A prolific writer of science fiction as well as drama, essays, and poetry, Orson Scott Card uses his energetic mind to plumb beneath the conventional notions of human behavior. Popular with the most inquisitive young readers of sf, his writings touch many, thrill some, and horrify a few. His sf novels tend to evoke passionate responses, including the highest praise of all: "That book changed my life."

Card's story lines are epic, and his probing character development draws the reader to speculate deeply about human motivations, definitions of good and evil, and the place of the individual in society; yet his work is also highly entertaining and readable. His various sf series include the Worthing saga (Tor, 1989; from stories of 1979), Ender (Tor, beginning 1985), Alvin Maker (Tor, beginning 1987), and Homecoming (Tor, beginning 1992). They build on Card's earlier writings, thus revealing a maturing philosophy. Recurrent themes are the influence of religious discipline, the relation of individuals to their communities, and the specialness of some individuals.

Personal Background

Born on 24 August 1951 in Richland, Washington, Orson Scott Card was the third child of Willard Richards Card, a schoolteacher, and Peggy Jane (Parks) Card, a secretary. They reared Orson as a member of the Church of Jesus Christ of Latter-day Saints, commonly known as Mormonism. After graduating in 1975 from Brigham Young University, Card did graduate work at the University of Utah before beginning his career as a teacher and a writer.

Card's religious training is an important aspect of his writing. He published several plays and various other writings about Mormon culture, including *The Folks on the Fringe* (1989), a sf collection of linked short stories. Card's first story, "Ender's Game," published in *Astounding Science-Fiction* in 1977, was nominated for a Hugo Award and later served as a nucleus for the interplanetary Ender series. As with Frank Herbert, author of the Dune series, much of Card's work is allegorical, cloaking his version of Mormon philosophy in sf metaphors. Card and his family continue to work actively as members of the Mormon church; during the 1970s he served for two years as a missionary in Brazil. Card's Mormon background is evident in the mythic complexity of his plots, the messianic nature of his protagonists, and the moral seriousness of his themes. His attractiveness to young readers may indicate their need for resources deeper than mere information or entertainment.

The Worthing Saga

The saga of Jason Worthing, which builds on the short story "Hot Sleep" (Baronet, 1979) and the stories in *Capitol* (Ace Books, 1979), eventually extends many centuries before and after the protagonist's extremely long life. An extended time span is one of several devices Card uses to give his stories a sense of religious epic. Like the Judeo-Christian Bible, his works stretch over many generations and contain episodes that mark significant events and also hint at other important happenings that occur in between. The first book of the saga, *The Worthing Chronicles,* introduces the telepathic Jason Worthing as he is shipwrecked on a planet. Using the knowledge his special mental ability gives him, he saves the lives of his ship's colonists, whose minds have been numbed to enable them to endure interstellar travel. Unable to restore the memories of his normal peers, Jason sets them up as a primitive society and uses the spaceship's powers to put himself into a life-preserving sleep, waking intermittently over the centuries to guide his fellow colonists as their civilization advances.

An important feature of Card's storytelling is the shifting point of view. The narrative is first told by Jason as he establishes his colony—a typical sf story of superpowers, intergalactic intrigue, and spaceships. Then the narrative shifts to the viewpoint of a newly born colonist, who despite being an adult has no memories of his former life. He puzzles through the basics of living, assuming that Jason is either his father or a god. Already, there is an important rift between the characters involved. The perspective widens as the society becomes bigger, and gradually, individual characters lose importance in the story. Characters who starred as protagonists become mythical to their descendants; Jason, now in hibernation for several centuries, is accepted as a divinity by most of the colonists. As the planet's history is related, what seemed visceral and immediate in the original version becomes conceptualized into myth. The book no longer focuses on individuals but on a social entity. Hidden from the others, Jason takes a wife and forms a family, which prospers until their inbreeding makes it apparent that they must merge into the larger society. Jason's genetic heritage gives the family remarkable powers, and they eventually dominate the planet.

Centuries later Jason's ship is found on the bottom of the sea, and he is awakened from hibernation and asked to judge the world he has helped create. The people of Worthing, having colonized all the planets, now control the universe. Benevolent despots, they heal all wounds and erase the memory of pain. When anyone dies of natural causes, their family's sorrow is softened until it barely exists. It is a universe without suffering.

Jason, still revered as a common ancestor, is dismayed by this turn of events. He argues that people whose lives are completely controlled, even if the intent is to banish suffering, are not really living. Because Jason is defined as God, the people of Worthing accept his judgment as valid and correct. But because they now perceive their lives as without meaning or purpose, they commit suicide on a planetwide scale.

The only people who remain from the original group are Jason and a woman called Justice, the lone dissenter to the decision to commit suicide rather than face pain. These two are left to explain to people of other worlds just why they are experiencing this new sensation called pain. A farmboy still learning to cope with this newfound sensation listens to their story and questions their decision. As a result, Justice decides to continue healing people's wounds but to leave their memories and fears intact.

The Worthing saga raises important questions about the assumption that cessation of pain is a worthy goal. Can one appreciate the joys of life without pain? Is life without pain possible . . . or desirable? These questions are also examined by Lois Lowry in *The Giver*.

The Ender Series

The Ender series begins with Card's most popular works, *Ender's Game* (1985) and *Speaker for the Dead* (1986), both winners of the Hugo and Nebula awards, followed by *Xenocide* (1991) and *Children of the Mind* (1996). *Ender's Game* focuses on the educational development of its protagonist, Ender Wiggin, before his life spreads out to encompass a community of characters. Ender Wiggin is a third child during a time when the government has imposed strict population controls, allowing a family only two children under normal circumstances. The government has sanctioned Ender's birth, however, because various factors lead it to believe that he could become the great military leader needed to defeat the alien Buggers, who had been conquered decades earlier only by chance and continue to pose a threat. Ender's education takes place in an orbiting station called the Battle School. Although Ender's two siblings share his intelligence, both have been denied admission. The eldest child, Peter, was deemed far too harsh to succeed as a leader, and the second child, Valentine, too compassionate, but in Ender the adult supervisors find a perfect combination of both siblings. A main motif of this series is Ender's constant struggle to live his life according to an idealized image of his sister, Valentine, whom he contrasts to the monster he sees in his older brother.

In a telling early scene, Ender tries to prevent further abuse from a school bully by defeating him so completely that the bully is afraid to attack again. Ender's cold calculation is tempered by a fierce compassion; after winning the battle, he cries. Ender's ability to manipulate people coupled with a lack of ambition for power destines him to become a great leader. As the story progresses, the extent to which Ender's life is being engineered by behind-the-scenes adult manipulators becomes chillingly clear. Ender's confrontation with the bully is just one of the ways he is being tested, isolated from other children, and challenged, often at great physical risk to himself. He responds with amazing resourcefulness, constantly achieving the impossible. Soon he becomes the leader of a squad of 40 children, who are pitted against each other in strategic battle games in zero gravity. Although the odds for winning are stacked against Ender by the mysterious supervisors, he perseveres, inventing new strategies and finding unimaginable strengths in himself.

But the stress is terrible. To relieve his mind, Ender becomes addicted to a game of artificial intelligence that is rigged to test the player's courage and drive; the last child who shared Ender's compulsion for the game eventually committed suicide. When Ender finally defeats the game with an utterly vicious move, it shocks him and the supervisors to the core. Yet still the adults drive the young man. The game adapts, and Ender finds himself in a whole new virtual world. In his real world he loses all of his friends when he is made their commander. He is physically attacked by a jealous rival in a battle reminiscent of his fight with his schoolyard nemesis, and when he uses violence to defend himself, he is again haunted by the fear of becoming his brother, Peter. Now, instead of engaging in the childhood games of his early education, he will be pitted against the Buggers, the enemy of the planet.

In what he thinks is a virtual reality game, a fantasy engineered by his mentor to simulate future battles against the Buggers, Ender finally overcomes the enemy, despite the bizarre nightmares of guilt that disturb his sleep during this time. In a final "virtual" battle, Ender sends all his ships on a suicide run that destroys the enemy planet. Tired of playing the violent war games that cause him so much guilt, he uses this strategy to retaliate against his adult teachers for the immense pressure they have imposed on him as part of his military training. He thinks he has destroyed their game.

When he discovers the authorities celebrating, however, he realizes he has not been playing a game. He really has sent the fleet to its destruction, dooming an entire intelligent species to extinction. The troubling dreams have actually been telepathic communications from the Buggers, who are trying to negotiate with Ender to prevent further attacks and formulate peace. The Buggers' first "invasion" had been a cultural misunderstanding. Organized as a "hive mind," the species is a collective consciousness that views individual lives and deaths as unimportant events, on a level with toenail clippings. Their first attack, which humans viewed as the merciless destruction of life, was just an indication of the Buggers' natural curiosity about another species, a mere lab experiment involving some dissection. As Ender's ship approached the Buggers and they realized their danger, they had tried to extend their consciousness to Ender through nightmares. Ender's "virtual reality game" thus had real consequences. At the end of the book, Ender finds an unhatched Bugger Queen, the repository of the Buggers' cultural memory. Saving her will rescue their race from extinction, but it will preserve a terrible threat to the human race. Ender must decide whether to endanger the humans who have been training him all his life, or to retain his self-respect.

Ender's rigorous education depends not on a single event marking his "coming of age" but on a series of smaller exercises that mercilessly test his ability to thrive by adapting to new knowledge and new experiences. Those who fail to adapt, fail. Ender succeeds because he is more imaginative, more persistent, and fiercer than the others. He learns to examine his own strengths and weaknesses as well as those of his enemies and is ruthlessly honest in his assessment of both. To win the confrontations that Ender thinks are training games, he learns to strike early and viciously, but he also learns the heartbreaking consequences. He is an empathetic killer. He knows his enemies well enough to realize that none are completely evil, merely misunderstood. Ender's exquisite sensitivity to the pains of others is his curse. Never does he forget the intense embarrassment and pain caused by his older brother's cruelty and his friends' teasing. The pathos of this book is Ender's anguish in realizing his greatest fear: in the process of inflicting such agony on his victim, he has become just like his brother, Peter. Ender mourns both the loss of his own innocence and the lost lives of those he kills. The clarity of his vision about the evil he has done is more painful than any other hurt he has ever suffered.

To atone, Ender becomes Speaker for the Dead, traveling from planet to planet with his sister, Valentine, writing and speaking about the people who have died, particularly the alien Buggers, and explaining their lives. At first his brutal honesty shocks his audiences, but his stories are so compelling that a sort of humanist religion evolves, with Ender as an anonymous participant. As a result of Ender's confessional writing, the public, unaware of Ender's identity as Speaker for the Dead, condemn him for his destruction of the Bugger civilization and laud Peter, whom Ender has forgiven and whose actions he has justified in his writing.

The second volume, *Speaker for the Dead* (1986), extends the story of Ender Wiggin, who has traveled the planets with his sister for several thousand years spreading a gospel of tolerance toward alien races and forgiveness through understanding. Through the effects of faster-than-light travel, neither sibling has aged beyond 30. Now humanity encounters another intelligent alien species. Largely because of Ender's teachings as the Speaker for the Dead, most of humanity decides they have been given a second chance, a way to repent for the xenocide Ender has committed. Because of the aliens' porcine appearance and bestial behavior, the humans nickname them "Piggies," a term of derision also used in other literary works by humans who underestimate the intelligence and innate worth of others. Despite the generous intentions of human nature, the cultures clash, and several deaths occur. Once again Ender is called upon to intervene. Soon he finds himself defending the aliens from the humans' fleet of ships. This crisis extends for the three books that conclude Card's original plan for the Ender series.

In this volume Card explores the complex realization that understanding a foreign culture will bring about tolerance and reduce fear and violence. Using the pseudonym Demosthenes, Ender's sister, Valentine, establishes a hierarchy of types of alien groups to use as an ethical basis for human reactions toward them. Her distinctions are based not so much on biological differences as on how well the comprehension between two beings can evolve. A stranger from another land, an *utlanning* in Valentine's typology, can eventually be understood, though cultural conflicts may at times cause misunderstandings leading to war. War is inevitable, however, with the completely alien *ramen*, whose behavior and values are totally incomprehensible to humans. The premise of these books is that humans must determine which species are merely foreign and which are altogether alien.

This task is complicated by the number of species involved. Ender has been carrying with him the Bugger Queen embryo, with which he regularly communicates telepathically and for whom he is seeking a new home. He knows that humanity, regardless of its goodwill, is not ready to accept the return of the insectlike Buggers. Another alien species, with only one member, is an artificial intelligence that lives in the communications network between planets and calls herself Jane. Communicating with Ender through a small jewel in his ear, Jane joins in trying to stop the starship fleet that threatens the Piggies, though her efforts endanger her own existence. When humans do learn about Jane, they plan to shut down all computers in order to destroy her. Danger to the universe mounts. While these species plan attacks and defenses of each other, another threat arises, a disease that may destroy the whole colony. Then a biologist discovers that the bacteria themselves may be intelligent; they may have caused the Piggies to evolve into a species with enough intelligence to speak. The mixture of ethical and pragmatic decisions that confront everyone becomes ludicrously complex, though not unlike real life. Some critics have complained that the end of the third book, *Xenocide* (1991), wraps up the story too easily to be credible. Readers demanded that Card continue the story.

In the latest book of the Ender saga, *Children of the Mind* (1996), Peter and Valentine, who reappear as children through Ender's accidental cloning of his brother's and sister's remains, help save the planet Lusitania and its three racial groups from destruction by the Starways Congress. Jane, a sentient artificial intelligence with her own charm, transcends the light–speed barrier to assist. This novel delves deeply into the relationships between people, aliens, and the warring sides of Ender himself. Is this the end? A number of profound questions about the characters and their motivations remain to justify yet another sequel for Card's admiring readers. However, at least one fan of Card protests: "No way—Ender dies. It's very powerful. Card wouldn't dare!"

Ender's Game and its immediate sequel, *Speaker for the Dead,* were highly acclaimed by some critics for the impact of their language and for their antiracist message: "[*Ender's Game*] is direct, real, bedded in military ruthlessness and military values. It's the best sf 'military academy' novel I've ever read."[1] "*Ender's Game* and *Speaker for the Dead* succeed equally as straightforward SF adventure and as allegorical, analogical disquisitions on humanity, morality, salvation, and redemption . . . ; both novels are compelling simply as psychological studies of strong characters. Both are highly recommended for readers interested in the cultural complexities and ambiguity the best science fiction novels explore."[2]

Elaine Radford's review, however, raised a tempest of critical controversy by comparing Ender to Adolph Hitler:

> Let me tell you about a book I just read. It's the story of a young boy who was dreadfully abused by the grown-ups who wanted to mold him into an exemplary citizen. Forced to suppress his own emotions in order to avoid being paralyzed by trauma, he directed his energy into duty rather than sex or love. In time, he came to believe that his primary duty was to wipe out a species of gifted but incomprehensible aliens who had devastated his kind in a previous war. He found the idea of exterminating an

entire race distasteful, of course. But since he believed it was required to save the people he defined as human, he put his entire weight of his formidable energy behind the effort to wipe out the aliens.

You've read it, you say? It's *Ender's Game* by Orson Scott Card, right?

Wrong. The aliens I'm talking about were the European Jews, blamed by many Germans for gearing up World War I for their own profit. The book is Robert G. L. Waite's *The Psychopathic God: Adolf Hitler.*[3]

After noting the parallel incidents in the lives of Hitler and Ender, Radford accuses Card of exonerating Hitler by creating a sympathetic character who commits genocide: "Look at the fact that the Fuhrer was sincere and re-defined his life as dedicated rather than evil. Forgive Hitler? Card, from your privileged position as a white male American Christian, you have no right to ask us that" (Radford, 49).

In an impassioned and thoughtful response, Card asserts that a careful reading of his work refutes Radford's accusations, and most of Card's readers agree.[4] Ender, unlike Hitler, does not initiate the war games, and his enforced involvement is self-aware and anguished, qualities one does not sense in Hitler. As a talented wordsmith, however, Card wields great power with his exquisite use of language, and his depiction of the problem of power and violence has disturbed other critics and readers.

The sequels to the first two books of the Ender series received less-enthusiastic acclaim, not because they weren't good fiction but because they weren't as excellent: "At best, *Children of the Mind* would be a slightly better than average novel by an average science fiction writer. But Card is not just an average science fiction writer; he is very good, as his earlier Hugo and Nebula Award winning *Ender's Game* and *Speaker for the Dead* show. As a sequel to these brilliant novels, *Children of the Mind* is mediocre."[5] The Ender series is controversial precisely because it is such a powerful stimulus for critical thinking about the nature of humanity and about our cultural responses to those instincts.

The Alvin Maker Series

Another series focuses on tales about the powerful Alvin Maker and includes *Seventh Son* (1987); *Red Prophet* (1988); *Prentice Alvin* (1989); *Alvin Journeyman* (1995), winner of the Locus Award for best fantasy novel; and *The Crystal City* (in progress). It is set in a colonial North America as it might have existed had Native American Indians continued their traditions in a country where the American Revolution never happened. (Followers of this series can join an online community on the Internet: http://www.hatrack.com.)

This America is a world where folk magic really works. The story focuses on Alvin, born the seventh son of a seventh son, a mystically significant situation confirmed by Alvin's magical powers, which earn him the surname Maker.

Alvin learns the dangers of his powers at a young age. After his sisters play a prank on him by putting needles in his pajamas, Alvin seeks revenge by "convincing" cockroaches to terrorize the girls. However, in a mystical experience he is visited by Lolla-Wissiky, the Indian brother of Tecumseh, who demonstrates how Alvin is causing pain to the innocent cockroaches, a species as sentient as humans. Horrified, Alvin swears to use his powers only for the good of others. To assuage his guilt and to express his gratitude, he begins his good works by healing Lolla-Wissiky of alcoholism and enabling the Indian to become Red Prophet, the protagonist of the second book in the series. Alvin's powers attract a mentor named Taleswapper, Card's representation of the poet William Blake, who convinces Alvin to use his powers to "re-Make" himself, changing his original oath and swearing to use his powers against the "Unmaker," an evil entity that is the great threat to all that is good. So Alvin swears to become a "Maker," an enemy of all that is not good. As he matures, he realizes that he must find a teacher who will help him discover exactly what a Maker does.

In the second book of the series, *Red Prophet,* Alvin ventures forth to discover his identity. In this novel Card explores tensions between white settlers and the Indian population. Local politicians stir up hatred toward the Indians; one actually hires men to impersonate Indians and kill some local white boys. Alvin gets caught in the middle but survives the experience and becomes "apprenticed" to Tecumseh, the great Indian leader. The white settlers, however, are fooled by the ruse and end up participating in a large slaughter at the Indian town of Tippy Canoe. Tecumseh's pacifist brother, the Red Prophet, forces the settlers to atone for their mistake by confessing it to any stranger who happens by, or else their hands will be covered in blood.

In this book, which is more mystical than the first in the series, Alvin learns much about himself and the art of Making from his mentors Tecumseh and the Red Prophet. He decides his final mission as a Maker will be to create the Crystal City, made up of all races of people working and living as one. Fortunately, Alvin is apprenticed to a blacksmith to learn skills that prove quite useful in his mission.

The third book, *Prentice Alvin,* tells of Alvin's jealous master and of the girl with special powers who devotes her life to teaching Alvin how to be a Maker. It is also a story of slave trading, and Alvin's dealings with a young black boy named Arthur Stuart who has escaped slavery make him many enemies. A judgmental preacher who has condemned Alvin's powers of folk magic joins with a Southern plantation owner to plot Alvin's destruction. Meanwhile, Alvin develops his powers, testing them to end his apprenticeship by making an automated golden plow from ordinary steel, a first step toward creating the Crystal City. His master tries to claim the gold, but Alvin refuses to surrender the plow. Meanwhile, slave traders have tracked down Alvin's young friend, but when they use their powers to determine that he is in the town, Alvin uses his to change the boy's genetic structure so they no longer can recognize him. The slave traders die, but not before they kill the boy's mother, Peggy Guester. Alvin returns with the boy to his hometown and tries to use what he has learned to teach others. Here the fourth book, *Alvin Journeyman,* begins.

Having made many enemies, Alvin is eventually brought to trial for the death of the slave trader who killed Peggy Guester.

He is also accused of stealing the golden plow he had created. Ultimately he clears himself of these charges and continues to pursue his dream of building the Crystal City.

The fifth book, *The Crystal City,* still in progress, promises by virtue of its title to bring together the threads of this story, which by now have become a rich tapestry on the level of the folklore that it imitates. The story of this series was inspired by an epic poem that Card first published in 1981 entitled "Prentice Alvin and the No-Good Plow."

The Homecoming Series

In the Homecoming series, Card again explores the mythical and religious aspects of creating a global society with a single totalitarian government. In the first volume, *The Memory of Earth* (1992), a planet of settlers originally from Earth decide to prevent global self-destruction by surrounding their planet with a system of manned satellites that prevents any country from starting war. This warless society creates wonderful technology but is forever inhibited by the satellites from space travel and even air flight. Eventually the people forget the purpose of the satellite system and start worshiping them as the Oversoul. Failing to maintain an educational structure that transmits knowledge of the past, they lose the technical knowledge base to sustain the military and industrial superstructures of their forebears. The global technology of the past becomes mythology. Just as Europeans of the early medieval period forgot how to replicate the architecture and plumbing of classical Greek civilization and relegated faint memories of these wonders to mere story, the characters of Card's tale allegorize their own distant history.

The plot of the second and third novels of the series, *The Call of Earth* (1992) and *The Ships of the Earth* (1994), unfolds the story in the present tense as the Oversoul is leading a group of people who build a spaceship and travel to Earth. Once there, the group hopes to find an ancient being known as "Keeper of Earth," who will give them further instructions. The main protagonist is Nafai, a talented young boy who gradually accepts more responsibility for the mission as he matures. His older brother, Elemak, chafing at Nafai's reputation for righteousness, reacts by discrediting the Oversoul and everything that Nafai values.

Earthfall (1995) relates how the group reaches Earth and sets up a primitive society in order to survive while they await further instructions from the Oversoul. The settlers discover two intelligent races on Earth—the aggressive earth-dwelling Diggers and the Angels, a smaller race with a limited ability to fly. The colonists try to live peaceably with these remnants of genetic experiments engineered by the ancient human race, but Elemak's jealousy interferes. He joins with the warlike Diggers and declares war on the colonists, now led by his brother, Nafai.

In *Earthborn* (1995) Nafai decides, partially at the Oversoul's direction, to keep a record of all that has transpired. He wants to insure that his story, and the true story of his people, is preserved through the generations. But since his children are not interested in learning to read—a skill that has little practical use in this primitive society without books—Nafai worries about their ability to understand. He creates two separate documents, both written on metal. One version relates the complete story, with complicated details. This he hides away for future generations. The other Nafai tells in the simplest terms possible, even creating a new method of writing to make the tablets easier to decode. He begins a tradition of teaching the oldest son in each family how to read this simple script.

Like the Worthing chronicles, the Homecoming series progresses from an individual point of view to a mythic saga of settling a planet. The Cain and Abel story of Nafai and Elemak and the division of their descendants into different cultures adds a more complicated dimension. Like Jason Worthing, Nafai is deified when he uses special knowledge to help his people change. When the Oversoul presents him with the Starmaster's Cloak, imparting knowledge of technology, some of the more superstitious inhabitants of the planet elevate him to a godlike status. The magic disappears, however, when the cloak is passed on to another original settler who is less involved with Earth.

In this epic tale describing the history of a culture, Card again draws a great number of parallels to biblical stories. In the last volume of this series, the descendants of the original settlers uncover evidence that they are not the first group to return to Earth. Previous groups have failed to live in peace with the other races and have disappeared or self-destructed. Theorizing a time of great trial, these descendants struggle to come to terms with each other and with their new knowledge. In their attempts to improve themselves, they realize that the attempt to live peaceably is all that is humanly possible. Card sums up this philosophy in a dialogue between a racist king who regrets his former habits and his mentor: "I want to change my heart, and I don't know how," confesses the king. The comforting advice he is given could apply to us all: "Wanting to is the whole lesson, all the rest is practice" (300). The mission to find the Keeper of the Earth and fulfill his orders to the Oversoul is completed as the people examine their morality and strive to live peaceably.

Card continues to examine the implications of alternate history and time travel in his most recent science fiction, the Mayflower books. In *Pastwatch: The Redemption of Christopher Columbus* (1996), scientists try to alter history by traveling back to Columbus's time and changing the motivation for his journey from profit seeking to peaceful coexistence.

Like many other authors of science fiction, Card also explores the boundaries of fantasy, as in *Treasure Box* (1996). The novel starts as a romance between self-made millionaire Quentin Fears and his lovely fiancée, Madeleine, but soon slides spookily into a ghost story. This example of Card's work outside of sf focuses on subtle character development as Quentin tries to decide to what degree the elusive personality of his new wife is related to the early loss of his beloved sister.

Card's moral message is that gifted individuals bear the burden of living responsibly for the sake of their community, that one person and his or her followers can make a difference. His work exemplifies the best of that type of science fiction written to teach. Didactic science fiction, often intended for an audience of young people, can be preachy and self-righteous. Card's work isn't. His characters are endearing because he details their faults and their heroic virtues with sensitivity and honesty. His plots move quickly and contain intelligent surprises that stretch the reader's critical imagination and allow the reader to delve deeply into the issues he explores. His work inspires the intense examination of basic ethical and cultural habits, which many believe is necessary to preserve our planet through the twentieth-first century. Even readers who do not agree with all facets of his philosophic outlook are impressed with the scope and depth of the conversation he instigates in his works.

The popularity of Orson Scott Card continues to grow, especially among his young followers. His work is available to many on the Internet site named Hatrack, cited previously. In early 1997 Fresco Pictures bought the film rights to the entire collection of works by Card, beginning with *Ender's Game* and including the romantic ghost short stories "Homebody" (1997), and "Feed the Baby" (1997), about a singer looking for new inspiration after a long career that's getting tired.[6] Can Card's fictions, especially the compelling tales of Ender, be translated into film versions that will match the books' soul-shivering power and appeal? His devoted fans must wait and see.

Card is a teacher as much as a writer, practicing his craft through speeches to various organizations, in lively correspondence on the World Wide Web, and in the classes he teaches about literature and writing at a college in North Carolina.

Chronology: Orson Scott Card

1951   Born 24 August in Richland, Washington, to Willard R. and Peggy Jane (Parks) Card; reared according to Mormon church discipline.

1975   Receives B.A. at Brigham Young University, followed by graduate study at the University of Utah.

1977   Short story "Ender's Game" nominated for Hugo Award.

1985   Ender series begins with publication of *Ender's Game,* which wins the Hugo and Nebula awards.

1986   *Speaker for the Dead,* second book of the series, is published and wins Hugo and Nebula awards.

1987   Alvin Maker series begins with publication of *Seventh Son.*

1989   Fictions closely reflecting Mormon history, *The Worthing Chronicles* and *The Folks on the Fringe,* are published.

1992   Homecoming series begins with publication of *The Memory of Earth.*

1996   Mayflower series begins with publication of *Pastwatch: The Redemption of Christopher Columbus.*

4. Science Fiction Adventure: Douglas Hill

The science fiction adventure story is an important subgenre of science fiction, scorned as superficial and second-rate by most literary critics but slurped up in enthusiastic gulps by devoted readers. It's the stuff that spawned early writers and fed the initial popularity of the field. Space operas kept science fiction alive in magazines until it reached maturity in radio, television, film, and pulp fiction.

The author of science fiction adventure gets his hero into trouble and then saves him using hard science, giving a modern twist to the tradition of heroic literature. The use of technology and science, however, cannot disguise the characteristic features of the ancient quest. Like his literary predecessors, the hero, most often male, is brave, courageous, and bold, venturing from the safety of his childhood on a mission to protect the homefront or to capture a treasure. Whatever his purpose, his way is fraught with danger, excitement, and challenge. In this type of literature, the plot is fast-paced, suspenseful, and geared toward action rather than contemplation, achievement rather than relationship. Winning is all. The best of heroic fiction captures the imagination immediately and races off from crisis to crisis, always building up to the triumphant denouement when the hero miraculously jumps over all obstacles to make the world neat and right. The works of Douglas Arthur Hill (1935–   ) exemplify the attractions of science fiction adventure for young people.

From Canada to London

Born in Brandon, Canada, a town in the province of Manitoba, Hill was raised in the backwoods of Prince Albert, Saskatchewan. "Its main claim to fame," he says in an interview cited at the end of his ColSec series, "is that it's the second coldest town in North America." Dark woods, mysterious and foreboding in winter, broad grassy plains glinting with sun and wind in summer: these landscapes of Hill's youth reappear in his writing, along with the bleak, rocky deserts of the planets he invents. As a boy he loved his home; exploring the forests and fields, he undoubtedly exercised his imagination and developed his storytelling skills. In school he read traditional literature, learning the values and literary patterns of Western culture; an attentive student, he excelled academically. Perhaps he also learned the excitement of travel from his father, William, a locomotive engineer, and the techniques and wonders of science from his mother, Cora, who worked as a nurse. As an adolescent, Hill began to imagine life beyond the woods and plains of his home. "I was a dreamer. I devoured science fiction. Flash Gordon and Buck Rogers were comic strips in the newspapers in those days, and I read every one."[1] At any rate, Hill imbibed the lore of science fiction as well as the heroic adventure stories recommended in school. His interest in literature and his writing talents helped him earn a B.A. degree with honors in English from the University of Saskatchewan, Saskatoon, in 1957. He pursued further studies for the next two years at the University of Toronto, and during this time he met Gail Robinson, a fellow author and a poet. They married in 1958, produced one son, Michael Julian, but divorced 20 years later, in 1978.

Immediately after leaving the University of Toronto, Hill moved to London and began his career as a freelance writer. From 1962 until 1964 he worked as an editor for Aldus Books and began reviewing science fiction for the London *Tribune*. Soon he became a leading critic of science fiction in the British press; at the same time he was establishing himself as a writer. Hill's first publications were nonfictional histories, but the subjects he chronicled were not always the kind usually included in history textbooks. His first published book was *The Supernatural* (Aldus, 1965; Hawthorn, 1966), an overview of otherworldly phenomena written with Pat Williams, and his second, *The Opening of the Canadian West* (Heinemann, 1967; Day, 1967), recounted European settlement. Books written by Hill in the same vein as *The Supernatural* include *Magic and Superstition* (Hamlyn, 1968); *Fortune Telling* (Hamlyn, 1970); and *Return from the Dead* (Macdonald, 1970, written under the pen name Martin Hillman), reprinted in New York as *The History of Ghosts, Vampires, and Werewolves* (Harrow, 1973). He also edited *Warlocks and Warriors* (Mayflower, 1971). Many of his adult novels are historical surveys of British and Canadian subjects, including *John Keats* (Morgan Grampian, 1968), *Regency London* (Macdonald, 1969), *The Scots to Canada* (Gentry, 1972), and *The English to New England* (Gentry, 1975). Under the name Martin Hillman he edited and contributed to *Bridging a Continent* (Aldus, 1971; Reader's Digest Association, 1978, 1979). Prolific, knowledgeable, and talented, Hill has also edited several anthologies of history, supernatural tales, and science fiction and has written many children's books, fantasies, nonfiction magazine articles, book reviews, and poems for a wide variety of publications. In an interview for *Contemporary Authors,* Hill claims to work "an eight-day week and a twenty-five-hour day" to accomplish the wide variety of writing projects that keep him afloat as an author, "the best way to live and to earn a living that I know" (300). He is a busy man content in his choice of work.

Creating Science Fiction:
The Last Legionary Series (1979–1983)

Since 1980 Hill has focused mostly on science fiction for young adults, the genre for which he is best known. As early as 1966 Hill used his extensive expertise in science fiction to advise several publishing houses in succession, helping to select stories and themes for anthologies. He began publishing the first of his three series of science fiction adventures in 1979.

The Last Legionary series of five books focuses on one hero's search for the evil force that has already destroyed one planet and threatens the peaceful coexistence of others in a futuristic galaxy where humans, some of them slightly mutated, have set up colonies after the destruction of Earth. The series includes *Galactic Warlord* (Gollancz, 1979; Atheneum, 1980), *Deathwing over Veynaa* (Gollancz, 1980; Atheneum, 1981), *Day of the Starwind* (Gollancz, 1980; Atheneum, 1981), *Planet of the Warlord* (Gollancz, 1981; Atheneum, 1982), and *Young Legionary: The Earlier Adventures of Keill Randor* (Gollancz, 1982; Atheneum, 1983). The hero of these books, Keill Randor, is the last surviving member of the extraordinary legion of warriors from the planet Moros, a barren world with a harsh climate and few natural resources to support any but the hardiest of people. These inhabitants, grown strong and tough to survive and realizing that their skills are their only marketable natural resource, develop a race of extremely disciplined and self-reliant soldiers expert in a wide variety of martial arts. Over the years, these folk have quickened their reflexes and honed their muscles, making them legendary throughout the galaxy for their physical control and fighting skills. The inhabitants of Moros are also highly ethical. Refusing to use their strength and military expertise either to exploit or to overpower weaker people, they contract themselves as defenders of the righteous against aggression. They are the galaxy's protection against an imbalance of power. In recent history, however, a growing number of inexplicable wars have arisen, starting up suddenly in places that had been peaceable for centuries. The galaxy seems to be bubbling with trouble. At the beginning of this series, the planet Moros has just been destroyed by a mysterious force that not even the sophisticated military devices on these planets can detect. The only survivor is Keill Randor, whose ship has barely escaped the sweeping rays of radiation so swiftly and unexpectedly administered by ships attacking seemingly from nowhere. Randor escapes only because he happens to be in the last ship returning from a minor foray to investigate a report of violence. At the last minute, a recorded message from the pilot of the ship ahead of him warns him to turn back from approaching

Moros; this voice of his best friend, Oni, saves Randor's life and asks him to avenge the murder of his people. Although Randor has not been murdered outright with the rest of his people, he has received enough radiation from the outskirts of the planet's atmosphere that his bones ache, and he knows his life will not last much longer. Determined to use the remainder of his time to fulfill the last request of his friend, he eventually exacts vengeance on the murderer of his countrymen.

One problem in an adventure series is how to provide the necessary background information to the new reader of an individual book without boring those who are familiar with the hero's adventures from previous books. While some novelists use headnotes, Hill captures the reader's attention by flinging him or her into the middle of the action. The first three or four pages are dramatic and packed with crisis. When we first meet Keill Randor in the first book of the series, *Galactic Warlord,* he is walking along the tawdry streets of a planet foreign to him as he pursues his mission of revenge, trying to ignore the anguished loneliness of his mind and the terrible pain of his bones, weakened and wracked by the same radiation that killed the rest of his planet. Outwardly stone-faced and icily calm, he is desperately angry as he stalks the most recent feeble clue he has wrenched from an informant, about the possible whereabouts of other survivors from his planet. Just as he thinks he is about to succeed, he is drugged by a needle thrown from behind and is kidnapped and taken away to another planet. We learn about the history of Moros and its destruction in the second chapter through the dreams Randor has while he is drugged.

When he wakes up to find himself trapped in a strange room, Randor begins invisible exercises to retrain his muscles and tendons, carefully observing his whereabouts while exerting the extraordinary self-control his training as a Legionary of Moros has instilled in him. This ability to calm the impulses of fear and anger and to focus physical and mental strengths into carefully considered actions is the key to the Legionary's success. More wiry than large in bulk, Randor, like his fellow countrymen, has undergone lengthy training in stretching and developing his muscles to become a supremely quick and knowledgeable fighter. He is the epitome of the kind of fighter admired in judo and karate—always alert, controlled, and aware of his surroundings. Now, however, unable to find an escape, he confronts his captors, who claim to be on his side, pursuing the same enemy he is searching for. These hooded benefactors, who call themselves the Overseers, are the wise men of the galaxy who have come together because of their growing concern over the increase in gratuitous violence springing up on the planets. Led by Talis, they claim to have replaced Randor's irradiated bones with an unbreakable steel skeleton to keep him alive and able to carry out the mission that is both his and theirs. As befits a lifetime warrior, Randor is suspicious, but having no other choice, he accepts the mission as well as the mind-reading alien Glr, who is sent to accompany him. During his battle against the giant Thr'un, a mutant creature girded with fleshy ridges that sprout leathery protective tentacles, Randor learns that the Overseers had told the truth about the strength of his new bones, and about the existence of an evil force, a tightly organized army called Deathwing that is controlled by a mysterious warlord called the One. *Galactic Warlord* describes how Keill Randor learns to trust the Overseers and to accept the friendship of Glr, the alien from Ehrlil. This alliance against the evil Deathwing and the Galactic Warlord is the basis for the plots of the next three books in the series.

Deathwing over Veynaa begins as Randor, posing as a wandering mercenary wrecked on a foreign planet, meets Joss and Groll, two armed humans who take him to the council of their Cluster. Groll, as befits his name, is a large, grumbling giant who glowers at Randor, jealous of his skills and the apparent admiration of Joss, one of the few human women in this series (Glr is referred to as "her" but is also identified as an alien). In fact, of the three major female characters in this series, the first two appear in this book. Joss, an attractive woman, uses her dark eyes to flirt with Randor while retaining the cool, competent intelligence that earns his respect. The other female member of the council is the large, forthright Shalet, whose leadership arises from her plain-spoken honesty about the facts as she sees them. The Cluster, once a settlement of miners from the planet Veynaa, has recently begun to suspect the Veynaan government of treachery and has declared war; the leader of this war is a recent arrival, Quern, whose influence over the council is now supreme. The unnaturally tall albino Quern has developed a new weapon that he uses to reassure the leaders of the Cluster of their safety, a machine he is eager to test. He alone of the council distrusts Randor, binding him in a body shackle that would crush anyone else. However, the unbreakable bones provided by the Overseers allow him to escape relatively unharmed. Randor's uneasiness about Quern is echoed by the reaction of Glr, whose telepathic messages suddenly disappear. When she reconnects with his mind, she tells him that Quern, also telepathic, has such evil in his mind that she finds it necessary to shield Randor by cutting off communication with the Legionary when Quern is near. When a satellite containing over two hundred Veynaans is destroyed in the same way that Randor's home planet Moros was blown up, Randor no longer doubts that Quern is an agent of the Deathwing, the military arm of the Galactic Warlord. In the terrible struggles that follow, Randor learns that Joss may be pretty but is not as good a friend as Shalet. He also realizes how much he depends on Glr for companionship and how deeply he has come to care for her. The six-armed robot that almost succeeded in disabling Randor at the beginning of the book reappears in an ironic scene that would have the audience cheering if it were on film. At the end, all is almost well, though the Deathwing has escaped again and the Warlord has still not been met.

A raid on the unsuspecting planet Jitrell seems pointless, except to the Overseers, who connect this attack with other instances of unprovoked aggression throughout the galaxy as one more sign of the Warlord's plan to take over. So begins *Day of the Starwind,* in which Randor and his sidekick Glr continue to pursue the power-hungry murderer who is plaguing the galaxy. Their spaceship lands in a cave that is haunted by wormlike monsters; the claustrophobic space drives Glr, a creature of the light, away. She will help our hero from afar as he explores the central tower that rises so boldly on this empty land. Because of the starwind, the tremendously destructive winds brought by the wake of a star whose orbit periodically brings it close to the planet, the colonists have been forced to develop an underground culture. The tower has been built recently, with a force field around it designed to protect it from the starwind, which is approaching. Randor finds that the tower houses the planet's master power, a golden cyborg whose huge metallic body is not even dented by the Legionary's most focused blows. Randor is repulsed by the flesh-puffed face with its small, twisted features. He is more horrified when the monster reveals that he is the One, Altern, the Warlord, who now holds Randor in his power and whose tower is now swaying in the throes of the terrible starwind.

In this volume, there are no women characters who disappoint our hero like the disloyal Joss or the earnest but rather simplistic Shalet. Here, Randor is mentally tortured by clones that look like his former companions on Moros and remind him of the friendships he has lost. These mirror images, however, resemble the Legionaries only in their skills; they are no friends. Fortunately, one friendly human, Tam, assists Randor when Glr is unavailable and sustains Randor's faith in the goodness of humanity as he faces the horrible, evil power of the archenemy of the galaxy. As in the other books, it is the alien Glr who saves Randor from certain death in the final harrowing scene; again, their partnership proves equally symbiotic, for without Randor's physical strength and military training, Glr's telepathic powers have no focus.

Planet of the Warlord (Gollancz, 1981; Atheneum, 1982), purportedly the last volume of the Legionary series, opens at the annual Battle Games of Banthei as Randor, ashamed of this show of bravado, is preparing to end his misery by swiftly defeating the other contestants. Participating in these games was not customary for the Legionaries of Moros, for they were too earnest about their fighting skills to want to display them except to maintain peace or defend against aggression. But Randor is showing off his skills as part of a trap, a snare to draw out the One, the enemy of the Galaxy.. Sure enough, Randor is kidnapped from the arena. Gassed into unconsciousness, he wakes up on a new planet called

Golvic and is taken to the center of a huge, sprawling city. The technology he sees and experiences on the way to the central building amazes him, including the diabolical body shackle that tightens with his every movement of resistance. Again, he faces Altern, the cyborg with the external skeleton of golden metal. But his most disturbing discovery is the draining impact of the Warlord, a technological life-support system that sucks out the mental energy of 24 enslaved experts to provide energy for the enclosed system. The center of all the Galactic evil is called Arachnis, the Greek word for spider. Keill Randor becomes the vassal of this cyborg, forced by the machine to train Golvician soldiers in the skills he learned as a Legionary and to hunt down his telepathic ally, Glr. In a truly horrible dilemma, Randor's strengths are turned against his mentor Talis as well as his friend Glr, and the heroes must almost kill each other to save themselves. The close bonds that enable them to communicate across vast spaces are manipulated by the enemy so that each of the former allies cannot trust the other, or themselves. The final battle is long and complex, but ultimately Glr and Randor destroy evil and save Talis. After the hard-won victory, however, Randor is depressed. Having fulfilled the last request of his childhood friend Oni by avenging the destruction of his home planet, Moros, he no longer has a mission to drive him; his life now has no purpose. However, Talis and Glr have a solution for their friend. Glr promises to lead Randor to explore a new universe, the home of her alien people, the Ehrlil. The series seems to end with a hopeful grin.

Hill, however, was not done with Keill Randor. Rather than extending the adventures of his hero, he deepens our understanding of Randor and his people with a sort of prequel. *Young Legionary: The Earlier Adventures of Keill Randor* (Gollancz, 1982; Atheneum, 1983) is an episodic novel that depicts the training rituals of Moros and Randor's childhood before he became a full-fledged Legionary. This volume explains the origin and depth of the values of the Legionary culture. During the Scattering, an emigration of humans to a number of planets across the galaxy, the colonists of Moros selected the bleak planet in order to live out their beliefs "in equality, in mutual support and responsibility, in *communality*" (*Young Legionary,* 14). Their harsh environment necessitated that they learn tremendous self-discipline and develop physical strengths as well as expertise in fighting to survive. To stave off the attacks of the vicious life forms on the planet, which include thundering six-legged mammoths and eels with poisoned spines, the inhabitants of Moros became adept at using both technological weapons and karatelike skills of balance and muscular control. Eventually the mainstay of their economy became their legion of mercenary soldiers, hired out only for defense against aggression.

The extraordinary discipline of the legion was the basis for its fame. "Yet the discipline was not *imposed,* from above. It was *accepted,* as a religion is accepted, by every human inhabitant of that world. It was taught to the children before they were weaned. It became a basic reality of life" (*Galactic Warlord,* 19). The people of Moros are "fiercely independent, self-sufficient, at one with themselves" (20). It's the familiar stiff-upper-lipped courage of the Anglo-American races, whose controlled impulses and self-abnegation bespeak more honor than boasting and materialistic display. During an early adventure of the Ordeal that earns him a place as a Young Legionary, Randor remembers his father's words of admonition: " 'Your feelings are like wild creatures. Try to crush them, or to pretend they aren't there, and they'll fight you . . . . Let them come out where you can see them—and then master them, and make *them* do *your* bidding' " (*Young Legionary,* 17). At another juncture, Randor escapes being trampled by a herd of wild mammoths by exercising the value of suicidal risk taking, another necessary lesson for survival on this planet of crazed animals and impossible terrain. The value of risky enthusiasm is epitomized by his best friend, Oni, a slim young woman whose physical strengths match Randor's. Her forthrightness endangers the young Legionaries when she challenges Charrel, a young man whose mental control is fragile following the tragic death of his family. This scene allows Hill to provide another example of the tolerant large-mindedness of the culture: "There was no special shame attached to [mental illness] on Moros, the counsellors were deeply concerned—as they would have been if Charrel had a virus infection or some other physical illness" (54).

Lest the people of Moros sound impossibly priggish, Hill includes some youthful mischievousness. For two days Oni and Randor have acted as guides for three quite boorish visitors to the planet. After successfully repressing their disgust and anger at the leering sexism directed at Oni and the overtly aggressive posturing toward Randor, the two release their pent-up frustrations in a wild game of demolition in which the two young athletes pulverize a roomful of wooden and concrete barriers set up specifically for that purpose.

The inhabitants of the planet periodically release their tensions in the Martial Games of Moros. However, in contrast to the Battle Games of Banthei, which Randor attended only as a trap to draw out his enemy, these games are described as "a peaceful competition" (112) where the combatants vie not to prove that they are better than all others, but to enjoy realizing their differences, a point that appears moot. The ultimate purpose of these games is to test whether the young Legionaries can lose a competition gracefully, an experience that Randor, with all his skills, almost misses. In the end, however, he proves himself more interested in the fate of his friend than in his own success; he has used the competitive fighting to assess his own needs for further training rather than to assuage his ego. He proves to be a worthy Legionary because, while recognizing his own virtues, he also recognizes that luck has played a large part in his victory, and with no bitterness he gives credit to the strengths of his adversaries. Among the virtues of the people of Moros, modesty is one of the most valued, along with the quiet confidence that comes from constant effort and training.

Hill's characters reflect their values in their demeanors. The hero Keill Randor is muscular but not muscle-bound. He is described as dark haired despite the more Nordic image depicted in some cover illustrations. Oni, his best friend, is slender with brown hair; otherwise she is described only as "shapely." Hill seems to avoid, however, any sexual attraction based on appearances. Grl, the other significant female in Randor's life, is an alien who resembles a bat-winged falcon with large transparent wings and slender folded appendages. The descriptions of her blunt muzzle and huge round eyes remind this reader of the pert, cheerful face of Disney's equally compassionate voice of conscience, Jiminy Cricket, though others may envision a different image. An illustration by Bradley Clark on the back of *The Huntsman* (Atheneum, 1982) showing a batlike creature with long pointed ears might capture Hill's intentions, although in the text Glr has no apparent ears. Hill's imagination seems drawn to bats, with or without ears—best friend and inner voice in one series, worst enemy and mechanical guard in the next. Randor's relationship with Glr grows from mere appreciation for her wit and wisdom, which saves his life in the first book, toward a fierce affection and concern for her livelihood in the later books. As an increasingly internalized companion, she replaces his childhood cohort Oni. Besides Talis, Glr is Randor's only trustworthy friend, one who can sense almost all his thoughts. As such, she accompanies him in his journeys, acting as a guide and guard, translating the actions and thoughts of other humans for Randor and providing a record of his thoughts for the reader. She is the consummate partner.

Randor's mentors, Talis and the other Overlords, are elderly, wise, restrained, and tolerant of his first outbursts. With deeply hooded cowls hiding their individual features, the members of this benevolent council act in accord, melding their unique talents for the overall good but retaining their own voices. In contrast, the evil force that Randor finally uncovers is a conglomerate of bodiless minds whose expertise is sucked out by transparent tubes drawn into a whirling vacuum of greed and evil intent; all is drawn toward a plan of destruction and war. The power of this amorphous aggression is redistributed to soldiers whose intelligence and will have been evacuated. While the Legionaries are identified by necklaces with unique medallions that reflect the individual qualities of each wearer, the soldiers of the nameless One all wear identical necklaces, without color, that replace their individual minds and wills. They become slaves to the horrible centrifuged mind. How can Randor overcome this? He almost doesn't.

Settings in these novels are sparsely delineated. Only enough details are provided to give a context for the action, yet the pictures Hill paints are vivid and unique. Moros is sparse and desert-like, with few comforts and only the necessary technology; the cities where Randor finds information are tawdry, gray, and dirty, and the ultimate evil is a mere machine. The caves of Planet Starwind are dank and slimy with wormlike creatures. Hill is a master at filling his landscapes with imaginary creatures that resemble earthly horrors closely enough to elicit squeamish reactions. Even his most alien geographies contain enough familiar elements to enable readers to recognize and relate to former experiences. The settings are odd but not fantastic.

The Huntsman Series (1982–1984)

In Hill's next books, the Huntsman series, his childhood memories of Canadian woodlands are reflected in the loving details of the forest wilderness he paints. The series is set on a post–nuclear holocaust Earth a few hundred years from now, after the Forgotten Time when people "built huge cities out of metal and stone, spread stone roadways across the land, lived and worked and traveled with always a barrier of stone or metal between them and the outdoors" (16). After an apparent nuclear war, Earth's population has dwindled to a few thousand survivors. These have begun to band together to rebuild civilization, but their efforts are squelched by an invasion of metallic alien humanoids, who mine the earth for ore and kill off any interfering humans with laser guns in the same offhand manner we use to smack at insects. These coldly efficient aliens decimate humanity, scattering people into small primitive farming villages guarded by huge batlike creatures called spywings. Any sign of progress toward restoring modern technology or conveniences is quickly destroyed by one of the aliens' egg-shaped hovercrafts. Like the serfs of the early Middle Ages in European history, the villagers become fearful, dull, and vengeful toward anyone different. They huddle in settlements, fearful of the uncharted wilderness on one side and the desert wasteland, rumored to be deadly, on the other.

The Huntsman (Heinemann, 1982; Atheneum, 1982) introduces a hero who is different. Finn Ferral is the adopted son of Joshua Ferral, who found him in the forest near his frontier hometown while he was hunting. Like his father, Finn prefers to be in the woods, "wandering, drifting, idly turning the pages of the endless and ever-changing book of the wilderness" (9). One day, sensing a restlessness in the woods, he returns to find that his father, Joshua, his younger foster sister, Jena, and another young man from the town, Lyle, have been kidnapped by the alien ships he has only heard about in the town's legends. Instead of sympathizing with the loss of his family, the townspeople blame Finn, for he is a convenient scapegoat. His uncanny tracking abilities, his fearlessness in the forest, and the strange dotted pattern on his upper arm set him apart from the villagers, who huddle together near their homes, afraid of anything but the routine drudgery of daily life.

Shunned and lonely, Finn decides to try the unthinkable, to rescue his father and sister from the Slavers, as the aliens are known. His skills help him trace the whirling patterns the ships' blades have left in the grasses. Although the first settlement he reaches does not hold his kin, he learns much about the mechanical masters and their apelike servants, who use captured humans as poorly fed, barely clad, and badly housed beasts of burden in their mining and building operations. Doggedly, Finn renews his search for another camp where he might find Josh and Jena, following a trail even more difficult because of the passage of time. Just as he is about to lose hope, he meets Baer, one of the apelike creatures, who has miraculously escaped the Slavers and who is delighted to help Finn avenge the masters. The two make quite a pair. Baer is bulky, stolid, a knowledgeable good ole boy whose clumsy, crashing movements belie a warm and wily intelligence, while Finn is the energetic young woodsman who seems able to melt effortlessly into nowhere. His hotheaded recklessness sometimes needs the tempering of his older friend. In the long, drawn-out process of discovering and invading the alien lair that holds Josh, the two become fast friends and, more important, partners. Finn is silent enough and slender enough to penetrate the underground tunnels where the slaves are kept, but Baer's blundering bravado and bulky strength also play a crucial role in recovering the exhausted humans, including the wounded Josh. Baer helps Finn understand and accept the meaning of the marks on his arm; he has been constructed by the aliens from human cells, just like the apelike Baer and the other members of the Bloodkin clan. Baer and Finn were each aberrant laboratory experiments— Baer's animal appearance is tempered with human intelligence, and Finn's humanity is enhanced by the sharper animal sensitivities toward natural wildness that are part of his genetic makeup. Both are better suited for leading humanity out of slavery because of their unnatural inheritances. Finn and Baer guide the former slaves out of danger, including the wounded Josh and scar-faced Gratton, and set them on their slower journey toward the Wilderness while they search for Finn's foster sister, Jena.

In the next volume of the series, *Warriors of the Wasteland* (Heinemann, 1983; Atheneum, 1983), Baer and Finn trudge back to the Wasteland after failing to find Jena among the slaves of other Slaver centers. There they find not their own civilization, or Josh, or Gratton, or even the uninhabited wilderness they expect, but Indian horsemen who live on the desert, one tribe led by Rainshadow, a slim young man expert with a spear. A more welcome surprise is Jena, thriving among the fearless women who have saved her—a group led by Marakela, a broad-shouldered, tough-minded redhead. When the Slavers realize that Finn, marked with the mysterious message on his left arm, is on the desert, they attack, armed with the Claw, a dangerous mechanical warrior, and aided by a large spaceship. After a long and arduous battle, Finn and Baer help the Warriors, as the rugged natives of the Wasteland are called, defeat the Claw. But their victory has annoyed their enemy. Vengeance is inevitable.

Alien Citadel (Heinemann, 1984; Atheneum, 1984) opens with a nightmarish vision of the mechanical Slavers' mindless, unimaginative vengeance. Hundreds of vehicles called whirlsleds and thousands of spywings systemically scour the Wasteland for the "vermin that were human beings" (5). They keep formation because they lack the human imagination that allows for surprise and spontaneity. As the Slavers approach, burning everything in their path, the Warriors must retreat toward the dangerous Firesands, which retain the radioactive poisons from the time when the Earth destroyed itself.

Finn Ferral and his cohorts Baer, Jena, and Marakela, despairing of surviving this last onslaught, watch as a greater threat, a strange and much larger spaceship, scorches something at a nearby waterhole and then descends to claim its victims. From the ship emerge four of the mechanical Slavers and a huge metallic monster that seems to be their leader. After picking through the ash for the remnants of the creature they have just killed, they return to the ship and leave, like a party of scientists collecting specimens. The group of heroes, now equally skilled huntsmen, follow the ship until it lands again. While Finn remains to watch the spaceship, the three other heroes pursue the four Slavers into a thicket, where they kill them before they can collect two more specimens. The two injured and exhausted men turn out to be Finn's father, Josh, and his friend Gratton, the only surviving remnants of the enslaved humans rescued by Finn and Baer in the first volume of this series. But when they return to tell Finn, the spaceship is gone, with Finn captive inside. He is taken to the underground Citadel, the Slavers' central headquarters. As a slave he learns about the mazelike tunnels and experiences the cold cruelty of the Slavers and their Bloodkin, who manage them. When the strange marks on his arm are discovered, he is carried in a transparent cage to a special lab, where the slimy, gray-skinned metallic monster from the spaceship pokes and prods Finn as if he were a trapped rat. The monstrous scientist is Cacinnix from the planet Vlant, who is studying the "two-legged and sometimes violent vermin" (77) of Earth to prove that despite the predominant opinion of his peers, the Slavers, these Earth creatures do possess some primitive intelligence. For the proud, independent woodsman, this is denigrating enough, but when his passionate protestations are translated only as mindless squeaking, he uses his captors' arrogance to escape his trap. Outside, Baer and the others have decided to try the impossible, to storm the Citadel; they have banded into a loyal group that will risk sure death for the chance to save their huntsman leader. Inside, Finn, dehumanized, is surviving by using the instinctive animal reactions he has inherited. When all seems lost, the ghastly Cacinnix receives a message from the Ikkarok, the leader of his home planet. The message drones on and on, incomprehensible to our heroes. Just as the final battle seems to be coming to a fatal close, a number of the huge spaceships descend to Earth. Evidently they have come not to obliterate the pesky human creatures whose usefulness is hampered by their inconveniently violent nature; they have come to collect their machinery as they abandon Earth. They have found another planet just as rich in resources as Earth, and uninhabited. Smugly, with no thought of the human pests they leave behind, they soar off into the sunset.

In a warm and wonderful conclusion, Josh and Jena are reunited with Finn as a family, which will now include Baer, a Bloodkin with the blond pelt of a beast but with a human heart and mind. All is well.

The ColSec Series (1984–1985)

Hill's third series, the ColSec sequence, describes the struggles of young interspace travelers stranded on another planet: *Exiles of ColSec* (Gollancz, 1984; Atheneum, 1984), *The Caves of Klydor* (Gollancz, 1984; Atheneum, 1985), and *ColSec Rebellion* (Gollancz, 1985; Atheneum, 1985). ColSec, short for the Colonization Sections of the Organization, is the police force for the tyrannical Organization that has ruled humanity since the decades of the virus that destroyed the civilizations of the past. These enforcers are the dreaded Crushers, men trained to kill without a speck of mercy. Since most of Earth's resources have been depleted, the Organization has sent out ColSec to gather young troublemakers from the inner cities of Earth, the Highlands of Britain, or any outlying area where rebels appear. The Organization, as this government is called, rids itself of these pesky teens by sending them on spaceships to planets to fend for themselves; if the "scards," short for discards, succeed in civilizing the planet, the Organization can then exploit its new colony. The story recalls the founding of certain parts of North and South America, when European mother countries sent sailors, religious fanatics, scrofulous adventurers, and even petty criminals to risk the unknown wilderness in the hope that these ne'er-do-wells might succeed in establishing profitable colonies.

In *ColSec's Rebellion,* Hill introduces the 16-year-old heroes of his series by depicting their dreams as they approach the orbit of Klydor, where they have been banished from Earth. The story is told from the viewpoint of Cord McKiy, a sturdy Scottish Highlander of tremendous physical strength and courage. Isolated from the urban mainstream, he is socially awkward. He meets the slender Samella Connel, a bright young woman from the North American Midwest who has been sold by her communal family to a corporation that trained her in computer skills. Her intelligent good sense and Cord's experience in the wilderness of his homeland combine to make them leaders of the small group of survivors. The others in their group form a multicultural mix. Ivory-skinned Jeko, identified as oriental, is quick-tempered but quickly deflated; coffee-colored Rontal helps calm him down. The two have been part of the urban rebellion near the site of Chicago; their initials, implanted in silver in their bald foreheads, and their aggressive attitudes reveal their backgrounds as gang members. Slighter in build and even fiercer in temper than the others, Heleth has belonged to the Bunkers, who control the underground sewer system of old London; her pasty white face is marked with black tatooed stripes, and her eyes squint in the sunlight. This tough little band of five comes together against the threat of Lamprey, another survivor and a former Crusher turned outlaw who has become the leader of the Death Angels. From the wreckage, Lamprey has grabbed a laser gun, which he uses with dangerous frequency; his ugly taunts, constant giggle, and evident past as a torturer and murderer clearly type him as insane, and his subsequent actions verify this first impression.

Hill depicts different styles of leadership by contrasting Cord and Lamprey. Cord is reluctant to take on the role of leader when the others seem to look to him, though his knowledge of this forest terrain would help them survive. "He didn't want the responsibility, nor did he want anyone else to be responsible for him. He wanted the Highlands way, the free co-operation of equals, among people who most of the time went their own way" (42). Lamprey leers at Samella, sneers at Cord, and snarls out orders to all of them, squashing them into submission with vicious threats. He boasts superior knowledge, age, and skill. No one is foolish enough to challenge him directly, but Samella cleverly uses her technical knowledge and luck to drive him away from the wreckage.

Just as pressing is the challenge of the new environment. Samella gets headaches when she leaves the vicinity of the shuttle. Sluglike creatures, their tentacles tipped with poisoned barbs, emerge from the ground and devour the funguslike growths at the tops of the trees. Humanoid aliens armed with spears appear in great numbers, stirred into anger by Lamprey's quick trigger finger on the laser gun. Trees have brains and feelings; they employ the humanoid aliens to keep the forest cleared and to protect them from the slug creatures. Their collaboration resembles the real-life relationship between corn and the crows that eat insects and carry off dead leaves, except, of course, that corn is not so actively intelligent. Evidently Samella's headaches are caused by her receptivity to the trees' brain waves.

The aliens trap the five teens inside the wreckage of the spaceship. Out of concern for Samella, whose telepathic pain drives her to run wildly toward a battle between aliens, the four others decide to move elsewhere. As the group overcomes the horrible threats on their flight from the landing scene, they gradually grow closer, clan members who risk their own lives to defend one another. Seriously wounded by Lamprey, Jeko bloodies the ground with his tracks in an attempt to rescue Samella, who has been dragged off by the crazed Crusher. Before Lamprey can destroy Samella, however, the aliens, after killing her captor, tie her to a huge central tree-mind, which sends out brain waves of hate and fear that affect even Cord, Heleth, and Rontal. An equally gigantic slug-monster threatens them all. In a desperate final battle, the five heroes expend every ounce of their energy and individual talents to overcome seemingly impossible odds. The final scene is a melee of swords slashing at poisoned tentacles, poles bashing into slug innards,, and gushing slime as the giant finally thunders to an end. The aliens are quiet for the present, but the group knows that the peace is probably temporary. They decide to move on, toward a part of the planet they can call their own. Remembering how ColSec dumped them here with no real concern for their survival, the five friends rekindle their hatred for the Organization and vow to be prepared to protect their newfound freedom. In *ColSec Rebellion,* Cord's goal of claiming Klydor as a free world for other young rebels against the enslavement of ColSec is finally realized.

The values depicted in this series show that cooperative unity works better than traditional competitive rivalries. It is a message for the young who want to throw off the strictures of the old and begin a new society that they imagine will be freer and will allow more personal independence. It is the dream of the new frontier, where working hard and enduring rough natural conditions are preferable to living under restrictive laws and dictatorial leaders.

Another value this series demonstrates is that automatic aggression against a stranger or an alien is not moral; in confrontations between different species or cultures, peaceful communication should be tried first so that misunderstanding, fear, and hate may be avoided. Repeatedly in the ColSec series, the hero Cord tries to temper this fear of difference. He tries to stop the crazed Lamprey from shooting at the alien inhabitants of Klydor, and then understands their aggression when he realizes that the ColSec spaceship has, in effect, murdered the trees that the aliens worship. To appease the aliens during battle, he suggests that his cohorts retreat, allowing the aliens to withdraw from battle without losing. To a traditional hero, retreat would be equated with shame; here Cord's strategy to avoid unnecessary bloodshed and violence seems wise and virile.

This theme of trying to befriend aliens before offending them is reiterated in Hill's *The Moon Monsters* (Heinemann, 1984), a children's book written at about the same time as the ColSec series. Nine-year-old Paul Carder and his astrogeographer father are forced to land on a moon of another planet, a moon with many animal-like monsters. However, Mr. Carder does not carry a gun because he "hated the way that some spacemen from Earth would shoot alien creatures without a single thought. He believed that you should stay away from places that might be dangerous, rather than shooting your way out because you had been careless or stupid" (15). This same pragmatic attitude toward preventing violence is often expressed by Hill's heroes in his books for adolescent and adult readers, though these older heroes repeatedly prove they are able and willing to inflict quite a bit of damage on those enemies who don't relent, and to endure agonizing pain to stop the disruption of peace. Hill's writing indicates a preference for peace but a readiness for violence to defend those who cannot avoid being attacked.

Hill sometimes uses unusual images. His characters give a "meaty slap" as they "ghost away" into the shadows; spaceships "judder," and battles bristle and ooze with gruesome graphics. Although his heroes frequently approach the edge of death, somehow they totter onward until another surge of energy propels them to another victory. It is the age-old story of the almost-human transforming into the superhuman, the slumbering chrysalis squirming out of its cocoon into the freedom of flight, the ugly, awkward duckling growing into the triumphant swan, the adolescent emerging into adulthood.

Antczak's theory that science fiction forms a modern mythology for young people is borne out well in Hill's stories of space adventure.[2] Traditional values of Western European culture are reflected in his work. Heroes sacrifice their own comforts and endure hardship and pain to show courage against an enemy. Hill's heroes are individualistic, competitive, physically strong, disciplined, and clever. Although they are cautious about trusting anyone, they eventually learn to care deeply about at least one special partner.

The Turn to Fantasy (1987)

Most recently, Hill's fiction has veered into fantasy. *Blade of the Poisoner* (1987) won recognition as a winner of the Parents' Choice Award. A sequel, *Master of Fiends* (1987), continues the thematic pattern of extreme horror and terror ultimately banished by compassion.

Critics tend to dismiss Hill as a writer of typical space adventures, but these are books that reluctant readers, whose opinions are not published in journals, praise for the very qualities that make them space operas. These readers like the fast-paced action, the traditional characters, and the dramatic rhythm of the language. The reassuring message that peace is preferable to war, embedded within a roller-coaster plot told in vivid, ringing style, makes Hill's books a satisfying read for many young people who want the vicarious thrill of teetering on the edge of destruction before grabbing a victory that seems impossible. Hill's adventures may not garner critical praise from literary experts, but they earn the enthusiasm of readers whose praise for books is rare.

Chronology: Douglas Hill's Life and Works

1935   Born 6 April in Brandon, Manitoba, the son of Cora, a nurse, and William Hill, a locomotive engineer.

1952–1957   Attends the University of Saskatchewan, Saskatoon. Graduates with honors in English.

1957–1959   Attends the University of Toronto.

1958   Marries Gail Robinson, a writer and poet.

1965   First book is published.

1962–1964   Works as series editor for Aldus Books in London, England.

1971–1984   Literary editor for *Tribune* in London, England.

1978   Divorces.

1979   Last Legionary series begins with the publication of *Galactic Warlord.*

1982   Huntsman series begins with the publication of *The Huntsman.*

1984   ColSec series begins with the publication of *Exiles of ColSec.*

1987   First fantasy novel, *Blade of the Poisoner,* is published.

5. Other Visions, Other Worlds: H. M. Hoover

Like Douglas Hill, Helen Mary Hoover also writes primarily for young people, but her science fiction is more reflective than adventurous, centered around the exploration of character and relationships more than the suspenseful thrust of plot events. Her writing is often noted for its teaching qualities as well as for its value as entertainment. She was born on 5 April 1935, one day earlier than Douglas Hill, and like Hill, she also writes historical nonfiction as well as science fiction for young readers. Otherwise, however, their lives and works differ radically. Hoover grew up in Stark County, Ohio, where she attended Louisville High School and then Mount Union College in Alliance, Ohio. Her parents and three of her grandparents were schoolteachers who taught her to read reflectively. Like Hill, she read widely and indiscriminately, developing an early enthusiasm for adventure stories: Edgar Rice Burroughs's Tarzan, Jules Verne, Saint Exupery, Admiral Byrd, and the Lindberghs. When she was 12 years old she discovered Huxley's *Brave New World*, which she took as a serious prediction, worrying about a future where "both embryos and ethics are bottled and decanted."[1] Curious, she moved on to other kinds of speculative fiction, which formed a background for her writing.

Although Hoover didn't grow up in forested land like Hill, she reveled in the flora and fauna of the Midwestern farmland where her parents showed her how to appreciate the jewel-like gleam of a Japanese beetle and the timeless song of frogs at night. Just as Hill's childhood images of woodlands appear as scenery in his work, Hoover delineates in precise detail aspects of the wide variety of animals and plants she studied with her naturalist parents, often revising them into marvelously novel organisms, some comical, some wistful, some gruesome and dangerous. It is typical of Hoover to insert a great deal of historical and scientific information in her imaginative writing, for she values the kind of learning that can be applied and that provokes thought. While Hill's books include many technological inventions, Hoover focuses more on sciences like biology, chemistry, and basic physics.

The Lion's Club (Four Winds Press, 1974) is an example of her historical fiction. It is full of visual details about the lives of Moslem tribes of the Caucasian mountains near the Black Sea, who warred with the Russians in the early nineteenth century. The hero, Jemal-Edin, grows from a young Moslem whose father's harsh orders necessitate unquestioning obedience into a sophisticated consort of Czar Nicholas I in the Russian court. The novel received much critical recognition. It was named a children's book of the year by the Child Study Association of America and was listed as one of the best books for young adults by the American Library Association, drawing attention to Hoover as an author of excellent books for young adults. Her story of Medea, *The Dawn Palace,* also won several awards, including the Parents Choice Honor Award in 1988. In her historical novels Hoover uses other time periods and cultures as a context for teaching moral lessons relevant to youth today. In her science fiction novels she uses other worlds as backdrops for young people's struggles to escape from binding circumstances and to reach a more enlightened life of choices.

The Morrow Series (1973–1976)

Hoover's first two sf novels are both about a post-holocaust world where only two colonies survive. *Children of Morrow* (Four Winds Press, 1973) contrasts two different human reactions to an environmental disaster in which most of Earth's living creatures slowly suffocate in the polluted air (much like the predicted greenhouse effect caused by our current misuse of technology). One of the remaining groups, the Base, has rejected technology and tried to return to a primitive agricultural economy where survival is insured by grueling work regulated by the totalitarian rule of a religious master called the Major. The other society, planned by Simon Morrow and named after him, is run by a Council of Ten; because of a genetic accident, Morrow's descendants are telepathic, able to communicate mentally across great distances with other telepaths. Two members of the council, Ashira and Varas, reach out mentally to two children, outcasts of the primitive Base community. Tia, the older child, is suspected of witchcraft because of her prescience, while the younger child, a lad known as Rabbit, is shunned because of his stammering and shyness. Both share similar dreams in which they seem to communicate with another culture, which is how they explain their telepathic ability. When Rabbit's mental power kills an older man who is threatening Tia, the two are urged to escape by these telepathic messages. Tia burns down the hated schoolhouse to create a necessary distraction so she can rescue Rabbit. They trek through deep woods, float down a river, wander through the remains of a city, and discover the sea on a Huck Finn adventure that takes them away from the cruelties of their childhood. When they reach the sea, Rabbit is bitten by a sea snail, and the two are captured by the Major and his men. Before they are rescued, Tia discovers, in an intensely suspenseful finale, why the Major hates them with such passion.

Hoover's first science fiction is a satisfying adventure story that depicts the harsh and laborious lives of a world without technology. It is also a frighteningly realistic picture of a world laid to waste by the kinds of pollution we are now practicing, made especially convincing by the informative biological details woven into the story. Finally, it is an endearing image of friendship between two young people who care for each other with selfless passion. In this novel Hoover establishes herself as a writer capable of creating memorably complex characters who carry out their adventures in a setting made relevant and real by her deft hand at description.

The sequel, *Treasures of Morrow* (Four Winds Press, 1976), after briefly reiterating enough background for new readers, describes

Tia's resistance to accepting Morrow, with all its wonders, as her new home. Hoover explores the clash between the mistrust engendered by a totalitarian environment and the gentle innocence of a kinder, more technologically advanced and democratic upbringing. After a period in which the two children are immersed in the modern world of Morrow, a group returns to study the Base, taking the children with them. Ever the naturalist, Hoover takes advantage of the trip to describe the disastrous effects of algae-filled seas, to explain deep-sea phosphorescence, and to remember the details of camping experiences. When they reach the Base, only Tia and Rabbit can fully comprehend the vast differences between a highly educated and evolved civilization and these primitive people who cower in fear at anything new because their daily struggle to survive leaves them with little opportunity for imaginative stimulation or experimentation. Tia notices that the people's first reaction to their visitors is fear, but "none of them asked why" (123). Curiosity is a luxury available only to those who feel safe. The first response of these primitives to the assurances that their visitors approach peacefully is "Bullshit," a term so foreign to this articulate people that Varas has to ask, "What possible relevance does the excreta of male bovidae have to the current situation?" Tia explains that it's "a verbal bridge," a "vulgarism used in place of thought" (113). Trust is another luxury, available only to those whose chances for survival are greater than those for death.

Hoover gives thoughtful advice to educated readers who want to advise those with other viewpoints: "Don't destroy their faith if you have nothing to take its place. . . . You take all and give nothing. They have a system that enables them to live" (116). She also warns against self-righteous interference in social systems without providing for the consequences: "Better slavery than starvation" (116), she writes in the voice of Ashira, whose ethical concern is to keep balance in life. When Tia wants Anna, the elderly cook who has been kind to her, to accompany their escape, the old woman explains how her simpler mind and lack of education would make her feel like a cow that needs watching. Like many young people who have left homes that were not kind, Tia and Rabbit discover that while they have learned new ways of living and looking at their world, their childhood companions have not changed their prejudices and will not change their minds about the worth of Tia and Rabbit. The two children accept their new home in Morrow. Hoover dramatizes this message in a long, exciting battle scene at the end of the book in which Tia's heroic climb from a caved-in missile silo is misread as threatening. Even as she is being made the scapegoat, Tia shows great moral heroism by anonymously saving the village from total destruction by fire. Tempted by personal vengeance, Tia recognizes the greater need for balance, allowing the survival even of these humans she deems hopelessly evil and backward.

After this duo about Morrow, Hoover has written single-volume works that are connected only by her recurrent themes of environmental destruction, corporate greed and carelessness about humanity, and parents who spend more time and energy on their careers than on their children. In these subsequent books, Hoover perceptively explores the ramifications of power, colonialism, scientific study, and human love.

Growth of Awareness (1977–1979)

The Delikon (Viking, 1977) depicts a future Earth conquered by the Delikons, who are "powerful enough to be benign where practical" (4). From the first page, the reader realizes that something is different about one of the main characters: "Three children played in the garden; Alta was ten, Jason was twelve, and Varina was three hundred and seven" (1). The natural form of the Delikons is more gorgeous than lovable, like jeweled and intricately articulated insects, but centuries after their first conquest they send envoys configured to look and sound like the most beautiful humans; only their cinnamon eyes and immensely long life span make them different. Varina is one such envoy whose vocation is to raise selected human children to become administrators of the Delikon state. Looking like a child, she educates them in the central kingdom called Kelador, where all that is best in human civilization is retained to form a lifestyle of the utmost grace and innocence; she knows nothing about the world outside, and the children she trains don't return once they leave as teenagers for further training at an academy.

Varina and her two current charges are kidnapped by Aron, a former student now turned revolutionary because he and his fellow humans prefer the chaos of democracy to a benevolent dictatorship that guarantees peace but creates a chasm between the wealthy with their luxurious lives and the working poor. The more conservative Varina berates Aron and his companions: "You would destroy the order Kelador imposes and call chaos freedom. There is no freedom without discipline, no excellence without order, no life without purpose. You would eliminate the castes and call that equality. Equality does not exist in any living form, only in atoms or chairs! I understand your goal is self-rewarding destruction; our goal is the advancement of the species into a true social animal, with the time and discipline involved stretching over generations" (69).

A horrible and bloody battle ensues, from which Varina and her companions escape, first on foot, then on horseback and by bulldozer. Varina comes to realize how sheltered she and the other privileged rulers have been as she wrestles through mud and death and gore back to the beautiful palace where her fellow Delikons rule. Ironically, just as she begins to value the peaceful, elegant life of the Delikons, especially in contrast to the ugly cruelties of human war, and decides she is ready to return to her native land, Varina finds that she is stranded on Earth. Yet the book's ending provides hope for her eventual return.

The new leader of the palace is Aron, who shares the irony of Varina's fate. Like her, he has questioned the rightness of his upbringing, but as he tries to share the advantages of his childhood home with less-fortunate humans, its comforts and luxuries are destroyed, as is the security of his youth.

Hoover's subtle language gives depth to this book. Varina expresses profound ideas ranging from the universal spiral patterns that occur in sunflowers and the Milky Way to the relationships among friends and their teachers. When Aron admits his limited understanding of life, Varina is sensitive enough to "regret his pain" but honest enough to "resent his weakness" (62). The imagery of singing, in both the joy of soldiers going to war and the keening loss of goodbye, is deeply moving. Hoover tells a story that makes logical sense but also paints an achingly poignant picture of the loss of childhood innocence, when those early privileged and safe days are replaced with knowledge of the world outside. *The Delikon* is not a perfect book, for the interspersed chapters confuse the plot unnecessarily, and the repetition of the first chapter at the end fails to account for the destruction and death that have occurred, but it is a moving and memorable work that teaches much about both the joys and disappointments of life among caring humans.

The Rains of Eridan (Viking Press, 1977) explores a relationship similar to that between Varina and her young charges, whom she has come to love as her own. Biologist Theo, short for Dr. Theodora Leslie, is researching the wildlife of the desert planet Eridan and has spent over a month happily camping out by herself, exploring and notating the flora and fauna she sees. One morning she finds 12-year-old Karen Orlov, the only daughter of the highly ranked and respected second commander of the Exhibition, who has just been murdered with a laser. Apparently the troops have mutinied, driven by the vague mist of unnamed fear that seems to be floating through the settlements of Eridan.

Theo likes Karen immediately. She respects the self-possession of the child who has just witnessed the murder of her parents, and she identifies with Karen's courageous curiosity; both Theo and Karen admit to having taste-tested the gorgeous crystals that are so attractive to the human explorers. On the long trek back to the base, made especially grueling by the heavy rains, Karen discovers in a cave the body of a huge leathery-skinned, sharp-clawed creature. It resembles the creatures both she and Theo have seen that, like spiders, suck the fluids out of their victims, leaving only desiccated husks. Karen and Theo have nicknamed the creatures "cave bears" because their other habits are similar to those of bears they have seen on Earth.

When Karen and Theo return to the base, they discover that one of these huge creatures has attacked some of the staff while the other humans have been out gathering crystals. Theo and her old friend Tairas discover through lab work and research that the gemlike crystals are not, in fact, mineral but are organic, virus-carrying cells expelled from the bodies of the dangerous cave bears. The virus manifests itself as the free-floating fear that has caused so much paranoia, hate, and havoc throughout the human bases. Theo and Karen supply the antibodies to cure the virus, and all is well.

In *The Rains of Eridan* Hoover invents a wide array of fascinating animals, some grossly disgusting and others whimsical and pretty. The obsessive focus of devoted scientists is sweetly depicted, especially in the characters of Karen and Theo, as are the pleasures and tribulations of camping in the wilderness and experimenting in the lab. The book is a fond portrait of scientific scholars who enjoy the camaraderie of shared interests in a remote community while enduring petty jealousies and irritations. Karen and Theo seem very familiar and so does the world they are exploring, which is not so different from what Earth may have looked like before the Industrial Age and its concomitant technological explosion. In this book Hoover's teaching focuses on information about the natural world rather than on political power structures, and her depiction of working parents is more generous than in her other work. It is a warm picture of humanity set in a stomach-wrenching context of guts and gore. As such, it is perfectly aimed at many adolescent readers who like to think and learn but who also enjoy the physical frisson of blood-soaked horror.

In *The Lost Star* (Viking, 1979) scientists are not depicted so kindly. Lian Webster, 15 years old and already renowned for scientific work done with her astrophysicist parents, crash-lands on the planet Balthor. There she meets a group of archaeologists searching for artifacts of a civilization they assume was lost many years ago. Because Lian's mind is open to all possibilities, she can see beyond these assumptions, especially regarding the relative intelligence of the creatures they discover on the planet where they have landed. Some of the animals that resemble those on earth are deemed attractive by association, but others, like the grayish, slow-moving six-footed creatures, short and squat like mushrooms or rhinoceroses, are stereotyped by the earth archaeologists as lumpish and slow-witted. Ignoring the intelligence and spirit of these creatures, the archaeologists derogatively call them "lumpies." While these scientists search for the source of the various signs of advanced civilization, Lian's open-minded observation proves they have been blinded by prejudiced assumptions. Lian, mature for her years, soon realizes she has practiced the same type of prejudice—based on physical appearances and past associations—toward the Tolats, spidery robots with minds of "neat files of schematics, thought disciplined to linear simplicity, minds that did not dance but enjoyed a game called "Jump!" (115). The Tolats lack the emotional responses of humans or lumpies, but their law-abiding natures make them seem ethical and decent.

The lumpies have indeed been playing the fool; they are in actuality the Toapa, remnants of a civilization more advanced than humanity, their starship gradually eroded by flooding and their intelligence by isolation. A sophisticated computerlike central mind called the Counter has absorbed the best of seven generations of Toapa minds. Now it scans Lian and finds her compatible and trustworthy; the Tolats it finds too mechanically intelligent to trust. As the archaeologists clean off the mud and grime from the central glass dome of the buried starship, they increase the Counter's solar-powered energies, enabling it to remember and to function mentally. In one of her frequent flashes of humor, Hoover describes the Counter's first dose of power after all these years as "intoxicating. At three A.M., the dome lit up, an emerald glowing in the dark. It winked just once and then went out—the Counter sobered up" (118). As its self-consciousness returns, it becomes able to help the lumpies communicate their intelligence and their true name to Lian and her fellow archaeologists.

In *The Lost Star* Hoover depicts the less charming side of a scientist's absorption with study, the situation she so lovingly portrays in *The Rains of Eridan*. Lian's parents are astrophysicists, so devoted to their work that they keep themselves remote from their daughter. She has had to raise herself, learning affection from the lumpies, who have also been isolated from any home or parent figure. The Counter has chosen to reveal itself to Lian after many centuries of silence and lethargy, an act of desperate hope for the survival of the lumpies. As it regains power, it reflects that it has selected Lian, whom it calls Guardian, because it recognizes the kinship between the lonely girl neglected by her parents and the Toapa. Both "had lived in isolation and imposed innocence, enduring the present by memories of a secure past. And survived almost whole" (149). Through the voice of the Counter, Hoover advises parents of young people. At the end of the book, the Counter, now fully empowered, starts to plan the rejuvenation of the Toapa civilization but stops itself when it remembers how total control, though beneficial, in some ways had led to its ultimate destruction. The benevolent Counter "would watch and provide, not as much as it possibly could . . . enough to allow them to become independent and self-sustaining and whole" (149). By helping the Toapa protect their artifacts from further exploitation and by undercutting human prejudices, Lian has restored Toapa dignity. In the process she has also discovered her own. The lost star of the title refers to the loss of a false, self-centered idealism based on the prejudiced assumptions held by Lian, her fellow scientists, and the Toapa.

Return to Earth (Viking, 1980) explores the loss of another kind of false innocence and idealism, that of the elite, who are sheltered against the hardships of the poor and thus scornful of their desire to escape the mundane. When Galen Innes, who is nearing retirement from his service as Governor-General of Marsat, a nearby moon, returns to the now-neglected country estate that was his childhood home on Earth, he meets a young neighbor, Samara, the daughter of the director of a major corporation that holds great power over the land.

Galen and Samara first become acquainted at a religious service, cultlike in its adoption of traditional cultural symbols: red and green represent death and life, and the egg implies resurrection. Is Hoover raising questions about Christian ritual when she presents this historical insight? When Galen is recognized as someone who might ask impertinent questions, armed guards try to harm him until he is rescued by Samara's cool, quick interference; she demonstrates a confident authority unusual in one so young. When his home is burned, he appreciates the girl's tremendous control over her emotions and her courage as she joins him in raising his accusations against the Dolmen, leader of the cult. "Command was as much a matter of stage presence as it was of heritage or power. Like charm, or talent, Galen thought it something one was born with" (53). Samara's privileged life also carries responsibilities, and she welcomes Galen as a confidante and companion, especially after the murder of her mother, the director of the corporation. Returning from the funeral, Samara and Galen are gassed and jettisoned on the desert. After a painful trek across the barren landscape, Samara learns how normal people live, as she and Galen travel in tourist class to the moon, where a friend of Galen sets them up for a safe return to Earth. From the moon they carefully plot to undermine the Dolmen's powerful cult by revealing his financial chicanery and demonstrating that the religious euphoria he advertises is caused more by candy laced with stimulants than by spiritual leadership. The Dolmen's empire crashes in on itself.

Samara has resented the constraints of her privileged life, but she wonders why people living the comfortable life of her mother's corporation could be so attracted to religion or to the Dolmen's cruelty. Galen advises her that "Utopias breed a very special kind of boredom. Pervasive, soul corroding" (107). A perfectly controlled life is not a worthy goal if that control is based on self-delusion and subjection of others.

The relationship between Samara and Galen is a lovely example of how friendship can transcend differences in age, though perhaps not class or experience. Samara is never able to befriend the staff who have known her all her life, though she does finally recognize their kind natures and mutual concern. Evidently some differences are too great to transcend.

Suspenseful and exciting, this novel examines in depth and detail the uses of personal power to manipulate business and political enterprises. Raising questions about the value of technology for controlling human comfort makes this a science fiction novel as well as a mystery thriller. What more relevant issue to explore than the social ramifications of commercialized science and technology? Hoover continues to raise such questions in her subsequent books.

In her next novel she takes the viewpoint of the underprivileged. *This Time of Darkness* (1980) focuses on the callous separation of the haves from the have-nots in a post-holocaust world where resources are scarce. Amy, now 11, has never ventured beyond the five levels of her underground home, a crowded, dreary, dirty slum made dangerous by the "crazies" who sleep in the corridors. People's minds are dulled by opiates, recorded propaganda, and the sameness of their routinized lives. When Amy learns about how her classmate Axel accidentally entered this underground prison from the outside, where rain falls and real sunlight shines and food tastes and smells delicious, she decides that the two should try to escape. Hoover delineates their tortuous journey up from the ninth level to the ground floor, the cement path covered with glass, then outside across miles of brambles and broken glass that strew the surface of an Earth once leveled by nuclear war. The two are threatened by security devices, unfriendly authorities, hair-covered savages, and finally fire, but they are also aided by humans who have not forsaken all hope and kindness. Gradually Amy learns to trust Axel and become a friend; from Amy, Axel learns to persevere in the face of despair. As their relationship unfolds, Hoover, as in her other books, teaches us how human relationships work, explaining possible motives and reactions of individuals, given their previous experiences and present insecurities.

Most shocking to the young reader is the sharp contrast between the underground workers, whose short lives are spent laboring nonstop like machines for the benefit of an elite whose uncrowded, cleaner existences are pasteurized into mediocrity. Neither Amy nor Axel can imagine the long, loving lives of the outsiders who farm in the traditional way, gather in families and communities that value individual lives, and cry in sympathy and laugh in loving pleasure. Hoover's picture of an unthinking upper middle class that can survive only by totalitarian control is chilling in its realistic depiction of attitudes all too familiar today.

Another Heaven, Another Earth (1981), recommended by the American Library Association as a best book for young adults, winner of the Ohioana Award in 1982 and Central Missouri State College's award for outstanding contribution to children's literature, is a thoughtful analysis of the corporate world in the context of the traditional sf plot of the lost colony. In alternating chapters this novel contrasts the viewpoint of natives with that of visiting scientists intent on studying them. Gareth Mitchell is shunned by the villagers because she does not have to work in the fields. As medic of the central compound and a descendant of the Builders who founded this colony on the planet Xilan centuries ago, her responsibility is to preserve the healing crafts of her family and to hand them down to the next generation. Her work is arduous, for the remnants of the original colony struggle with frequent insanity, overdeveloped lungs resulting from the thin atmosphere, and increasing sterility, which threatens their future. While she is gathering the herbs she needs, using this as an excuse to visit the wilderness her parents described to her before their deaths, Gareth meets the biologist Lee from the starship Kekule. This starship is inspecting Xilan with an eye to its potential as a colony of Earth, which has grown too crowded and overdeveloped for humans to live comfortably, though modern medicine and technological engineering make communal standardized life possible for many. Lee finds a compatible personality in Gareth, who is also more comfortable with natural wilderness than with human society. Gareth is "too bright, too tall, too different from the other children" (17) to belong. As he helps Gareth discover the artifacts that explain the past history of the commune, Lee helps protect the Builders from the results of contamination from the Kekule and further exploitation by the greedy scholars and media experts who accompany them. Gareth and Lee become allied in understanding the disadvantages of modern life with its frenetic pace and standardized mediocrity and, concurrently, with its advantages of providing physical comfort and longevity. Hoover portrays in detail the complicated process of living with a corporate decision driven by profit making yet informed by personal involvement with individual participants. The guilt of inflicting suffering, even by accident, is matched by the pain of losing trust in a good friend who shows more loyalty to the company than to individual commitments. Neither the first colonizers, now "natives" barely surviving in an environment unnatural for their species, nor the new invaders, whose values are thrown into question, prove to be winners. The book raises complex questions about the ethical validity of business investment in colonization where any form of life exists.

More Human Relationships in Alien Guise

In *The Bell Tree* (Viking, 1982) Hoover describes the effect of corporate colonization on the family of the decision makers. This book portrays the way character warps when a person is forced to choose between self-aggrandizement and family responsibility. Dr. Sadler is inspecting his corporate holdings on a distant planet, accompanied by his 15-year-old daughter Jenny, with whom he has spent little time in his busy career. Although Jenny finds the people who greet them obnoxiously rude and false, she is fascinated by the strange birds and animals they see. Their guide, Eli, an outcast from human society, knows the land and animals so well he can predict what will happen as well as sense what is present. He avoids people because "people think inside their skins. Animals don't. If you touch an animal, it either likes you and moves closer, or it bites you and runs away. But it doesn't *think* about it" (70).

Despite the blunt honesty that makes him seem odd to others, Eli's sense of humankind is valid. When he first meets Dr. Sadler, he compares him to a bird called a wok, "a creature tall and gaunt with hunched neck, wings half-spread, eyes round with hunting as it stepped, deliberately. The beak speared, the eyes rolled dementedly" (34). Eli lets his attraction to Jenny Sadler betray his first impressions. Despite his instinctual distrust of Dr. Sadler, Eli leads the man and his daughter to the fabled treasure.

In the cave are statues wearing bluish stone amplifiers like halos that magnify and clarify sound, so that wearing them is "like having the ears of God" (59). The artificial lake and alluring bell trees, with leaves that gleam with perfect tones when rain strikes, are artifacts of a civilization that sought to understand truth through synthesizing sounds into perfect harmony. When Dr. Sadler spies these artifacts, he becomes insanely reckless in his efforts to possess them. Like the wok to which Eli has compared him, Dr. Sadler has become demented with greed.

Jenny has been attacked twice by a Ghema, a beast like a giant guinea pig, terrible enough with its huge claws and speed, but even more horrifying because it can transform itself into balled light and sear its victims to death. She has also been picked up by giant ants that also live in the caves. Though Dr. Sadler has seen these creatures himself, he brushes off their threat as a nightmare and rushes away without concern for the safety of his daughter and young Eli.

Like the heroes of Hoover's previous books about Morrow, the creatures in the cave have developed telepathic communication, and they try to explain to Sadler their resentment at being invaded and exploited. However, he is unwilling to listen, because for him reality is defined only by his past experiences and education; his mind is closed to new adventure. As Jenny and Eli save him from certain destruction, the cave collapses, sealing off the treasure from further investigation.

In summing up the lessons learned from this adventure, Sadler admits that his responsible behavior at home is a cover for the reckless adventurer he feels he is at core, not recognizing the limitations of his thoughtlessness. Both young people have learned that growing up often means letting go of old assumptions, especially about other people. Jenny decides that her "real" father is not someone whose capability or word she trusts; she loses the illusion that her father's world is wholly good. Eli finally trusts Jenny enough to promise to visit her on Earth; he loses his wholesale cynicism about humanity. The perfect harmonies of the bell tree are lovely in gentle rain that lasts forever, but too painful to bear when played hard and fast. So too is the experience of knowing and caring about people. Moderation is the appropriate key.

Hoover displays her sophisticated knowledge of natural history in this work by depicting the varied subtle senses of the creatures she describes, alluding to the theory that although humans once shared the sixth sense of animals (which feel a ripple of energy when another sentient being approaches), their "instinctive sensitivity" has been "shorted out from overload" (130). In the guise of Eli, she expresses disapproval of the manners and motives of many humans, especially those in business. On the first page of *The Shepherd Moon* (Viking, 1984) is a sentence typical of Hoover's thought-provoking style: "The woman was waiting for the world to change. The girl wanted to see the moonrise" (3). The surprising contrast of age and youth hooks the reader into wondering about the author's own perspective: Is it romanticized fantasy or tough-minded science fiction? Set firmly in the context of technical and social possibilities, Hoover's work is always more science than fantasy, but it focuses its careful scientific purview on social, psychological, and ethical questions as well as on technological possibilities and hypotheses about the material world. Her work includes quite a bit of scientific theory based on validated facts, like most other science fiction, but the inclusion of political and social themes makes the tone of her writing differ from traditional sf. In this case Hoover contrasts the concerns of the privileged 12-year-old Merry, who sits on the cold beach for the aesthetic pleasure of watching the rare concurrence of five of the manmade moons rising together, with the more pragmatic concern of Worth, a servant who, like others of her station, has known too much hunger, filth, and cold to enjoy the sight.

Tonight only four moons rise, and a strange, stinking capsule falls from the sky onto the beach. Inside, Merry discovers Mikel, a beautiful young man who frightens her despite his apparent charm. As the story is told by the alternating voices of Merry and this young newcomer from the heavens, the reader recognizes a connection between the two. Both have been raised as privileged members of their race, but while Merry is gentle and kind, innocent of the hard lives of the poor, Mikel has learned to be hard, sophisticated, and deceptive in order to survive. He uses pied-piper-like powers to attract children and other innocents to hear promises about the Shepherd Moon, where they will receive sustenance and care. As Mikel wreaks great havoc on those who befriend him, Merry tries to track down the reasons for his vengeful nature. When she adopts a young runaway in an attempt to rescue her, Merry discovers the horrible conditions of the servant class in her own world. She subsequently realizes that being sheltered from knowing about cruelty does not make her less culpable than Mikel, who knows the world firsthand. Ignorance does not equal innocence. Like her grandmother for whom she is named, Merry decides to take responsibility for her world and try to change it. The nursemaid she had scorned for her insensitivity has martyred herself to make life better for the poor, and Merry will take up her cause.

Like many of Hoover's other protagonists, Merry is ignored by her mother and father. None of this would have happened to her if her parents hadn't forgotten her while they enjoyed the social luxuries of the privileged class, blissfully unaware of the suffering of workers who make their comforts possible and doggedly unappreciative of their daughter's intelligence and ethical strength.

Orvis (1987), winner of the 1987 Parents Choice Honor Award, features a robot whose outdated appearance and eccentric nature have made it seem useless to adults but a perfect companion to Toby, a 12-year-old girl mourning yet another move away from friends and schoolmates, from Earth to Mars. Toby prefers Earth because she likes the security of a breathable atmosphere and the variety of the environment. Centuries earlier, humans had almost destroyed Earth's atmosphere by causing holes that let in too much sun, necessitating artificial shields over the few areas that were still populated. In the twenty-fourth century, however, the atmospheric gases were rebalanced so that humans could live outside again. Like Toby, her friend Thaddeus is also the child of well-educated and well-heeled ruling-class parents who are too busy to pay much attention to their offspring. In this book as in others, Hoover expresses disapproval of the privileged classes, comparing them to "the aristocrats of old who sent generations of their too young sons away to exclusive boarding schools famous for poor food, cruel social structures, cold water, and primitive sanitation—all of which were thought to be character building deprivations"(29). Feeling dumped at school and constrained by their parents' expectations, Toby and Thaddeus empathize with the robot, named Orvis, who has been ordered to deposit himself at the landfill. Created to obey, Orvis realizes that this has been the last order programmed into him; now he is free to make his own choices. He soon realizes, however, that "[one] liberty leads to another, one choice to another, until self-discipline must be imposed to avoid mental chaos. Freedom is frightening" (50). But Orvis chooses freedom.

Orvis's intelligence is immense, including not only the logical data entered by a variety of previous owners but also input from an electronic nerve net that helped him become self-educating. Through this character, Hoover dispenses a great number of memorable observations: "Humans smile to avert threat" (42); "Humans believe they have a soul and non-humans do not" (55). Fortunately Orvis has also learned practical tasks, like making a fire from brush and identifying poisonous plants. After he and the children are kidnapped en route to Toby's great-grandmother Goldie and then abandoned in a forest, Orvis's skills save the children's lives, just as they have saved him from the landfill. After a brief visit to a community of older humans who also feel displaced in the modern world, Orvis, Toby, and Thaddeus find acceptance and caring in their respective new homes. *Orvis* explores family relationships, children's need for their parents, grandparents' need for their children, and friends' ability to substitute for family bonds. Hoover's lessons are more explicit in this book than in others; her style is more didactic, but the straight-faced wit of Orvis's statements lightens the seriousness of her teaching. This book, appropriate for middle schoolers, is fun to read.

Away Is a Strange Place to Be (1990) is set in 2349, when Earth is only one of the habitable planets in a galaxy of colonies crafted to resemble the most lovely resort areas of Earth but without the annoyances of real dirt, bacteria, or animal life. Abby Tabor lives with her Uncle Mochi, manager of the elegant seaside country inn at St. Anne's, a luxurious mansion that entertains visitors to Earth who are amused by the quaintness of the ducks, deer, and other natural life now considered old-fashioned. Twelve-year-old Abby loves most of her work at the inn, guided by her beloved

elderly uncle, who is preparing her to inherit the elegant livelihood he has created, but she sometimes wishes she could choose
another life. As the story begins, she is putting up with Bryan, a
spoiled brat of a guest who is the only other child at the inn. Obviously lonely and bored, Bryan follows Abby around, making trouble and turning up his nose at her and the homeliness of Earth.
Suddenly the two are kidnapped and taken to work as slaves for
VitaCon, a corporation experiencing a shortage of the cheap labor
needed to finish the development of another habitat for profit, a
future home for five million human colonists that is being made
Earthlike through the inclusion of hand-planted gardens and
hand-painted skies. VitaCon, short on robots, has contracted with
orphanages and a few parents, including Bryan's father, to provide a disciplined environment for "vocational training"; taking
Abby was merely a mistake. The young people are put to work,
dressed in vibrant pink robes, housed in shabby cell-like dormito-
ries, drugged into submission, and monitored by guards armed
with stun guns. Quickly Abby realizes how sheltered her life has
been as she watches young Cleo, a former ward of the state, react
with gratitude for the mediocre food, the daily routine of work,
and the bright pink costume. Another inmate is hostile to Abby,
envious of her former life in a privileged home. While the garden-
ing work is not unpleasant, Abby realizes that once the habitat is
finished, she and the other children will be a dispensable embarrassment to the corporation. She foresees a future as a "crispy
critter," the name given to trash that is freeze-dried and inciner-
ated to save space and keep the spaceship's orbit clean.

Threatened by increasing fear and vacillation, Abby runs from
the work site with only a mere shadow of an escape plan. Bryan
follows her. The success of their escape depends more on luck
than on skill, but the two suffer great suspense, never sure of
their success until the end. Abby remembers a line from a play
that summarizes their situation: "If you want to destroy a man,
first cause him to despair, then give him reason to hope, then
destroy all hope" (111). This pattern epitomizes not only the story
of their escape, but also the lives of the other imprisoned children
set adrift by inept parents or unfortunate circumstances, awarded

entrance to this institution that promises education for a better future but dispenses with them when they are no longer cost-efficient.

When Abby meets Bryan's mother, she finds a woman driven by ambition for great wealth and status who has succeeded in becoming the Comptroller of Triark, another development corporation. Bryan is delighted to be back home in the habitat ruled by his mother; it is a beautiful, clean residence without the mess of animal or insect life—the ultimate synthetic resort for the rich. Bryan's self-centered, manipulative behavior obviously results from this luxurious life where the abundance of material goods hides the lack of warmth and attention from parents or friends. Bryan's mother is so cold natured that she even threatens to kidnap Abby from her uncle to suppress the publicity that might embarrass VitaCon, a corporate world closely allied to her business interests. For her, her son, Bryan, exists merely as a link to future investments.

In contrast to the cool restraint of Bryan's return to Triark, Abby is greeted with tears and celebration by not only her uncle but a great number of the inn staff as well. She uses the bribe money that Bryan's mother has finally forced on her proud uncle to help arrange the rescue of the other children from VitaCon. Some of these children have been so abused that even though they are emaciated and weak, they do not want to be rescued, valuing the relative security of their present circumstances over the uncertain challenge of Earth life. Hoover contrasts the privileged life of Abby, who enjoys her work at the lovely inn, with the lives of the lonely children spoiled by well-to-do but neglectful parents and the other lonely children who are neglected because they are poor. The story line is quick and suspenseful, and the characters are motivated by a realistically complicated mesh of circumstance and passion. Abby loves the secure elegance of life at the inn but resents its constraining routines. Bryan irritates her with his snobbish remarks and elicits her sympathy for his loneliness. Even the minor characters have developed personalities: Mr. White, the guard who bullies and taunts the children with sarcasm and his stun gun, turns out to be only 16. Cleo, the younger girl who befriends Abby in VitaCon, has a past that makes her pathetically grateful for small favors. Even Pat, the girl who threatens Abby, is driven to cruelty by fear as well as natural orneriness. This novel is a deceptively light read, but its social commentary runs clear and deep. Even the spoiled brat Bryan recognizes how he may have learned from his experiences with Abby. In a phone conversation with this girl who has taught him to care for her as a friend, he asks: "If I promise to try to be a nicer person, will you promise to put up with me until I am?" (167). Abby accepts the deal.

Only Child (1992), an environmental novel, puns on its title phrase. Twelve-year-old Cody was born on a spaceship two light years from Earth while traveling outward toward Patma, a frontier planet. His mother, Dr. Olivia Palcheek, is a neurobiologist who relates to her son more as a subject of study than as an object of affection. As he is the first child born in the artificial environment of a spaceship, his initial reactions to solid ground, gravity, and open-air spaces are valuable data for science and the media. Cody's real source of affection is Dr. Emily Avichenko, affectionately known as Avi, who has acted as mother to him from his infancy. As the only child among a crew of adults, Cody grows up like a favorite pet, content with the only life he has ever known.

Patma is owned and managed by a corporation as a source of gems and seashells and as a recreational stop for the crews of its ships. The seaside hotels have all the amenities of a luxurious tropical resort; the white sandy beaches edge a blue-green sea, and bright flowers and birds flourish. After Cody adjusts to gravity and learns to ride an air scooter that skims over the beautiful land, he begins to explore. Lying in a cool beachside cave, he overhears a conversation between two creatures—each with five green eyes on a large oblong face with brown velvet skin atop a large body with six jointed legs. After some incomprehensible conversation, one of the creatures captures Cody and takes him into their community. Cody learns from their leader that these "skippers," named for their mode of locomotion, are intelligent beings who hide from the humans of his spaceship because humans have traditionally killed them as specimens or captured them for study. This practice violates the law of the universe that maintains that no one can claim land already inhabited by intelligent beings. When Cody wonders why this law has not been respected, one creature explains human ethnocentrism in the language he learned as a youngster when he was captured by humans and kept as a pet.

The book's theme is reminiscent of *The Lost Star*. As with the lumpies in that story, the heavy, squat appearance of the skippers is assumed to indicate mental dullness. Though these creatures use tools, make decisions, and cooperate socially, their intelligence is not recognized. As the leader tells Cody, "Your kind does not listen to others. Pets. To them, only humans can think or feel" (47). Recognizing that experience of not being heard by adults and of being treated as a curious specimen, Cody, like Lian in *The Lost Star,* becomes the guardian of the creatures' future.

This book, slight and readable at an elementary level, nevertheless clearly delineates the thoughtless and arrogant exploitation of animal species by humans. Cody's solution to protecting the aliens without exposing them to further exploitation is simple yet practical. Using the video camera given to him by his mother to assuage her guilt at using her own child as a research subject, Cody films the lives and artifacts of the skippers as proof that despite corporation claims to the contrary, intelligent life does exist on the planet Patma. The skippers allow Cody to film them because he respects them as equals; he tells them all he knows about humanity and corporate law. In return, the leader of the skippers listens and promises to pray for him.

Cody reminds him, "You told me each one thing is special, that one affects all the rest. If you truly believe that, then even though I'm human, I have to matter to you. And you have to listen to me" (114). " 'Yess,' it hissed. 'You do well to remind me. You matter, young human. I may not understand why, but there is a reason you came to this world' " (115). The leader admires Cody for endangering his own safety for the sake of preserving another civilization. The wise leader appreciates the innocent clarity of Cody's ethics that allows him to blame even his own people for disobeying a natural law. They take Cody to the Sacred Caves where the aliens' prayers warm Cody, filling him with courage to return to the Earth he has never seen and to step out from the security of the familiar closed-in space of the ship that has been his home. He knows that even though he is only a child, his actions can matter to the world. His experience reiterates the theme that a single strong person can bring about change, "like the keystone to an arch" (*Return to Earth*, 110).

Hoover sprinkles her work with wonderfully profound epigrams like this one to express her views about humanity. Children are often portrayed as lonely—their parents, especially mothers, are too busy with high-powered careers to attend fully to their children and sometimes use material goods as bribery against guilt. For individuals with political or economic power, friendship is suspect, often based more on motives of profit and status than on honesty. This pessimistic view of humanity is tempered by Hoover's portrayals of wonderful friendships developing between beings of different ages and even between different species— bonds based on equal respect, similar intelligence, and a commitment to consider the other's viewpoint. In *Return to Earth* Hoover stresses this commitment through the voice of Galen, who admits that he loves more people than he likes. He explains, "Loving doesn't require thought, just acceptance" (35).

Similarly Hoover differentiates between ethical practice and religious ritual or creed. Many of her protagonists spend much energy reflecting on the morality of their actions, exploring the ramifications of what they do and say by imaginatively entering the heads of whatever sentient beings they affect. Organized religion, however, is at times portrayed by Hoover as an institution used by immoral leaders to shield the masses of people from recognizing their oppression; religion can be used to prevent them from seeking free choice in their lives. Generally, corporate institutions tend to make harmful decisions, whereas individuals who think independently raise questions that lead to fairness, peaceful existence, and environmental balance. For Hoover the good life seems to be a rural community near the ocean where individuals practice their crafts in harmony with the natural world, yet retain enough technology to ensure comfort and good health. It is a vision similar to the utopia described by Ursula K. Le Guin in *Always Coming Home*, where technology is used sensibly to store knowledge and permit universal communication but does not replace the pleasure of handcrafts, cooking, and the natural pace of life based on the sun and the seasons. To many adults as well as young people, this sounds like a good vision to share, one that can transform the future.

While Hill's space adventures encourage universal government to preserve peaceful coexistence among all kinds of civilizations, Hoover's alternate worlds explore ways to live harmoniously among individuals. Is it a coincidence that Douglas Hill uses physical prowess, self-control, and military ingenuity to conquer evil by winning war games, while the female H. M. Hoover discusses ways various individuals and cultures can attend to one another's views and compromise to get along together? The differences between Hill and Hoover may epitomize many of the gender-specific stereotypical comparisons made by readers and critics of science fiction since women became visible players in the field. Yet important shared views between the two writers must not be overlooked. Both Hill and Hoover protest our cultural tendency to judge the intelligence, character, and worth of organisms by their exterior appearance, and both emphasize the preeminent value of personal relationships in working toward a future existence worth living. Hill and Hoover differ in their metaphorical imagery and the shape of their plots, but the motivations of their protagonists to pursue peace and connection are alike.

Chronology: H. M. Hoover's Life and Works

1935   Born 5 April in Stark County, Ohio, daughter of Edward Lehr and Sadie Schandel Hoover, both teachers.

1952–1955   Attends Mount Union College and Los Angeles County School of Nursing.

1973   *Children of Morrow,* her first science fiction novel, published.

1974   *The Lion's Club,* her first historical fiction, published. Selected as a children's book of the year by the Child Study Association of America and chosen for the American Library Association's best books for young adults annual list.

1981   *Another Heaven, Another Earth* selected for the best books for young adults list.

1982   *Another Heaven, Another Earth* selected for the Ohioana Award.

1984   Receives the Central Missouri State College Award for outstanding contribution to children's literature.

1987   *Orvis* receives the Parents Choice Honor Award.

1988   *The Dawn Palace* is selected as an ALA best book for young adults, receives the Parents Choice Honor Award, and is included on Enoch Pratt Library's "Youth to Youth" books list."

1989   *The Dawn Palace* is named to the Library of Congress best books for children list and is designated a notable children's trade book by *Social Education.*

1990   *Away Is a Strange Place to Be* is published.

1995   *The Winds of Mars* is published.

1997   *The Whole Truth . . . and Other Myths,* Hoover's retelling of myths that inspired several artistic masterpieces, is published by the National Gallery of Art.

6. Feminism and Science Fiction: Pamela Sargent

In an autobiographical article in *Language Arts* (1980), H. M. Hoover describes a phone call she received from an editor after she submitted her first book, *Children of Morrow,* to Four Winds Press: "The first thing she said was 'You're H. M. Hoover?' And I said yes, and she said 'I won! I won! We had a bet on here as to whether you were a male or a female' " (Hoover, "SF—Out of This World," 428). What made the editor, who reads many books, so sure? What made her risk money on such a bet?

Women Writers and Pseudonyms

Women writers of sf have felt so rare and unwelcome in the field that many have resorted to using initials, genderless pseudonyms, and even male names to receive an unbiased reading. Early-twentieth-century writers C. L. Moore and Leigh Brackett assumed a male voice and ambivalent names to avoid prejudice from the publishing world. Even Ursula K. Le Guin, long accepted as a premier sf writer, published a story in *Playboy* magazine as U.L.G., and Alice Mary Norton wrote both as Andrew North and, more recently, as the ambiguous Andre Norton. The most famous case of a woman writer fooling the public is the story of Alice Sheldon, who borrowed her pen name from a marmalade jar and, at age 52, started publishing widely respected science fiction as James Tiptree Jr. Few readers suspected that Tiptree was female because the writing was forthright and clever and the stories' male characters were decent, likable men. A year before Jeffrey Smith revealed her gender in 1976, Tiptree was asked to withdraw from a written symposium, *Khatur 3 & 4,* because the nine other women in the group resented the defiant maleness of the author's writing. The readers who praised Tiptree's particularly sensitive portrayal of characters (a trait supposedly unusual in science fiction, which is more plot-centered) were admiring a characteristic traditionally attributed to women writers. Critics who try to classify sf written by females claim that it focuses more on the network of characters' interaction than on the linear unraveling of events, and that it uses the "soft" sciences of sociology, psychology, and biology more than physics and chemistry. Whether this is a valid contrast is difficult to judge without careful study of individual works side by side, but this stereotype certainly makes sense in light of social history of the genre.

Reasons for the Dearth of Women Writers

Science fiction has traditionally been a man's field because it focuses on the male-dominated subjects of science and technology. In her foreword to *Women of Wonder* (1975), a collection of sf stories written about women by women, editor Pamela Sargent notes that "publications for science fiction readers have at various times reported that most of their subscribers are men; a readership of 90% male and 10% female is not unusual."[1] Reasons for the traditional dearth of women sf writers are not easily validated scientifically, but logic suggests that because women were discouraged from entering the fields of technology and science before the 1960s, they were also not encouraged to become readers and writers of science fiction. Traditionally considered more intuitive than logical, more social than intellectual, women were not deemed capable of understanding the technical jargon of sf or enjoying its plot-centered nature. Although the Hugo Award was first given in 1953, there were no female winners until 1967. Although both feminism and science fiction flowered in the 1970s, there were only 11 female winners of the many sf prizes awarded in the 16 years between 1968 and 1984. Not until 1974 was the topic of women and sf seriously discussed in a major public forum, when Susan Wood led a panel discussion at the World Conference.

During the two decades since then, feminism in science fiction has waned, denigrated by some critics as a tiresome fad, and then, in more recent years, waxed again. In her introduction to *The Norton Book of Science Fiction* (1993), Ursula K. Le Guin, herself only a recent convert to feminist ideology, describes her view of the present status of women sf writers: "I wish science fiction were not as male as it is, but it isn't as male as it was, not by a long shot. The strong and brilliant female presences in this book give me joy, and that so many of them are young gives me confidence. We have regendered a field that was, to begin with, practically solid testosterone."[2] There were notable exceptions, women whose provocative tales proved that fine science fiction could be written by females, and their works help define gender differences as well as broaden the definition of the genre.

First Women Writers of Science Fiction

The first great female writer of science fiction wrote one of the most important works that define the field. Many students of sf have noted the irony of the fact that although Mary Shelley was one of the genre's main progenitors, no major female characters appear in her book *Frankenstein*. Other early sf works were written by women, but they are few. In Rhoda Broughton's "Behold It Was a Dream" (1873) the main character, Dinah Bellairs, sees the death of friends in a dream before they die. This emphasis on dreaming seemed "soft" to the hard science males, who placed more value on mechanical gadgetry.

Not until almost fifty years later was another sf work by a woman published. In 1917 "The Nightmare" by Francis Stevens (aka Gertrude Barrows) appeared, and two years later her novel *The Heads of Cerberus* (1919) introduced the concept of parallel time, in which a world much like ours develops along another historical path because of different choices or events. An example of the parallel time concept is in Philip K. Dick's alternate history *The Man in the High Castle,* which describes what the world might have looked like had the Nazis won World War II. Francis Stevens herself mysteriously disappeared from history after moving to California in the mid-1930s.

Another female who initiated a modern sf convention is Catherine L. (published as C. L.) Moore, who in *No Woman Born* (1944) explores the yearning of her cyborg heroine Deirdre for social contact with other humans, echoing Mary Shelley's portrayal of her mechanical hero's need for human contact in *Frankenstein.* In Moore's book the brain of a former dancer who has been badly injured in an accident is placed in a mechanical body that is unable to dance with conventional grace. However, Deirdre overcomes the public's acceptance of only certain conventional movements and invents a new kind of dance. As with other sf writers who published in the pulp magazines of the 1930s and 1940s, many of Moore's protagonists were he-man heroes, like Northwest Smith, a traditional adventurer of the solar system. After marrying Henry Kuttner in 1940, C. L. Moore wrote collaboratively with her husband until his death in 1958.

Female Characters in Science Fiction

During the heyday of pulp science fiction in the 1940s, women were portrayed more as pets than as humans. Pamela Sargent notes that "sf became a neighborhood clubhouse where the boys could get together away from the girls (or parents or the short-sighted culture at large), who were a nuisance anyway" (Sargent, xxxvii). There, the males could freely enjoy the adventures of science and technology, which they considered their own proper domain. At worst, the attitude of these writers toward women is summed up in Lester del Rey's "Helen O'Loy" (1938), which describes a robotic woman programmed to be the perfect wife, selfless and loyal to the extent that she chooses to die with her husband-inventor. Isaac Asimov did portray a female scientist, Dr. Susan Calvin, but she, like other working women in his stories from the 1940s, is single;

the reader can assume that she would be more fulfilled as a wife and mother. "She writes like a man" was high praise for female writers in this era of heroic adventurers and solar system cowboys. For most writers of sf, however, women were just not relevant to the future they envisioned. Speculative fiction designed worlds invented by men and dominated by men.

In the 1950s, women characters often reflected that decade's assumption that women's roles were best limited to housewife and mother, sheltered enough from the outside so as not to comprehend the complexities of science and technology. Men who had been to war wanted to maintain the security of their childhood homes as remembered through a rosy haze. The postwar preference for a virile but cynical and emotionally insulated male hero is embodied in the work of Robert Heinlein. Sargent, in her introduction to *Women of Wonder,* discusses at length Heinlein's complex attitudes toward women. Perhaps his portraits of women as sexually provocative, focused on getting a man and keeping him, are a result of "cultural spillage," where an author has subconsciously absorbed the values of his environment (xliv). But is this an appropriate attitude for a speculative writer? Sargent's answer is negative: "A science-fiction writer, because of the distinctive nature of his or her work, must be on guard and ready to assume a skeptical or questioning attitude" toward the status quo (xliv). She then wonders if Heinlein's public liberal persona is at odds with his fictional portrayal of women as people who, although they may display superior intelligence at times, prefer protection, sexual subjugation, and the role of wife and mother after their youthful adventures. In this lengthy passage carefully delineating all of Heinlein's virtues, Sargent seems to be encouraging Heinlein, and other sf writers who wish to emulate him, to examine their consciences and reconsider their portrayals of women.

The Growing Numbers of Women Writers

Since the early 1960s when the Civil Rights and Women's Liberation movements heightened public awareness of those who had been marginalized by mainstream society, science fiction has been slowly generating a more inclusive view. More women writers of sf have been published, more women characters appear as active protagonists in science fiction, and more women are active in the field as critics, scholars, and authors. One of the most active of these women whose careers have made a remarkable impact on the field of science fiction is Pamela Sargent.

Life of Pamela Sargent

Pamela Sargent (1948–   ) enjoyed her early years in Ithaca, New York, a "child-sized" city[3] enlivened by the intellectually curious people attracted there by Cornell University, where her parents had met as students. As a child she swam in the Cayuga River, wandered through the downtown area, and explored the university's hilly campus. She still touts this area of New York State as an ideal place to vacation—lovely, green, and serene. Her inner life, however, was not wholly at peace.

Like many people who become science fiction aficionados, Sargent had a unique view of life from her early years. Nearsighted almost to the point of blindness, she first experienced the world as a "chaotic place, full of unseen dangers and events I could not predict" (Elliot, 74). In her essay cleverly titled "Through the Looking Glass," printed as an afterword in Jeffrey Elliot's bibliography of her work, she reminisces about how her early confusion over the world outside herself led her to seek order, first in the stories she invented herself and then in those she discovered in books—books she could see better than the fuzzy television screen. Before entering school she taught herself to read and write, "crouched over paper, my eyes only a couple inches from the pencil" (Elliot, 74).

Her life was chaotic in other ways as well. While both her parents were artistically talented and mentally energetic, her father's early heart attack, while he was only in his twenties, curtailed several of his attempted careers, and he became known as quirky and undependable. Sargent's mother worked to help support the family, and Pam was often responsible for taking care of her younger sister and brothers. This emotional burden led her to decide at an early age that she could never depend on a husband for economic security. For her, life was sometimes a frightening challenge. She manipulated these anxieties and insecurities into stories that she used to entertain her siblings. At summer camp her ability to titillate the imagination of her fellow campers terrorized them out of sleepiness, and the camp counselor begged her, unsuccessfully, to stop. When Sargent was 9, she wrote two plays for her schoolmates to perform at Elsmere Elementary School, which she attended after her family moved to Albany. At 12 she discovered science fiction, when E. Everett Evan's *Man of Many Minds* was included by mistake in an order of paperbacks. "Here was a protagonist who could read other minds, who boarded a spaceship and traveled to another planet, who met aliens—it all struck me as terribly original" (Elliot, 5). It reminded her of how, when she got her first pair of glasses in the second grade, she suddenly saw the world differently, more sharply focused. As a writer of science fiction she provides new lenses for her readers so they too can see a different version of life.

Science fiction can also be a way for intellectual young people to escape from the psychological pains of adolescence. When she was 14, Sargent attended the Albany Academy for Girls, an institution for troubled youth where she became desperately angry and discouraged. At a particularly low point, she read Alfred Bester's tale "The Stars My Destination," which she now considers an "emotional lifeline."[4] In a letter written in 1990, she describes how it affected her: "I read "The Stars My Destination" in a very unsophisticated way. I identified with Gully Foyle, imagined being able to teleport, as he did, out of the hellhole I was in. In a weird way, the book gave me some sense of a possible future, because I'd try to imagine myself leaping past that experience and looking back from a time when I'd finally escaped it (Engel, 10)." The uncomfortable lessons Sargent learned in her childhood appear in her younger protagonists, who tend to be unusually independent, distrustful of authority, and emotionally distant. Sargent is pleased that her own science fiction often elicits letters from teens who also have suffered and who have found solace from her writing, identifying with characters who face life alone.

Even after succeeding academically and winning praise for her dramatic scripts, which were performed in school, she did not consider herself a writer. In 1990 she admitted: "The earliest serious ambition I had was to be an actress, largely because the only other kinds of jobs apparently open to women at the time—namely, being a secretary, nurse, teacher, or hair stylist—all required you to be reasonably respectable and work long hours for not much pay. It made more sense, at least to me, to dream of something that might provide money, fame, and a chance for lurid love affairs" (Engel, 3). Her mother's gift of Betty Friedan's *The Feminine Mystique* encouraged her rejection of the traditional homemaker role.

After graduation from high school she entered the State University of New York at Binghamton, where she majored in philosophy, taking courses that challenged her to think clearly. During her first year there she met a fellow student, George Zebrowski, whose determination to become a writer of science fiction encouraged her to consider writing as more than a diversion. She and Zebrowski remain together, keeping close contact with another sf buff from their college days, Jack Dann. In her senior year she began her career as a published writer with the sale of two short stories, "Oasis" and "Landed Minority." Sargent describes how her academic interests meshed: "I was finishing a paper on Aristotle's *Nicomachean Ethics;* in a fit of exasperation, I set that aside and wrote 'Landed Minority' which Ed Ferman bought not long afterward" (Engel, 3). She joined the Science Fiction Writers of America (SFWA) in the following year and with Zebrowski and their friend Jack Dann edited the *SFWA Bulletin* until 1975. More of her short stories were published in magazines such as *Fantasy and Science Fiction, Universe, Protostars,* and *New Worlds.*

First Anthology of Women's Science Fiction

In 1975 Sargent's *Women of Wonder,* an anthology of science fiction stories written by women about women, appeared. Amazingly, it is the first work of its kind. After its rejection by many other publishers, Vonda N. McIntyre, a prominent writer who finally convinced Vintage to publish a collection by women, suggested that Sargent submit her stories, which received enough acclaim to warrant four subsequent collections. These include reprinted sf stories by Sonya Dorman, Ursula K. Le Guin, Joanna Russ, Josephine Saxton, Chelsea Quinn Yarbro, and Joan D. Vinge.

In her introduction to *Women of Wonder,* Sargent extensively explores the history of women writers of science fiction and issues the challenge to Heinlein cited previously. This first volume of the series, often used as a text in science fiction and women's studies courses, was an important step in bringing the growing number of women writers of science fiction to the public's attention. In the process of editing *Women of Wonder,* Sargent recognized herself as part of a long tradition of women writers of science fiction and decided to commit her life to writing.

Early Work of Pamela Sargent

Sargent's first novel, *Cloned Lives* (1976), received praise for its realism and accessible style. Astrophysicist Paul Swenson agrees to be cloned as part of an experiment and raises the five infants cloned from himself as his own, which, of course, they are. Isolated by the scorn of the general public, the five have an especially difficult time establishing individual identities separate from their genetically identical siblings. Sargent had explored this theme in three previous short stories, "A Sense of Difference," "Clone Sister," and "Father." "Clone Sister" is about erotic feelings between two siblings, an exploration of androgyny: Is the protagonist who imagines herself sexually involved with her cloned "brother" really in love with herself? Sargent's research for this book led to a second feminist anthology, *Bio-Futures: Science Fiction Stories about Biological Metamorphosis* (1976), a collection of stories that raise questions about the ethical and social impact of biological technology, an issue particularly relevant to women because of their role in bearing children.

Starshadows and Blue Roses (1977), a collection of Sargent's own short stories, including "Clone Sister," contains inklings of themes that underlie most of her subsequent work. In "Shadows" the prisoner Suzanne breaks the bonds of stereotypical thinking that control her and her friends when she is able to approve of the ultimate goals of their captors. Formerly a weak-willed, whining sort of person, this woman who has always played a traditional role finds her own voice, independent of her friends and former lover. She finally speaks her mind, a virtue inherent in Sargent's outspoken protagonists. The use of empathy to understand how the world works is also important to Sargent, as it is to many feminist writers. Perhaps it stems from females' traditional interest in understanding the motives of the people around them, once necessary in tribal or village living to protect the young and weak. In any case, feeling and understanding the minds of others is an important theme in the writing of Ursula K. Le Guin, where it is called "mindspeech," and in Octavia Butler's Patternist series. Empathetic powers are just one aspect of the global connection that most modern sf worlds assume. In her next book Sargent explores the dangers of a single totalitarian rule.

In *The Sudden Star* (1979), because of cutbacks by the central governments a virus has spilled out of the laboratory kept on Earth. Sargent plays with multiple points of view as a prostitute and an ex-con doctor travel from New York to Miami Beach through a nation badly frayed by overpopulation and a recent bout with nuclear war. Greed for power has undermined the safety nets against the kinds of accidents that could destroy humanity. This complicated struggle pits the values of individual status and power against communal preservation and compassion. Sargent is hardly a simple humanist protesting the use of science, however. In *The Golden Space* (1982), humans, now immortal, try to create better lives by applying analytic logic to human problems. As in *Cloned Lives,* the theme deals with biotechnology.

Sargent's Works for Young People

Sargent's books for older children continue themes established in *Watchstar* (1980). Empathetic Daiya is a traditional hero in that she undertakes a daring adventure and brings home new knowledge as the prize, but she is also a compassionate female, using her mental talents of empathy, telepathy, and telekinesis to comprehend a person rather than using a sword to slay him. The mysterious stranger Rieho, a descendant of the Earthfolk, holds knowledge that can both harm and heal. Daiya must learn to use the knowledge she senses in him without getting fatally hurt.

Sargent's first young adult novel, *Earthseed* (1983), reflects her early habit of doubting her first perceptions. Always suspicious of what parents and other authorities teach their young, Sargent encourages her readers to question deeply with minds as independent as possible of preconceptions. Before the orphaned adolescent protagonists, led by Zoheret, may leave the spaceship where they have been raised by a computer named Ship, they discover that much of what they have learned in their childhoods is false. They must learn on their own to judge what is true and trustworthy. In *Eye of the Comet* (1984) Lydee, originally from Earth, has grown up on a lush, technologically advanced comet controlled by the computer Homesmind. Now she is sent on a mission to help the people of Earth regain the knowledge they have lost through the generations. The third book of the trilogy, *Homesmind* (1984), focuses on a telepathic meeting between generations. On Earth Anra and some friends try to establish communication between the Earthfolk and the people of the comet that seems so threatening. This union proves fortuitous when another enemy comet invades the solar system.

In *The Shore of Women* (1986) Sargent depicts a hunter-gatherer society where a small group of powerful, intelligent women dominate the men. Sargent calls this her "love story for feminists" (Elliot, 8), though the book, highly praised by many readers, has been damned both by ardent feminists, who feel that her female characters should be more humane and fair-minded, and by traditionalists, who feel that men are depicted unsympathetically. The novel's premise resembles that of two other sf feminist novels: *Motherlines* by Suzy McKee Charnas and *The Gate to Women's Country* by Sheri Tepper, in which women and men live separately on an Earth ruined by nuclear war. In Sargent's book the women, determined to prevent more war and destruction, have walled themselves inside cities that they control through their technological superiority. Told in several voices, the story delineates the experiences of three young protagonists: Laissa, who is part of the urban dominant class; Arvil, a young hunter who lives with the rest of the men in the wilderness; and Birana, a rebel who has been banished from both societies. Sargent portrays women who protect their dominance defensively, afraid that sharing power will lead to oppression in the future, but she also depicts women who are willing to reconcile as long as they can maintain the personal freedoms they have gained. This is a radically feminist novel, appreciated by many readers unfamiliar with science fiction, yet scorned by readers who resent the implicit attack on the male establishment. In this work Sargent engages in social criticism rather than scientific theory or futuristic technology. In her next books, she reverses that focus.

The Venus Series

Venus of Dreams (1986) and *Venus of Shadows* (1988) describe a near-future world ruled by an Islamic cult that wants to spread its domain beyond Earth to the planet Venus. Based on Thomas Mann's *Buddenbrooks,* which traces a family's growing wealth and refinement yet moral decline, and on the theories of "terraforming," whereby other planets are modified for human survival as discussed in James Oberg's *New Earths,* the book combines the sociological depth of the nineteenth-century novel with futuristic science. In *Venus of Dreams,* readers watch the preparation of colonists from Earth who will be able to survive on Venus by changing the temperature and chemistry of its atmosphere; *Venus of Shadows* continues the story through the generations as Risa Liangharad, daughter of Iris, reacts to the evolving social and political texture of this new settlement. Although many readers rank this series as an all-time favorite, the Venus books fall through the cracks for those sf readers who define themselves as either "new humanists" who focus on character development and social criticism, as in Sargent's previous works, and those who prefer the technical, hard-science fiction of cyberpunk literature. The Venus books are a saga, detailing a fully developed world and peopled with complex characters, yet the imagery is the ultramodern technology of physics-based "space age" science. Sargent calls the cybernetic Habbers who inhabit the Venus worlds "cyberutopians" rather than cyberpunks because they escape the mechanical aspects of Earth's urban jungle in order to create a more stable society. The feel of the book calls to mind the traditionally male arena of courageous exploration and bold conquest, but the themes and the pace are feminist.

Alien Child (1988), written for young people, poses questions about the future of the human race. Nita is a young girl born into the alien world of a future where humanity has become extinct. After she realizes that she is the last of the human race, Nita tries to discover what happened. This chilling theme, verging on horror, is made more terrible by the philosophical depth of Sargent's style.

Feminist Issues

In 1993 Sargent's first departure from science fiction was published by Crown, the publisher of Jean Auel's historical sagas. *Ruler of the Sky* is a massive tome that relates the previously untold story of Mongol women in the era of Genghis Khan, again bringing once-ignored female accomplishments from the shadows of male-dominated history.

A summary list of the feminist issues Sargent has addressed in her writing would not only include the themes of empathy, independence, and cooperation for safety but also describe the following roles:

> *Women Ignored by History:* Neither women writers of science fiction nor the women of outer Mongolia have been noticed by historians or other publicists.
> *Women as Wives and Mothers:* are marginalized in roles that involve psychological servitude.
> *Women as Sex Objects:* Science fiction portrayed women as mere sexual playthings both on their covers and in prose, in the past and in the current cyberpunk literature.
> *Women as Dominant:* Several feminist utopias imagine a society where the establishment is female.

Women as Equally Competent: Especially in literature for young people, female characters act with intelligence, emotional control, and physical prowess equal to that of male characters.

Androgyny: The Disappearance of Gender Differences: As in Ursula K. Le Guin's *The Left Hand of Darkness,* the disappearance of gender differences raises interesting questions about the necessity of differentiated sex roles.

Some Prominent Women Writers of Science Fiction: Since the 1970s women writers of science fiction have begun to achieve recognition from this field traditionally dominated by males.

A paraphrase of another list may indicate the reasonableness of Sargent's feminist visions of science fiction. In 1990 "The Martin scale," measuring levels of feminism, was composed only somewhat satirically by Diane Martin, the editor of *Aurora,* a radical journal that defines sf as "speculative feminism."

Level One: Women are victims of male dominance.
Level Two: Women and men are equal.
Level Three: Women are better than men in some aspects.
Level Four: Woman are better than men.
Level Five: Men are necessary but a pain to live with.
Level Six: Poor pathetic men . . . what can you do?
Level Seven: Men make good slaves.
Level Eight: Women need to separate from men to survive.
Level Nine: Lesbian/feminist utopias are pretty good!
Level Ten: Parthenogenesis or scenes of castration are a conceivable answer.

Joanna Russ

One of the earliest women writers of science fiction recognized as a radical feminist is Joanna Russ (1937–   ). Professor of

English at the University of Washington since 1977, Russ began to publish reviews and short stories in the *Magazine of Fantasy and Science Fiction* in the late 1950s. The Alyx series begins with *Picnic on Paradise* (1968) about a "time-travelling mercenary, tough, centered, autonomous and female," indicating a kind of quiet tacit feminism (Clute, 1035). This proved an effective and comfortable precedent for later adventurous female protagonists, nonthreatening to both publishers and traditional readers. Her next novel, *And Chaos Died* (1970), is more explicitly feminist, but her most famous work, *The Female Man* (1975), is blatant feminism. Based on "When It Changed," which won a Nebula for Russ in 1972 for best short story, the novel is set both in New York in the 1960s and on a utopian planet called Whileaway. Russ describes four alternate lives of a single protagonist, ranging from a traditional male-female relationship in which she plays the passive role of psychic servitude to a role where she is completely independent of male approval on the utopian Whileaway. "Savage and cleansing in its anger, the book stands as one of the most significant uses of sf instruments to make arguments about our own world and condition," claims sf critic John Clute in his recent encyclopedia article (1035). But 20 years earlier sf writer Poul Anderson called her writing "shrill," a word used pejoratively against women but rarely applied to male writers.[5] Since then, Russ has continued to figure prominently in the field of science fiction, writing about women and religious oppression in third-world societies. In 1983 her story *"Souls,"* appearing in the collection *Extra(ordinary) People* (1984), won the 1983 Hugo for best novella.

Suzy Charnas

The most radically feminist work, according to Martin's scale, is exemplified by *Motherlines* (1978), written by Suzy McKee Charnas. Charnas, one of the most outspoken feminist writers of sf and fantasy, describes attitudes toward female speculative writers during the 1980s: "When a woman author invented science (telepathy, teleportation, shape-changing, etc.) her book was pegged as 'fantasy.' When a male author did it (electronic or chemical mind-augmentation, Faster-Than-Light travel, bioengineering), his book was 'science fiction.' The categories are largely based on illusory distinctions."[6] Like many other sf writers, Charnas imagined an end of the world as we know it so she could start from scratch, imagining sexism pushed to its furthest extreme in *Walk to the End of the World* (1974). *Motherlines* (1978) describes the mythical Amazonian world as if it were unchanged by the male-dominated Greek culture. Neither particularly scientific nor suitable for sensitive readers, it depicts a female-dominant culture where men, valued only as submissive helpers, are castrated to reduce their aggressive behavior. Charnas's most recent novels veer toward the usual definition of fantasy, which stretches the imagination beyond what scientists define as reality.

The Present Status of Women in Science Fiction

Has the attitude of other sf writers changed toward women? Since so many writers now incorporate science fiction in their work, it is more and more difficult to delineate sf from mainstream writing. Generally, all thinkers assume equal capabilities and rights for women, and many issues once labeled as "feminist" are now taken for granted. Traditional stereotypes about gender differences are melting, albeit slowly in some quarters, and science fiction is increasingly used to experiment with a wide range of social possibilities. However, the same issues described in 1914 by Charlotte Perkins Gilman in the feminist utopia *Herland* (republished in 1979) were considered outrageous when Pamela Sargent wrote about them in her novel *The Shore of Women* (1986). Progress is unequal. Most of Sargent's work is feminist in the sense that it values women and their traditions, the kind of feminist creed delineated by Sarah Lefanu in her study *In the*

Chinks of the World Machine: Feminism and Science Fiction (1988).

In her introduction to *Women of Wonder* Sargent recognizes that until the 1970s most women were limited to passive roles in literature. "Only sf and fantasy literature can show us women in entirely new or strange surroundings. It can explore what we might become if and when the present restrictions on our lives vanish, or show us new problems and restrictions that might arise" (Sargent, ix). Science fiction could speculate on better cultural attitudes toward human rights. Those sf works written for young adults could offer role models that could also serve for adults. Sargent asks readers, writers, and publishers to fight against damaging stereotypes.

Vonda McIntyre

Vonda McIntyre, author of the feminist *Dreamsnake,* also writes for younger readers. In *Barbary* (1986) a young orphan, toughened by years spent in foster homes, smuggles her cat, Mick, aboard the research station Einstein. The head researcher, a U.N. diplomat for the Native American tribes of North America, and all but one of the other main characters are female. McIntyre preaches in only one brief passage: "Things are better than they used to be. A lot better. But there are still people in power who don't think women in general and women of color in particular have what it takes to run things" (122). McIntyre's feminist consciousness surfaces more subtly in her description of the gentle aliens or "other things," whose achingly lovely voices and crystalline appearance belie their superior strength. The aliens teach two rules: "Beyond your own planet, you may create, but you may not destroy. You may observe, but you may not interfere" (180). This protective attitude toward worlds and cultures as they exist intrinsically against an authoritative assumption about "how things ought to be" is essential feminism, for it nurtures and preserves, just as mothers and wives have done for centuries. It is the underlying ethic of all feminist science fiction.

Chronology: Feminist Science Fiction

1914   *Herland,* a feminist utopia by Charlotte Perkins Gilman, is first published. Reprinted in 1979.

1975   *The Female Man* by Joanna Russ contrasts several possible roles of her female protagonist.

Women of Wonder: Science Fiction Stories by Women About Women, edited by Pamela Sargent, is published.

1976   *Woman on the Edge of Time* by Marge Piercy depicts a woman driven to insanity because of her social role.

1978   *Motherlines* (1978) by Suzy McKee Charnas describes a radical matriarchy that includes male castration.

1987   *Mindplayers* by Pat Cadigan creates a cyberpunk world deemed by critics as powerful as male depictions.

1988   *The Gate to Women's Country* by Sheri S. Tepper suggests that genetic male traits be selectively bred out of humanity.

The Handmaid's Tale by Margaret Atwood, a mainstream writer who uses sf to depict a misogynist future, is published.

Chronology: Pamela Sargent's Life and Works

1948   Born 20 March in Ithaca, New York, daughter of Shirley Anne (Richards) and Edward H. Sargent Jr.

1968   Receives B.A. at Harper College at State University of New York at Binghamton, where she meets George Zebrowski. Begins graduate work in philosophy. "Oasis" and "Landed Minority" are published.

1970   Receives M.A. in classical philosophy. Becomes managing editor of *The Bulletin of the Science Fiction Writers of America* with George Zebrowski.

1975   Edits *Women of Wonder: Science Fiction Stories By Women about Women,* cited by the American Library Association in their annual list of best books for young adults.

1976   *Cloned Lives,* a novel, is published, as well as two more anthologies, *Bio-Futures* and *More Women of Wonder.*

1977   *Starshadows,* a collection of her own stories, is published.

1978   *The New Women of Wonder* is published.

1979   *The Sudden Star,* her second novel, is published.

1980   *Watchstar,* her third novel, is published.

1982   *The Golden Space,* her fourth novel, is published.

1983   *Earthseed,* her first young adult novel, is cited by the American Library Association as a best book for young adults and by *Booklist* as a young adult reviewers' choice.

   The Alien Upstairs, a fifth novel, is published.

1984   *Eye of the Comet* and *Homesmind* end the *Watchstar Trilogy.*

1986   The Venus trilogy begins with *Venus of Dreams* and *The Shore of Women.*

1987   *The Best of Pamela Sargent,* short stories, is published.

1988   *Venus of Shadows* continues the Venus trilogy. *Alien Child,* a second young adult novel, is published.

7. Beyond Gender and Racism: Octavia Butler

The emerging role of women in science fiction has raised challenging issues that have expanded the dimensions of the genre, offering alternate visions of heroism, social relations, and the quest for survival or fulfillment. This feminist elaboration of the fictive worlds created for young adults is reinforced and expanded still further by the work of other new sf writers of different ethnic and racial backgrounds.

Most sf authors are driven more by the desire to create a gripping, adventurous plot and compellingly heroic characters than by the preferences of the audience they are supposedly reaching. Women writers of science fiction for young people generally focus on character development more than on technology, battle plans, or plot adventures; their themes often center on the process of maturing, the coming of age that can happen more than once and at any age. For many young readers this universal process of becoming an individual is the most familiar and attractive thread in the uniquely strange settings and circumstances of science fiction. While sf written specifically for older children and young adults can be didactic and preachy, sounding like parental advice woven sometimes ineptly into a story, the better works can be read with lasting pleasure by young adults and by anyone who remembers the experience of being young.

Two Writers for Young Adults:
Louise Lawrence and Sylvia Engdahl

One such writer often recommended for teens interested in science fiction is Louise Lawrence, an author based in the United Kingdom whose actual name is Elizabeth Rhoda Wintle (1943–). Her intelligent fictional works, such as *Calling B for Butterfly* (1982), *Children of the Dust* (1985), and *Moonwind* (1996), reveal a mind that thinks deeply and widely, and they are also appealingly romantic.

Another such author is Sylvia Louise Engdahl (1933–). From 1957 to 1967 she pursued a career in computer programming, which no doubt influenced her fictive comparison of technologically superior cultures with those whose outlook depends less on science. *Enchantress from the Stars* (1970) and *The Far Side of Evil* (1971), her best-known works, describe the dilemmas of anthropologist Elena, who must protect a more primitive culture from being overrun by a scientifically modern power. Like Ursula Le Guin, Engdahl uses anthropological study to explore the consequences of cultural borrowing. In a second series that includes *This Star Shall Abide* (1972), *Beyond the Tomorrow Mountains* (1973), and *The Doors of the Universe* (1981) Engdahl shows how religion can be used to overpower another culture, with useful consequences but also with the sacrifice of free choice. This important theme, the conflict between authority and individual freedom, is also examined by a writer of more recent fame, Octavia Butler.

Octavia Butler: Her Early Life

Since the late 1970s Octavia Estelle Butler (1947–) has emerged as an sf author who addresses issues of race and gender at a most profound level, though without making them the sole focus of her writing. The daughter of Laurice and Octavia M. (Guy) Butler grew up in Pasadena, California, where she spent much of her youth reading "whatever was in the house . . . a lot of odd stuff . . . a lot of science fiction with absolutely no discrimination . . . good, bad, or awful."[1] Like many young readers, she would latch onto a book and read everything else she could find by that writer. John Brunner, Theodore Sturgeon, and Robert Heinlein were her favorite sf authors. She also remembers novels by John O'Hara and other writers who describe an upper-middle-class, white male world of manners and muffled passion, a world completely different from the life Octavia led in Pasadena: "It was Mars for me" (Potts, 334). This literary world of a privileged elite, an exclusionary social hierarchy based on definitions of status stemming from past traditions, is foreign to many young sf readers who prefer to hope for a more democratic future. Butler's works tend to expose the subtle, intricate wounds left by social hierarchies and to explore the far-reaching implications of erasing borders among sentient beings. While social injustice is not a new theme, Butler explores it in remarkably inventive and provocative ways; she even gives it a cosmic dimension, challenging the usual assumption that Earth-born humans should rule the universe. She explores the range of prejudicial viewpoints we consider normal against people who look different, reproduce differently, and have different ideas of privacy and ownership.

From the age of 10, Octavia wrote down her thoughts, much like the young girl in *Parable of the Sower* who develops her beliefs in a journal. In college Octavia began to write seriously, entering and winning several contests for short stories, including a national competition sponsored by *Writer's Digest*. After she graduated from Pasadena City College with an associate of arts degree in 1968, Butler studied at California State University and the University of California, both in Los Angeles, where she still makes her home. One of her writing teachers was Harlan Ellison, renowned for his sf stories. He encouraged her to join the Clarion Science Fiction Writers Workshop, where she produced a story later published in the collection *Dangerous Visions*. Since 1970 Butler has worked as a freelance writer, producing science fiction with a strong psychological and social emphasis. A private person who tends to keep her personal life separate from her work, she writes in the hours before dawn, a time when few people intrude upon her thoughts. In what may well be an autobiographical passage in *Kindred* (1979), Butler describes a writer who supports herself with temporary blue-collar jobs: "It was nearly always mindless work, and as far as most employers were concerned, it was done by mindless people. Nonpeople rented for a few hours, a few days, a few weeks. I did the work, I went home, I ate, and then slept for a few hours. Finally, I got up and wrote. At one or two in the morning, I was fully awake, fully alive, and busy working on my novel" (53). Butler obviously writes with a wholly alert mind, aware of the subtle nuances of complicated issues.

Her first published sf story is "Crossover," anthologized in *Clarion* in 1971. Butler didn't receive much attention, however, until the publication of the Patternist series. This sequence of novels takes great liberties with chronology. The first, *Patternmaster* (1976), envisions a world of the future that takes place after the timeline in the later books in the series. The third volume, *Wild Seed* (1980), set in 1690, moves back to the earliest scenario, providing much information about origins of characters and motives. Doro, a 4,000-year-old body changer, is trying to breed a race of humans with whom he can settle. He and his son both breed with a shape changer, Anwanyu, called a "wild seed" because her genetic abilities to send and receive messages telepathically are superior to those of her contemporaries. The complicated relationship between the older Doro and his daughter/lover is somewhat reminiscent of stories about slave masters who became deeply attracted to the bondswomen on whom they forced sex but who then had to adjust to a society where explicit friendship across the hierarchic divide was not acceptable. Eventually Anwanyu and the son Doro (Doro altered by time?) form a new community, first in New England, then in Louisiana, where their mutant children can develop in a setting that does not scorn them for their inherent differences. This volume gives an overview of the whole series; the subsequent volumes explain how this idealistic goal could be accomplished. The series explores not only the powers of empathy, but its responsibilities as well.

The next stage of the story, *Mind of My Mind* (1977), takes place in contemporary California and explores the founding of the Patternist community in which individuals submit to a central will, which periodically calls upon them to focus their mental powers. Mary, a daughter of the original Doro specially bred by him to another mind reader, discovers that other telepaths are bound to her in a loose network; she is the unwitting node of this web through which the others communicate thoughts and feelings as well as give over to her some control of their mental energy. Though worried about a lack of privacy, Mary also takes pride in her power to connect, the same pride she has respected in Doro.

On another level this story traces the maturing of a childlike servant whose adoring relationship to the powerful master changes as Mary evolves into an independent source of her own strength, with the courage and ability to challenge her former oppressor and to form her own community. Butler's perceptive descriptions guide the reader as Mary and her fellow servants discover their own powers, delicately unwrapping each part of their personalities and piecing them together into a collective tool. The chapters alternate between Doro's reminiscence and explanation of his social project, and Mary's description of how she is weaving a mental web of secret knowledge and trust among peers to thwart him.

In *Patternmaster* Butler describes Mary's tool as "a vast network of mental links that joined every Patternist . . . to give the Patternmaster strength he needed" (19) to combat enemies. Like many complex relational systems initially designed for emergency use, this network is increasingly used for satisfying personal curiosity more than for its original purpose; participants tune into the pattern to judge each other's mental strength and compatibility as much as to communicate urgent practical news. Like other feminist writers, Butler recognizes the human need to forge unique links and to assuage individual insecurities as much as to attend to the corporal body. Human motivations are more often driven by complex personal problems and bonds than by simplistic, overgeneralized communal ideals.

The tone of this book harkens back to the radical communal projects of the early 1970s, when individuals sought to share themselves totally. In many of those utopian experiments, as in the book, a hierarchy develops, with much of the decision-making power and resources being subsumed by a single leader and his cohorts.

In *Survivor* (1978), the Earth of the future has become dominated by these Patternists, who have inherited in varying degrees the amazing ability to communicate mentally, establishing a complex network of family relationships. Humans without empathy—"mutes"—have been sent to serve a planet where the aliens do not particularly want to be saved. The story is told in alternating chapters by Alanna, a wild human orphan raised by the more civilized Missionary settlement, and Diut, one of the hair-covered Tehkohn, enemy aliens who now threaten to overpower the Missionaries and other humans. The story opens with Alanna, after two years as a captive of the Tehkohn, returning to the Missionary settlement run by Jules. As the story unfolds, she tries to walk a tightrope of tact, hoping to bind the two races into friendship against a larger enemy, the Garkohns. The stiff, self-righteous pride of the Missionaries makes it difficult for them to recognize the Tehkohn as human, much less as sources of good advice. To complicate matters, Alanna is grieving the loss of her daughter, conceived while she was held captive by a Tehkohn she came to love. In his chapters Diut describes the captivity of Alanna from his point of view, and at the end of the book they again meet in the present. The novel sensitively portrays the emotional complexities of mixed-race meetings and more intimate relationships. The hair-covered Tehkohns indicate their status and their emotional responses by flashing different colors, thus sharing a language the Missionaries never bother to learn. As a subordinated race, the Tehkohns have become masters of camouflage (though not as skilled as the Garkohns), analogous to the "invisible men," the devalued or ignored people and races, of our human society.

Farther into the future, *Clay's Ark* (1984) describes a plague from another planet that infects a few humans with an aggressive drive to touch, to connect with other humans who in turn also become infected. Set in a California desert that has become an enclave of criminals and of the rich, who build walled homes to protect themselves from crime, this book describes a group of the plague's survivors who attempt to control the bestial hunger for sex, raw meat, and touch so that they can consider themselves human. When their offspring appear more like quadruped apes than human bipeds, the group strives even harder to protect itself from outside contact and interference. So strong are the descriptive details of these survivors' desperate measures to survive that the reader experiences the story almost viscerally. The book is horrifyingly realistic; Butler captures the inexplicable strength that comes to both animals and humans when their own or their children's survival is threatened. Butler also examines how various people react to children who are born with physical differences; some are repulsed at any abnormality, while others focus more on their charms as children.

In *Patternmaster* (1976), the futuristic conclusion of the Patternist series, the Clayarks have become a faceless, nameless mass whose racial difference is universally considered disgusting—a dangerous social force that must be destroyed as efficiently as possible. This depiction varies greatly from the original sympathetic portrayal of individual hapless victims of a plague contracted through no fault of their own. Butler's contrast is caustically instructive.

In this future world the Patternists dominate the direction of Earth's cultural development; the person who holds the pattern in his power can control all, partly because of his sensitivity to the slightest ripples of mental activity by those connected. Patternists can not only send and receive telepathic messages but can even borrow the memories of other Patternists from the vast network of awareness. Individuals try to protect their privacy against such invasion by activating a mental shield that varies in effectiveness according to each person's inherited mental strength. Those with the strongest sensitivity interbreed to maintain their superiority and to strengthen the overall pattern. In fact, Rayal, the present Patternmaster, is married to his sister, who is alive because she alone among their equally sensitive siblings did not strive to compete with Rayal to hold the power.

Since disposing of his rival brothers and sister, Rayal has maintained peace, but his imminent death and the increasing strength of the Clayarks threaten a chaotic upheaval when his two strongest sons vie for the title and the power.

The younger son, Teray, is not ambitious to be Patternmaster until he realizes that his brother and rival, Lord Coransee, will not trust him to remain harmless. Butler's portrayal of Rayal and Coransee suggests that desire for power is normal to most human males and that only immature youths and women who prefer to be valued for their expertise in healing and nurturing refuse the opportunity to dominate. Neither brother is willing to trust the other. Coransee will guarantee Teray great wealth and subsidiary power only if he can hold ultimate control over his mind, a control he promises not to misuse, but Teray cannot bring himself to accept these terms, even though he would receive all he ever wanted in return. What could have been a sensible compromise for both, and what could have saved not only Teray but the women who protect him in great pain and danger, is not acceptable. His macho pride endangers him.

Butler also contrasts two levels of commitment between lovers. When Teray first leaves school, he is engaged to marry Iray, a familiar relative with whom he is comfortable. But soon after she is forced to be the concubine of the rich, powerful, handsome Lord Coransee, she transfers her loyalties and affection to the man who seems so strong. Teray salves his wounds with an undemanding erotic affair, which he ends when he meets Amber, a healer who more than matches him in intelligence, courage, and desire for independence and equality. This mature relationship will not be an easy one, but it will never be dull.

The two brothers, Teray and Lord Coransee, eventually fight it out and Teray wins, just barely and only because he uses the skills learned from the healer Amber, who has taught him how to fight more efficiently against the savage Clayarks. When it comes to battle, she is the tougher of the two, though Teray proves to be more sensitive and better able to work the pattern. Although the novel includes features of the traditional heroic adventure, Butler tweaks our intelligence through the interaction of main characters who quickly grab our attention and affection. This and the complex metaphor of an interconnected mentality raise interesting questions about our current society.

Kindred (1979) is related to the Patternist series only thematically. Dana, a contemporary black woman married to a white man, is involuntarily pulled back through time to a slave plantation in the American South of the 1800s, to a moment of crisis when Rufus, the young white son of a plantation owner, is about to drown. Knowing that Rufus is fated to be her great-great-grandfather, she returns from modern-day life to save his life, enduring beatings, danger, rape, despair, and fieldwork for which she is not prepared—all the horrors of slavery—to preserve the generational line that will result in her own birth. The novel thus questions how a twentieth-century black female, raised in relative freedom, would confront the indignities of inescapable slavery and the dangers of nineteenth-century wilderness. Dana's relationship with Rufus changes, as does her attitude toward her modern husband, who accompanies her back in time so he can try to protect her from the worst tortures. Butler's vivid and detailed portrayal of life on a plantation captures the horrible effects of the slave system on both whites and blacks, but her picture is not overly bitter; flashes of humor, caused by the juxtaposition of memories of modern culture with conventions of the past, and also by ingenious revolutions of plot and character development, make this story impossible to put down, even for a reader who is repelled by the historical truths. This novel is categorized as sf mostly because of time travel, which raises the usual questions about what consequences would result from changed events. These issues become especially charged through Dana's central choice of whether to keep alive the man who would become her master. Each time she returns, she faces the terrible dilemma of how best to use her powers, and this dilemma affects both her servitude and the lives of other slaves whom she has come to love and know as family. Feminist sf writer Joanna Russ notes that "Butler makes new and eloquent use of a familiar science-fiction idea, protecting one's own past, to express the tangled interdependency of black and white in the United States," for the plot addresses modern relationships as well as the roles of master and slave complicated by the nurturing instinct of women toward children and the sexual curiosity of men toward the black women they owned. [2]

Butler's special strength is her characters, whose lives are so real that they haunt the reader's mind, forcing a sympathetic participation in the anguish and long-term pain of powerlessness, especially for individuals who are personally strong. Among readers and critics, Butler is honored for offering insights into racial, sexual, and family relationships to a degree that is rare in science fiction. Because so few sf writers are black, her work is greatly treasured by black women readers who appreciate finding their own experiences reflected in her writing, though in a style uniquely hers.

Butler's work has won wide acclaim. Her short story "Speech Sounds" won a Hugo in 1984. In 1985 the novelette "Bloodchild" won a Nebula Award, a Hugo Award, a Locus Award (from *Locus* magazine), and the award for best novelette from *Science Fiction Chronicle Reader*. In 1987 her novelette "The Evening and the Morning and the Night" was nominated for a Nebula Award. In 1995 Butler won a grant from the MacArthur Foundation to continue her writing. Although Butler does read the literary criticism and reviews of her writing, she tries to keep them from affecting her work; she values her originality and her unique style.

The tone of her language, however, often draws from the voices of other science fiction because she addresses issues larger than personal relationships. The range of her themes reflects an awareness of not only her own racial history but of colonization in contexts outside of known history.

"Bloodchild" (1984), first printed in *Isaac Asimov's Science Fiction Magazine,* portrays a young man kept by an alien female because she needs him to produce children. In this invented world men are used as breeders for an alien race just as human women once were valued for their reproductive capabilities in our own history. In an interview in 1996, however, Butler points out that although critics often notice the tie to American slavery because she is a black writer, this story focuses as much on the forceful power of love (Potts, 334–35). Although the alien looks like a centipede, hardly a sexually attractive creature to most human sensibilities, Butler gives her such sensuous, caring qualities that the human male victim is able to overcome his initial repulsion and develop a loving and erotic relationship. Butler questions our dominant cultural definition of sexual attractiveness as one of clichéd and superficial appearances that ignores more basic qualities.

Butler has been quoted as declaring, "Civilization is the way one's own people live. Savagery is the way foreigners live" (Rotsler, 136). She continues to explore this widespread attitude toward cultural and racial differences in her more recent series, Xenogenesis. In *Dawn* (1987) Lilith is one of the few human survivors of a planetary invasion of an Earth made almost unlivable by war, radiation, and waste. Kept alive but isolated over a vast period, Lilith finds her craving for touch and contact has become almost unbearable. Still, the first time she meets an adult she is repelled by "his alienness, his difference, his literal unearthliness" (11). Tall, thin, gray, and wraithlike, this sexless creature, Jdahya, communicates through sense organs that hang in thick ropelike locks. This figure recalls the most horrifying apparition of Greek myth, the snaky-headed Medusa who turned viewers to stone; yet, as Jdahya's sensors writhe in response to environmental stimuli, he speaks gently and kindly. In this strange figure Butler challenges our deepest visual and psychological stereotypes in exploring the anxieties of cultural-racial difference.

Jdahya is a member of the Oankali race, which is compelled by a deep-seated instinct for survival to mix genetically with other races, thus renewing themselves and evolving as a race. Jdahya's purpose in preserving Lilith and other human survivors is to borrow genes, to repopulate Earth but without the flawed genetic combination that has proved fatal to the planet. "You are intelligent, . . . the newer of the two characteristics," Jdahya informs Lilith, but "you are hierarchical. That's the older and more entrenched characteristic. . . . When human intelligence served it [the hierarchical tendency] instead of guiding it, when human intelligence did not even acknowledge it as a problem, but took pride in it . . . , that was like ignoring cancer" (37). In the Xenogenesis series Butler explores the oppression drawn from competitive individualism, which seems inherent and natural to modern American readers but partly accounts for the practice of ownership and aggression that has almost destroyed Earth. Can humans give up these qualities at the behest of an alien race that represents their only hope for human survival, or has the habit of war for land become too deeply ingrained? Perhaps Butler's critical concern about these human qualities harkens back to her early reading of British mysteries, Robert Heinlein, and John O'Hara, where the worth of characters is judged according to a hierarchical caste system that excludes anyone not born white, male, rich, and educated by a few selective institutions. At any rate, her work is a strong critique of the dangerous tendency to stratify.

Ironically, the Oankali are most interested in obtaining the human ability to grow self-reproducing cancer cells, an advantage for a race that desires perpetual self-renewal through continual evolution. *Dawn* traces the eventual adoption of Lilith into an Oankali family and the lessons they learn about each other. Finally Lilith becomes a sort of imprisoned trustee, able to wake other humans from their stasis and compelled to do so by her urge for freedom. One by one she introduces 40 humans to their new environment because the Oankali realize that people can overcome fear and revulsion toward differences more effectively and safely as individuals than as part of a larger group. When people are given the opportunity to exercise choice and free will, they are generally more able and willing to reach out, to accept racial and ethnic differences. Most, however, must be forced into close contact so that the choice to communicate becomes preferable to isolation. In the end, Lilith decides to cooperate fully with the Oankali, accepting their need for genetic diversity in order to preserve the remnants of humankind.

Adulthood Rites (1988) opens with the birth of Lilith's son, who has a fully human appearance but also the Oankali's superempathetic memory and ability to both heal and kill. He is a bridge between the two races. Butler slyly slips in an example of her subtle humor when she introduces his name; after a short chapter describing his first consciousness of pain and identifying his familial relationships, she begins the second chapter with "He was Akin" (6). As the child grows, he becomes aware of his differences from both his human forebears and the more sensitive aliens who share his parenting in their community, called Lo. It is from the Oankali that he mainly learns civilized, kindly motivations. When he is kidnapped by a group of human resisters who live a desperate savage life in the woods, he comes to understand how their urgent desire for individual independence from genetic engineering drives them against the very aliens who have the ability to preserve the human race. The dilemma becomes personal as Akin must trace a delicate path between his human sympathies and the alien part of his biological makeup that can assist his captors. Like Butler's other books, *Adulthood Rites* is a compelling adventure story that provokes the reader to reflect on important human and cultural issues, especially the numerous ethical and practical questions surrounding current technological advances in genetic engineering.

Imago (1989) continues to explore these themes, bringing to fruition the xenogenetic cycle—the birth of something new and foreign. Jodahs, a construct who looks human but has the genetic abilities of Oankali, ultimately prefers his/her ooloi parent Nikanj, who gives him/her the ancient memories of his long experience. Jodahs lives the Oankali dilemma of wanting to help humans survive on Mars, where they have escaped from a transformed Earth, but knowing that humanity unchanged will eventually destroy itself. Jodahs's life becomes complicated, however, when metamorphosis into the adult form reveals that Jodahs is, in fact, a genetic mistake dangerous to other humans because of the ooloi ability to genetically distort or destroy others simply by touching them. On the positive side Jodahs can also generate cells for beneficial purposes. The dilemmas Jodahs faces as he/she tries to decide between the Oankali need to control human reproduction and the human desire for genetic independence make fascinating reading. The Xenogenesis series returns to its beginning place in the cycle when Jodahs selects and nurtures a single seed cell from within his/her genetic memory, retained through the gift of Nikanj, to begin a new colony.

Parable of the Sower (1994) continues the imagery of the seed. The sower is Lauren Olamina, an 18-year-old girl whose family tries to help her cope with her empathetic mind through which she can feel the pains and joys of others, an ability that almost cripples her when the people around her engage in violence or sex. The story takes place in Los Angeles during the next century, from 2024 to 2027, a time similar to that described in *Clay's Ark*, when overpopulation has caused a breakdown of the safeguards of current modes of civilization. Organized families wall themselves within protective colonies to resist individuals driven to violence or insanity by the lack of drinkable water and adequate food, shelter, and social connection. Lauren's younger brother, Keith, gets involved with the wrong people and is left to die a grisly death. After a fire destroys their neighborhood, Lauren travels on foot up the highway north, meeting other victims and survivors. In the end a small group forgives each other their mutual wrongdoings, accepting each other's differences in order to establish a community farm, a place where they can live in some security without participating in the slavelike labor system that remains from the former capitalist system of the United States. Lauren believes that "God is Change" (298), perhaps the only hope a young person can have in the face of the social destruction portrayed in this novel. The earthseeds are those useful plantings—squash, corn, melons, tomatoes, beans—that offer an investment in a viable future. *Parable of the Sower* is a bleak prophecy too predictable and realistic to be comfortable, but the end offers a hopeful view of humanity, an affirmation that people will exist who dare to trust each other, to sustain each other as a community despite racial, ethnic, and economic differences. It is a prime example of science fiction as social speculation. Ironically, in this work the social machinery that once sponsored the production and use of sophisticated technology is coming apart. The scarcity of oil-based fuel has made even automobiles a rarity, and the lack of control over violence and crime has made private ownership of anything, especially good clothes, more a danger than an advantage. Only the system of using money still works. Besides setting this novel in the future, the only element of science fiction Butler uses is Lauren's mental sensitivity, a trait she attributes to the drug abuse of the child's mother.

Butler describes herself as "a pessimist if I'm not careful, a feminist always, a black, a quiet egoist, a former Baptist, and an oil-and-water combination of ambition, laziness, insecurity, certainty, and drive" (*Parable of the Sower*, cover). As one of the very few African-American women writers of science fiction, Butler has been particularly honored for the depth with which she has explored racial and feminist themes, and she has been welcomed by women readers of color who find a familiar chord in her work. Her writing, however, is deservedly lauded on its own merits for the vivid details, spare rhythms, and powerful imagery of her style, and above all for her sensitive treatment of the most important human dilemmas: the quest to understand human nature and the complexities of relating to others.

Chronology: Octavia Estelle Butler

1947   Born in Pasadena, California, to Laurice and Octavia (Guy) Butler.

1968   Receives associate of arts degree at Pasadena City College; studies at California State University and UCLA, including a writing course with Harlan Ellison.

1971   Short story "Crossover" is anthologized in *Clarion*.

1976   *Patternmaster* begins the Patternist series.

1977   *Mind of My Mind*, second Patternist volume, is published.

1978   *Survivor*, third Patternist volume, is published.

1979   *Kindred* is published.

1980   *Wild Seed*, fourth Patternist volume, is published.

1984 "Speech Sounds" wins the Hugo Award for short stories.

1985 "Bloodchild," a novelette, wins the Nebula, Hugo, Locus, and *San Francisco Chronicle Reader* awards.

1987 "The Evening and the Morning and the Night," a novelette, is nominated for a Nebula Award.

Xenogenesis series begins with *Dawn,* then *Adulthood Rites.*

1989 *Imago* concludes the Xenogenesis series.

1994 *Parable of the Sower* is published. Selected for the American Library Association's list of best books for young adults.

8. Science Fantasy: Pamela Service and Piers Anthony

Science fantasy creates worlds that exist mainly in the imagination and often only lightly intersect with current scientific theory. Many fantasies are founded on magic and wish fulfillment, whimsical combinations of the more attractive aspects of reality and the alluring suggestiveness of scientific inquiry. At present the line between "fantasy," which exists only in the imagination, and "science fiction," which draws upon science and technology and may become reality, is so blurred that any distinction must be vague, with many exceptions easily argued. "Science fantasy" is often used to designate, though fuzzily, the tone of a work more than its actual subject matter or purpose.

In the last few years science fantasy has become increasingly popular with many readers. Perhaps one reason is that it allows a more complete escape from reality and satisfies the desire for novelty. Some readers of fantasy enjoy the elements of whimsy and surprise more than the intellectual exercise of playing out the logical speculation "what if?" Fantasy can be more romantic and seem more playful because it deals with talking animals, cute aliens, and arbitrary social laws. While science fiction extrapolates new inventions from technology to address and solve the larger issues of humankind, fantasy often uses a smaller focus and explores more-personal issues in a more playful manner.

Another reason for science fantasy's recent popularity is that science and technology have been redefining "reality" and breaking through former boundaries at a fast rate. Phenomena that seemed fantastic only a few short years ago—cloning a sheep, exploring Mars by remote control, reading brain waves—have now become scientific history. Fantasy allows writers and readers to push beyond current definitions of the possible without the careful justifications required by scientific fiction.

A third possible cause for the tremendous appeal of science fantasy for young people is described by Pamela Service in an article for *The ALAN Review*.[1] A writer of science fiction and fantasy herself, Service explains that the freedom of these genres is particularly appropriate for sensitive adolescents who generally avoid any literature that discusses potentially embarrassing situations too directly or deeply. When fantasy and sf allow young people "to identify with characters who are not human or don't even live in our world or time, then they can do so safely—without giving away too much of themselves" (Service, 17). More than just an escape from the confusion and discomfort of adolescence, this kind of reading also gives young people a way to begin sorting out questions about life's patterns and interpersonal relationships in the privacy of their own minds; where difficult meanings are cushioned by imagery and metaphor, self-awareness can emerge gently and comfortably.

Defining Qualities of Science Fantasy

Service believes that science fantasy must be believable and consistent to be effective in helping readers relate the embedded principles and lessons to their own lives outside the story. Fantastic elements must flow smoothly from a kind of reality that the reader already accepts as valid, and the events of this invented world must develop logically according to the author's first descriptions. Fantasy is not so much a divorce from the reader's perception of the real world as an extrapolation of familiar psychological or social principles told in new language.

Pamela F. Service and Mind Travel

Pamela F. Service (1945–   ) grew up in Berkeley, California, with her parents, Leroy Forrest and Floy Horner, in an environment of new ideas and intellectual exchange. Summers spent in the mountains of the Sierra Nevada taught her to appreciate the dramatic rocky land and the mysterious relics of past lives. After receiving a bachelor's degree in political science from the University of California in 1967, she traveled to England with her husband, Robert Gifford Service. By 1969 she had earned a master's degree in African prehistory from the University of London. While she and her husband lived in England, they kept pace with contemporary issues by working in political campaigns and explored the past by assisting with excavations in Britain and the Sudan. During these years Service acquired the knowledge necessary to re-create the historical past in several of her novels where characters living in contemporary times relate empathetically to events and people of long ago. Besides writing, Service has combined her interests in archaeological history and political science by serving since 1978 as curator of the Monroe County Museum and since 1979 as a member of the city council in Bloomington, Indiana, where she lives with her husband and her daughter, Alexandra Floyesta.

In her novels Service combines lessons learned from the past with her concerns for the future, writing literature for children and young adults so she can "make a real difference in shaping a reader's interests and attitudes."[2] Her first book, *Winter of Magic's Return,* was published by Atheneum in 1985. Since then she has written more than one volume every year, producing science fiction that unfolds quite logically once the reader has accepted a few of the author's imaginative twists of fantasy.

Many of Service's works focus on the possibility of humans sharing lives across boundaries of time, space, and consciousness. In *Under Alien Stars* (1990) a routine rite of passage for adolescents is to participate in the work of their parents in a sort of apprenticeship. Jason Sikes is horrified that his mother must work side by side with the Tsorians, whom he has been taught to consider alien enemies. One of these Tsorians, a young female named Aryl, shares the same sort of jaundiced viewpoint toward different peoples; she considers humans rude and uncivil. Both learn about tolerance and the responsibilities of adulthood by sharing adult work experiences. In *The Reluctant God* (1988) Lorna Padgett of today's world helps solve a mystery by communicating across time with Ameni, the son of a pharaoh who ruled 4,000 years ago. In doing so, she learns how the present monumental ruins of Egypt relate to political situations that occurred many centuries ago but are not so different from present-day world events. *Vision Quest* (1989) is also a time-travel novel in which minds communicate across time. Determined to isolate herself after the pain of her father's death, Kate begins to see visions from the past superimposed on a dusty mining town of present-day Nevada, where she has just moved. These visions seem connected to a pair of charm stones that suddenly appear in her pocket and that hold an emotional power over her she cannot explain. To relieve the desperate yearning she feels through the stones, Kate must overcome her self-centered bitterness and befriend a fellow student, Jimmy Fong, who transports her on a wild motorcycle journey to the place where both Kate and a figure she envisions from the past who seems to share a similar loneliness can assuage their grief. In this story, mind travel can be translated as a metaphor for wisdoms that recur through time, and Kate also engages in a vision quest that reaches beyond human measurements of time. The power of religious fantasy is another underlying theme. But despite these deep symbolic dimensions of Kate's struggle with grief, this book is as full of wit, personality, and adventure as other novels by Service. A lighter treatment of shared lives is *Stinker from Space* (1993), which combines the consciousness of space warrior Tsyunq Yr with that of a skunk who has been sent into orbit to carry information vital to the planet's survival.

Being of Two Minds (1991) explores the possibility of two people with identical brain waves sharing each other's consciousness. Fourteen-year-old Connie Hendricks has suffered since birth lapses of consciousness during which she inhabits the mind of young Prince Rudolph, son of the kindly monarch of a tiny central European country called Thulgaria. Often Connie becomes aware that Rudolph is also mentally visiting her, keeping her company in the same way. By sharing the same sights and sounds—literally the same viewpoints—the two learn about each other's cultures and develop a friendship that feels as intimate as family. Although Connie and Rudolph are not telepathic, they communicate by speaking aloud or by writing notes visible to the mental visitor. This comes in handy when Rudolph is kidnapped in an attempted coup of his father's government. Service's thought-provoking exploration of shared minds develops into a fast-moving adventure novel toward the end; its speedy denouement leaves the reader wondering about the implications of such a close personal relationship as these two share, especially as they mature. Although this book might have seemed fanciful even a few years ago, the recent cloning of mammals that necessarily share identical brain configurations makes the possibility of shared brain waves more intriguing.

In *All's Faire* (1993) a young man of the present returns to the period of the English Renaissance, allowing Service to demonstrate her expertise as a historical researcher. *Storm at the Edge of Time* (1994) combines an Irish setting with the fantasy elements of animals who communicate like humans, with fully developed personalities and individual wills.

Like other science fantasy writers, Service is focusing more on fantasy in her recent work, as readers allow themselves greater imaginative freedom from the constraints of scientifically plausible settings and plots.

Chronology: Pamela F. Service

1945   Born in Berkeley, California, to Leroy Forrest and Floy Horner.

1967   Receives bachelor of arts degree in political science at the University of California.

1969   Receives master of arts degree in African prehistory at the University of London. Works in British political campaigns and in archaeological excavations in Great Britain and the Sudan.

1985   First book, *Winter of Magic's Return,* is published.

1988   *The Reluctant God* is published. Cited as an American Library Association best book for young adults.

1989   *Vision Quest* is published.

1990   *Under Alien Stars* is published.

1991   *Being of Two Minds* is published.

1993   *All's Faire* is published. *Stinker from Space* cited as an American Library Association best book for young adults.

Other notable writers of both science fiction and fantasy for young people who have gained notable popularity include Anne McCaffrey, Diana Wynne Jones, and Peter Dickinson.

Anne McCaffrey

Anne McCaffrey (1926–), an American citizen who lives in Ireland, is best known for her books about the planet Pern, threatened by parasitic spores called Thread and protected by genetically produced dragons that live in an extinct volcano. The main character is Menolly, a young girl who faces problems like other young people and solves them with intelligence and courage. The Harper Hall trilogy, McCaffrey's most widely read young adult work, includes *Dragonsong* (1976), *Dragonsinger* (1977), and *Dragondrums* (1979), though the world of Pern is first described in the adult novel *Dragonflight* (1968). Although the use of dragons and the medieval setting and tone of these books would indicate that they are fantasy, the scientific rationale for the existence of dragons and the logical basis for the plots and settings of these books neatly fit the definition of science fiction. McCaffrey uses music as a constant motif in her novels, a metaphor that wonderfully combines her ability to create mathematically based systems and her talent for coloring them with imaginative artistry. Her work continues to attract readers who appreciate the connection between today's science and the symbols of a psychological reality that existed before written history, a time when our most basic cultural instincts were formed. These meanings exist now as memories so deeply rooted as to be inexpressible except through symbols and stories outside the realm of science and logic. Dragons and their wisdom cannot be explained in our current language, which depends on polarities and comparisons with the visible, tangible world, so fantasy is the only appropriate language. Science-fiction fantasy acknowledges a connection to our present-day logical sense that is still unarticulated except through artistic means.

Diana Wynne Jones

Diana Wynne Jones (1934–) of the United Kingdom now creates primarily fantasy for older children and young adults, but she began her career as a playwright. Her writing is sharply honest about the ways humans can hurt each other, but her humorous edge makes the painful realizations bearable. One of her novels, *Dogsbody* (1975), which features the soul of the star Sirius now revisiting Earth in the body of a dog, is only marginally scientific. *The Homeward Bounders* (1981) involves a child trapped in parallel worlds, unable to synthesize into a single being. In its exploration of selves fractured into seemingly irreconcilable parts, this novel predates the more graphic novels of Pat Cadigan, whose work is not called fantasy perhaps because of an increasing acceptance of psychic phenomena. Wynne's complex comedy *Archer's Goon* (1984), dramatized in 1992, again describes parallel worlds and time warps. *A Tale of Time City* (1992) also explores questions about time and the human ability to slide back and forth using memory or imagination. Currently Wynne is recognized more for her fantasies, especially the Chrestomanci sequence.

Peter Dickinson

More scientifically realistic in tone is the work of Peter Dickinson (1927–), also British, though he was born in Zambia, Africa. His novel *Eva* (1989) explores the ramifications of using borrowed organs and even animal bodies to ensure the survival of human individuals. In an overpopulated Earth of the future when large animals have become so scarce and the environment so industrialized that the remaining specimens are preserved in special enclosures like zoos, 13-year-old Eva survives an accident only through having her nervous system implanted in the body of a chimpanzee. She finds that her mind connects not only to her own past but to some of the "natural" instincts of her host as well. *A Bone from a Dry Sea* (1992) moves backward in time, depicting an apelike girl who lives with her tribe both in and out of water. Some of Dickinson's work occupies the other end of the spectrum from McCaffrey's fantasy worlds, as when he tries to support a theorem that is based on scientific logic but cannot be proved. Using the theories of anthropologist Elaine Morgan, he tells a story that while highly imaginative, is also quite realistic and scientific. The apelike characters of his book have been forced to move from an area of dry plains into the shallow waters of the sea. Over generations, they lose most of their body hair to facilitate swimming, develop a more upright posture to keep their heads above water, and develop patterns of body fat to help keep themselves afloat. The female protagonist, more curious and experimental than her peers, develops the first humanlike tools.

Other books by Dickinson focus less on scientific theory and more on myth and magic. For example, *The Gift* (1973) is about a Welsh mind reader and uses contexts traditionally attributed to fantasy, and the award-winning *City of Gold and Other Stories from the Old Testament* retells mythic stories. Dickinson has also authored a nonfiction work, *The Flight of Dragons* (1979), justifying the existence of dragons, a book of which McCaffrey would approve. His wife is Robin McKinley, a well-known writer of fantasies for children and young adults.

Although many of these writers' works are marketed as sf fantasies for young people, their work is also satisfying to adult minds open to wandering beyond the conventional world into a realm where anything can happen and surprise abounds. Piers Anthony is a prime example of a writer marketed for adults who has invented many such worlds for thousands of readers both young and not so young.

Piers Anthony: Invitation to Belong to Separate Worlds

Piers Anthony Dillingham Jacobs, who writes under the name Piers Anthony, was born in England on 6 August 1934. His American father, Alfred Bennis Jacobs, had come to England to study at Oxford University, where he met and married a fellow student, Norma Patricia Sherlock. Anthony's father was head of the British Friends Service Council mission in Spain during the years that the dictator Franco was gaining power as World War II approached. In 1940 Alfred Jacobs was forced to leave Europe suddenly to protect his family from increasing harassment by Axis officials. Piers, with his mother, father, and younger sister, Teresa Caroline, left on the ship *Excalibur* for the United States.

After a brief stay with Anthony's grandfather, Edward H. Jacobs, a Quaker whose wealth stemmed from mushroom farms, in Media, Pennsylvania, a suburb of Philadelphia, the family moved frequently as his father sought a suitable position. These moves through five New England states in fewer than five years may help explain why Anthony, who would one day be the author of hundreds of thousands of published paragraphs, had such a problem learning to read and write. In later life Anthony realized that he must have been dyslexic as a child, like his daughter Penny. At any rate, it took him three years to get through first grade. These frequent moves also prevented him from forming deep friendships; his memories of these early childhood years are tinged with feelings of rejection. Perhaps Anthony's later fondness for designing fantastic worlds where he has the security of imaginative control results in part from the early insecurities he remembers.

After these early forays into public education, Anthony attended two notable Friends schools, Rose Valley and Westtown. In his autobiography, *Bio of an Ogre* (1988), he depicts himself as a serious child particularly sensitive to injustice, with a persistent courage and determination to protest—characteristics that may stem from the American Quaker tradition.[3] When a cousin near his age died of cancer at 16, Anthony developed an aversion to death that led to a lifelong habit of vegetarianism. When he was a student at Goddard College, slim finances and an appreciation for naturalness caused him to quit wearing shoes for several semesters. Although Anthony does not claim any religious affiliation, his strong ethical stances against unnecessary violence and his insistence on straightforward honesty in both personal and business matters seem rooted in his early experiences, and perhaps in his family connection with Quakerism.

The academic and moral climate of Goddard, known as one of the most liberal institutions of higher education in the United States, allowed Anthony to meet many like-minded people, including Carol Ann Marble, whom he married in 1956, the same year he graduated. Before the wedding the couple and two friends, all nearly six feet tall, drove down the coast from Vermont to Florida in four days, an adventure Anthony remembers with delight. After a two-year stint in the U.S. army, where he learned about weather balloons and wrote for the battalion newspaper, Anthony worked as a technical writer, a high school teacher, and a social worker before becoming a full-time writer of fiction.

Anthony's first introduction to science fiction came from discovering an issue of the magazine *Astounding Science Fiction* in his mother's office when he was 14 years old. He was immediately attracted to the "array of wonderful worlds, each of which was better than his own" (Anthony, 83), where life's problems could be solved vicariously. Goddard permitted him to write a science fiction novel for his senior thesis, which needed years of improvement before it was published.

Anthony, however, is a determined writer, and his rich emotional life and excellent education served as wonderful resources for his kinds of fiction. In the years between 1954 and 1962 he submitted to magazines 16 pieces that were not published, but in his first year as a full-time writer, "Possible to Rue" was accepted for publication by *Fantastic Stories Magazine*. Only four years later, during which he worked outside the home, his short story "The Message" was nominated for the 1966 Nebula Award by the Science Fiction Writers of America. Since that year he has devoted all his time to writing fiction.

Piers Anthony's allegorical fiction, beginning with *Chthon* (1967) and *Macroscope* (1969), shares the intricacy of detail and the mythic themes of fantasy, yet includes elements of science fiction.

The Science Fiction Allegories

Chthon is a coming-of-age novel in which the character Aton Five, imprisoned within a planet, contacts the "mind" of the planet Chthon and eventually emerges metaphorically from his subterranean constraints. Conceived while Anthony was in college and in the army, *Chthon* unites numerous episodes into an intricate structure, like a doubled hexagonal puzzle. Three of the six sections pair the novel's present with a future time, and three match the past. Anthony believes that most readers did not appreciate the extent of artistry in this work, where every set of numbers matches and the stories parallel in both a literal and a figurative sense (Anthony, 192). It may be that science fiction readers and critics, who were attracted to the outer trappings of this psychological study, are less attuned to formal literary patterns than scions of fantasy. In the sequel, *Phthor* (1975), Aton's son Arlo conquers the planetary intelligence of Chthon, demonstrating an individual hero's conquest over a massive machine.

The theme of a universal order is also played out in *Macroscope* (1969), a complex but well-structured space opera where scientific devices are so imaginatively logical as to seem fantastic. People travel through space by melting through temporary black holes and then solidifying on another galactic layer, an idea that also occurs in *Star Trek* as "transporting." Four heroes are led to another universe, where their lives change and their minds are captured by Anthony's suggestive astrological images. The line between sf and fantasy genres is magnificently fuzzy here. *Macroscope* was nominated for the Hugo award in 1970, and came in third.

Science Fiction Series

The complex allegory of *Macroscope* was followed by simpler adventures, whose characters move quickly through situations drawn to speed the action more than to foster thoughtful analysis. *Sos the Rope* (1968) (which won an award from Pyramid Books), *Var the Stick* (1972), and *Neq the Sword* (1975) make up the Battle Circle trilogy (1978). Anthony's plots sound ordinary, but he weaves a magical world with his skillful use of language.

Omnivore (1968) captures the damp, cloying mystery of a fungoid world on the planet Nacre. The sequel, *Orn* (1971), depicts the author's theory that the dinosaurs' extinction is related to the breakup of the continents, a theory the scientific world has not disputed. *Ox* (1976) captures the powerful logic of inanimate intelligence by using the metaphor of a three-dimensional game; this notion was especially inventive, as this book was published before the preponderance of computer technology in our thinking.

Anthony crafted the Apprentice Adept series to be precisely half fantasy and half science fiction, bridging a gap that usually separates readers into mutually intolerant camps. The series begins with *Split Infinity* (1980), its title a pun on the grammatical habit of inserting a modifier between the word "to" and the verb of an infinitive phrase. *Blue Adept* (1981), *Juxtaposition* (1982), and *Out of Phaze* (1987) continue the series, which also includes *Unicorn Point* (1989). These volumes unite unicorns with robots, computers with magic, and androids with dragons, trolls, and vampires. The model for the unicorn Neysa is Sky Blue, a small black horse Anthony bought in 1978 for his daughter Penny; it is also the model for Nightmare Imbri of Xanth.

Soon after Anthony started his popular and lighthearted *Xanth* series, a lingering illness spurred his decision to address serious issues in his writing, challenging his many readers to consider the political implications of their uninvolvement. He decided to launch a two-pronged discussion, one focusing on positive aspects and using science fiction as a framework, and the other a fantasy series presenting a roughly parallel view from the negative side.

The Bio of a Space Tyrant series is the science fiction part of the project. *Refugee* (1983) is an exposé of the plight of refugee boat people from Vietnam and from Haiti, a serious social commentary "spiced up considerably by blood and sex" (Anthony, 210). The Incarnations of Immortality is a dark fantasy series, beginning with *On a Pale Horse* (1983), where death is more popular than the life that the boat people yearn for.

The Fantasy Series

The Tarot series (1979–1980) returns to the themes of *Macroscope,* as does the Incarnations of Immortality series. The occult imagery of the Cluster series (1978–1980), including the Kirlian auras, is continued in the Tarot series in order to address the important religious question about the existence of a single omnipotent God. In his *Bio of an Ogre,* Anthony states that he considers the novel *Tarot* (1987), which compiles the three earlier novels of the series, "the most important one of [his] career" (200). It is less a galactic battle than an inward fight to resist temptations, to accept companions, and to face personal failings.

In contrast to these serious-minded moral epics, Anthony's most popular works are infinitely more superficial and lighthearted—full of puns and invention. Xanth was born while the author was walking with his daughters through their wooded land in central Florida and Cheryl got snagged by a blackberry thorn. "Instead of live oaks, there were tangled trees whose tentacles not only dangled, they grabbed. The cacti could literally shoot their needles. Paths were magic, sometimes being one way: existing only in one direction. And there was a huge forgotten chasm in the center. I had in fact transformed the entire state of Florida in the Land of Xanth" (Anthony, 204). The Xanth series of fantasies includes *A Spell for Chameleon* (1977), *The Source of Magic* (1979), *Castle Roogna* (1979), *Centaur Aisle* (1982), *Ogre, Ogre* (1982), *Night Mare* (1983), *Dragon on a Pedestal* (1983), *Crewel Lye: A Caustic Yarn* (1984), *Golem in the Gears* (1986), *Vale of the Vole* (1987), *Heaven Cent* (1988), *Man from Mundania* (1989), *Isle of View* (1990), and *Question Quest* (1991). The titles reflect Anthony's affection for punning. In *Roc and a Hard Place* (1995) and *Yon Ill Wind* (1997), the 19th and 20th volumes of the series, he incorporates over a hundred puns suggested by his many young fans of Xanth. *Piers Anthony's Visual Guide to Xanth* (1989), written with Jody Lynn Nye, helps readers keep all the various settings straight. Anthony selected the name Xanth from a name book; it means blond or yellow-haired. When the fifth novel of the Xanth series, *Ogre, Ogre,* was selected for the *New York Times* best-seller list, Anthony began calling the month of its publication "OctOgre" in its honor. Soon other puns followed: JamBoree, FeBlueberry, . . . NoRemember, DesMember. These, like the puns in many of his titles, endear him to some readers but elicit raised eyebrows from those who think public punning is beneath human dignity. This split assessment of Anthony's writing is generally indicative of readers' attitudes toward including fantastic elements in science fiction—they are either charmed by the imaginative lightheartedness of a story that ventures beyond everyday life or repelled by the frothy silliness. Like general attitudes toward science fiction, the tendency to either love or loathe fantasy is usually very strong.

The Dragon series of fantasies, written by Anthony with Robert E. Margroff, includes *Dragon's Gold* (1987), *Serpent's Silver* (1988), and *Chimaera's Copper* (1990). The Mode fantasy series describes travel between differing realities: *Virtual Mode* (1991) explores the roots of 14-year-old Colene's suicidal habit of slitting her wrists and her search for unconditional love as she finds relief in one of a great number of parallel realities that exist outside the world. *Fractal Mode* (1992) continues the story of Colene and the mind-reading horse, Seqiro, on a planet that glows with joy and beneficence but is threatened by the slave-trading people called Gaol. *Chaos Mode* (1993) relates a number of episodes in the various alternate realities of this series. *Balook* (1990) uses science fiction to travel to the past as a lonely young man, Thor, befriends a science project reconstructed from clones of past beings who introduce him to other prehistoric characters.

Historical Space Fantasies

Anthony admits that although he prefers to write thought-provoking fiction, his historical space adventure *Steppe* (1976), which necessitated months of research, sold no more than his other novels that took less time to write. In *Steppe,* the hero, Alp, revisits through a massive computer game the great empires of the Turks, the Mongols, and the Huns, who inhabit Asiatic plains. As Genghis Khan he conquers much of this world by clever manipulation of the rules of the game. Intelligent and fast moving, the book is singularly successful as an adventure unencumbered by any weighty proselytizing.

Like *Steppe* (1976), *Isle of Woman* (1993) is a work of fiction "based on research on the derivation and nature of the human kind," the first volume of the Geodyssey series (Anthony, 441). Rather than dividing this series chronologically, each volume moves from the beginning of humanity into the future, and each addresses a different aspect of the human condition. The first volume addresses the problem of overpopulation. Why are the human genitalia proportionally larger than those of other animals? How will we face a future without adequate food and land? Anthony traces a fictional family through the ages from the time of Lucy, the oldest "human" figure identified by anthropologists, to a future colony along the coast of Mexico when food is so scarce that cannibalism has lost its horror. The same characters reappear in each time frame as if reincarnated, until in the last chapter they are united as lovers, fulfilling the vague sense of longing they have felt through the ages. This is the only fantastic part of an otherwise plausible account. As in many of Anthony's other works, *Isle of Women* contains many references to sexual arousal and erotic pleasure, but he never uses language that is commonly called offensive. Like Dickinson in *The Bone of the Sea,* Anthony uses the theories of Elaine Morgan in *The Aquatic Ape* to extrapolate an explanation for the "missing link" between animals and humans. *Shame of Man* (1994), the second volume of the Geodyssey epic, continues the adventures of the characters Hugh and Ann, focusing on multicultural themes as they are reincarnated in different times. The ambitious project continues in *Hope of Earth: Geodyssey 3* (1997). Is this science fiction, or historical fiction, or fantasy? As usual, Anthony mixes genres to send a message, to relate personally to his audience, and to speculate on the future using the tools of logic and science. He is an engaging writer, but readers must pick and choose carefully among his books to rescue the gems from mere blocks of stone. However, the number of gems is amazing, considering his prolific output and the intricacy and length of many of his books. By his 50th birthday on 6 August 1986, he could (and did) list 50 novels in his autobiography. In 1994, with Richard Gilliam, he edited a highly praised collection of fantasy stories with Indian themes. *Letters to Jenny* (1993), the collection of selected letters he sent to a disabled fan at the behest of her mother, reveals a person who can be closely attentive and thoughtful.

Up to this point in his career, Anthony has chosen to focus more on his best-selling light fantasy in order to make money. Now that he is financially secure, he can spend more time and effort on more careful work, especially with the help of his research assistant, Alan Riggs. On the other hand, his loyalty to the many fans who prefer his escapist fantasies encourages him to continue in that style. A large part of Anthony's tremendous charm is his strong loyalty to his readers and his genuine concern about those who write to him. Each of his later novels includes a lengthy author's note in which he chronicles his life and his thoughts about subjects related to the novel. In these notes he establishes a personal relationship with his readers—a generous gesture, especially from a writer so prolific and popular. Anthony is controversial, having had several public battles with publishers and critics. The prominent sf critic and scholar John Clute notes that many of Anthony's popular books are "helter-skelter. . . ; only when he embraces a complex mythologizing vision of the meaningfulness of things [does] he become fierce" (Clute and Nicholls, 40). This comment reflects the opinion of those readers who prefer pure sf to this mixed genre; often they find the whimsy and playful silliness a disturbing detriment to the desire to treat sf as serious literature. Nevertheless, Anthony's writings, especially his fantasy series, are tremendously popular. His plots flow easily, his wit surprises with puns and other stylistic devices, and his ideas draw from wide-ranging research and a deeply thoughtful nature. Some detractors are irritated by his sexist humor and the cuteness of his punning, especially in the various series. Admirers, however, note the complex mythic power of his novels, and they appreciate the kindly humor, the beguiling imagery, and cheerful language that make them so readable.

For many traditional readers, the mix of science fiction and fantasy is uncomfortable, taking rationalists closer to the boundary between logic and imagination and threatening the comfort of readers who seek escape from literal reality. The most successful writers of science fantasy, however, have been able to stretch the parameters of both kinds of minds, a feat to be admired.

Chronology: Piers Anthony's Life and Works

1934   Born 6 August in Oxford, England, to Norma Patricia Sherlock Jacob and Alfred Bennis Jacobs.

1940   Moves with his family from Europe to Pennsylvania.

1956   Graduates from Goddard College and marries Carol Marble, a computer programmer.

1957–1959   Serves in the U.S. army.

1964   Earns teaching certificate from the University of Florida.

1966   Begins career as a full-time writer. "The Message" nominated for Nebula Award.

1967   *Chthon* nominated for Nebula Award.

1968   *Sos the Rope* and *Chthon* nominated for Hugo Award.

1982   *Ogre, Ogre,* fifth novel of the Xanth series, is the first original paperback fantasy novel to appear on the *New York Times* best-seller list.

1985   Publishes his 50th novel, *Politician.*

1993   Publishes *Letters to Jenny,* selected letters to a fan.

1994   Collaborates with Richard Gilliam to edit *Tales from the Great Turtle,* a collection of fantasy stories with Indian themes.

1996   Twentieth volume of the Xanth series is published.

9. Humor in Science Fiction: Douglas Adams

Much of science fiction is written as a complaint about the way humanity conducts its life on Earth or as a warning of what will happen if humans don't correct their ways. So it is not surprising that the genre is not particularly known for its humor. Perhaps there is little humor in sf because its writers are creating a world readers need to enter wholeheartedly, committing serious attention to re-creating a new context. Much sf creates the illusion of total escape into a new reality, and humor often depends on a connection with the familiar.

Types of Humor in Science Fiction

Exceptions to the serious tone of most science fiction are works for young adults that use a lighthearted approach. Space-travel adventures like Ruthven Todd's *Space Cat* (1952), Lester del Rey's *The Runaway Robot* (1965), and Douglas Hill's books for older children invest less authority in their plots or in the worlds they create. Another important exception is satire, which cuts away comfortable assumptions about the rightness of life-as-we-now-live-it by capitalizing on the actual connections of all speculative fiction with present-day reality. Satire mocks the status quo, eliciting a smile of recognition if its descriptive metaphors are accurate, and a grin of appreciation if its language is particularly clever.

While satire depends on its accuracy and intellectual cleverness to succeed, humor is more elusive; it delights because it speaks lovingly of humanity and life. We laugh because we recognize bits of ourselves and our friends in a picture so exaggerated as to become ridiculous. The coincidental nature of good puns and repetitions surprises us, and most humans like surprises—unless those surprises are too sharp to be comfortable. Some writers of science fiction do use puns to add humor to their work. Piers Anthony is famous—well, perhaps infamous is a more accurate term—for his puns, which he uses even as titles in many of his novels. Kurt Vonnegut's work is satirical but often has a silly edge that makes it fun. Harry Harrison's *Bill, the Galactic Hero* and *The Stainless Steel Rat* are similar to Vonnegut's work in tone, though not as political in their targets.

Remakes of the Frankenstein myth and endless jokes about it are successful because having a mere man create a machine that walks, talks, and acts like a human fascinates us. What makes a human? If a machine can appear human, what is the missing link between it and an actual human? Perhaps it is a profound uneasiness about the close relationship between humanity and nonhuman beings that makes humanoids seem so funny. Robot jokes were introduced in the early twentieth century by Edgar Franklin's *Mr. Hawkins' Humourous Inventions* (1904) and J. Storer Clouston's *Button Brains* (1933). The TV show *The Addams Family,* produced in the 1960s and still popular in reruns, depicts at least one character reminiscent of Frankenstein's creature.

Aliens visiting the human world often misinterpret the purpose of our customs, waxing enthusiastic about a phrase or an event we accept as mundane and normal. Robin Williams's portrayal of a well-meaning alien trying to act human in the 1970s TV series *Mork and Mindy* foreshadowed the more recent popular TV series *3rd Rock from the Sun,* in which four characters experience the modern American way of life through equally innocent eyes. What is so funny about these and similar characters is that their explanations of ordinary events are so logical, yet so different from the conventional meanings we humans generally assume. Few of us particularly welcome sneezing, but Sally, the alien in *3rd Rock from the Sun* who has been chosen to play the role of a female, immediately recognizes that the physical sensation of suddenly releasing the urgent tension that precedes a sneeze is similar to an orgasm. How ingenious to note the coincidence!

Early Background of Douglas Adams

This alien viewpoint is the heart of the delightfully wacky comedy invented by Douglas Adams (1952–   ), whose *Hitchhiker's Guide to the Galaxy* (1979) has reached cult status and continues to attract avid readers. Adams was born in Cambridge, England, where his father, Christopher D. Adams, studied theology for a short while before moving on to other odd jobs. His mother, Janet Donovan Adams, was a nurse. Unfortunately, the couple was not happy and divorced in 1958, when Adams was five and his sister was two. Perhaps this disruption of his family is part of the reason for Douglas's early reticence; he did not speak or show much intelligence or emotion as a child. At the Brentwood School, which he attended from 1959 until 1970, he was self-conscious, much taller than most of his peers. His brand of dour, self-deprecating humor colors his memories. He describes himself as socially backward and physically awkward—breaking his nose with his knee during his first game of rugby, losing his model airplane collection to a falling mirror, and having to abandon his love of nuclear physics because he could not perform the required arithmetic. His reading focused on comics and science fiction by Eric Leyland—with hero David Flame—and Captain W. E. John, popular British writers for young people.

One of the comics, *Eagle,* published two letters and a short story written by Adams when he was 11 years old. This very short story, titled "short story," was actually an extended joke, fairly sophisticated for an 11-year-old. Mr. Smith seeks help from a policeman for losing something very bad—it turns out to be his memory!

Adams liked the idea of writing more than the practice of writing, so he had more ideas for pieces than finished pieces; deadlines were as much a problem in his youth as in his adult career. However, his acting experiences in school plays and his exposure to John Cleese via *The Frost Report,* a popular TV show, fanned a spark in him: he would become a writer-performer.

Inspiration for the Hitchhiker's Series

The years 1970–1971 were pivotal for Adams in reaching this goal. First, he got an idea that would make him famous as a writer, although it seemed preposterous at the time. After an assortment of jobs to earn funds for the journey (cleaning chicken sheds; working as a porter in a mental hospital and in an X-ray department), Adams hitchhiked to Istanbul. Unfortunately, he contracted food poisoning and returned home by train, moaning and groaning as he slept in the corridors. In a subsequent effort in 1971 to make up for this fiasco, he drank too much in Innsbruck, lay down in a field to recover, and thought about a book he would like to write, describing six different reasons that the world should end. In trying to design a motive for an intelligent alien to peaceably visit Earth without letting people know his identity, he thought, "OK, he's a roving researcher for *The Hitchhiker's Guide to the Galaxy.*"[1] Adams hasn't yet written his book *The Ends of the Earth,* but the idea he tucked into his brain then became cult history.

Adams entered Cambridge in 1970 and joined several acting societies, first CULES (Cambridge University Light Entertainment Society) and then Footlights, where he met Simon Jones and John Cleese, who later became part of the British TV show *Beyond the Fringe.* The next step was a "guerilla revue group" formed with Martin Smith and Will Adams called Adams-Smith-Adams. The group wrote and performed two popular shows, *Several Poor Players Strutting and Fretting* (very successful) and *The Patter of Tiny Minds* (Gaiman, 11). Martin Smith subsequently applied his talents to the field of advertising, and Will Adams joined a knitwear company. The 1974 Footlights performance used some of their material and included Martin Smith but not Douglas Adams, an oversight that still leaves a bitter taste in the author's mouth. Adams's show *Chox,* however, was televised; Adams was paid the sum of a hundred pounds, and Graham Chapman of the *Monty Python* team, impressed with Adams's sketches, invited him to collaborate as a writer. The pair worked together for the next year and a half; they also drank a lot of gin. Ultimately the partnership dissolved, but by this time Adams had met many influential people in the field of radio and TV writing. In 1976, when Adams was at the depths of failure (or so he felt), radio producer Simon Brett offered him a show, which was to be comedy science fiction. This is when he remembered *The Hitchhiker's Guide to the Galaxy* and wrote the first radio science fiction the BBC had produced since the 1950s. As the deadlines became too much for him, he collaborated with John Lloyd for the last two of the six episodes. Wildly popular with fans of both sf and humor, the show also attracted attention for its special sound effects, though most of them were actually produced more naturally than technologically. The show placed second to the movie *Superman* in the 1979 Hugo Awards for best dramatic presentation, where actor Christopher Reeve, who starred as Superman, received great applause when he generously intimated that Adams's script should have won instead.

The First Hitchhiker Book

In 1979 Adams wrote the script into his first book, *The Hitchhiker's Guide to the Galaxy* (Ballantine, 1979). The unlikely hero is Arthur Dent, a muddleheaded British clerk of about thirty living a quiet, orderly life until he discovers that his house outside of London is about to be demolished to make way for a bypass. When Arthur decides to protest, he considers this the most exciting event that will ever happen to him. Before the afternoon has waned, however, Vogon spaceships have destroyed the world in a parallel move to make way for an interstellar hyperspace route, and Arthur finds himself aboard one of these ships, along with Ford Prefect, a casual friend he has known for about a year. Actually Ford is an alien from the vicinity of the star Betelgeuse whose job it is to research the planets of the universe for a hitchhiker's guide. He has chosen his name because it seems so unobtrusively human. Unbenownst to many American readers, it was also the name of a car common in Europe at the time.

When stowaways Arthur and Ford are discovered, their punishment is being forced to listen to the worst poet in the universe.

When Adams first submitted his script, the poet was a male named Paul, but he renamed the poet Paula Nancy Millstone Jennings after a school friend, Paul Neil Milne Johnson, complained to Adams. Perhaps the similarity was too painful.

Fortunately Arthur and Ford are soon rescued by two-headed, three-armed, too-cool Zaphod Beeblebrox and his sweet girlfriend, Trillan, on their starship, the *Heart of Gold.* Eventually the group reaches the planet Magrathea, where they find the designer of planets, Slartibartfast. Adams invented this name to tease his secretary, who first protested its similarity to a common vulgarism. From Slartibartfast, Arthur discovers that Earth and its human inhabitants have no particular purpose for their existence except as an experiment designed by the computer Deep Thought, which is seeking the Question to "the Great Answer of Life, the Universe, and Everything." Administering this experiment in behavioral psychology are white mice, in revenge for their treatment by Earthly scientists. What is the answer they find? Readers will find it too simple to understand. The book ends rather suddenly as Ford and Arthur decide they are hungry and need to eat. The sudden ending occurs because Adams was so late with his deadline that his publisher finally sent around a motorbike to collect whatever pages Adams had finished. Fortunately, the book was wildly successful despite its abrupt ending, partly because sf shows such as *Star Wars* and *Close Encounters of the Third Kind* were opening the market for space-age fiction, making it seem less alien to the popular audience.

Subsequent Hitchhiker Books

The second Hitchhiker book, *The Restaurant at the End of the Universe* (1980), begins as Arthur tries to teach the computer how to make a cup of tea and almost kills their entire group by jamming the controls at the crucial moment that they are being attacked by a Vogon starship. The phrase "dying for a cup of tea" takes on a rather literal meaning at this point. They do survive, however, and continue their quest for a meal. Zaphod Beeblebrox, former President of the Universe, is delayed and is sent to the evil planet Frogstar as punishment for his sins, along with Marvin, the manically depressed robot. The two survive and meet Ford and Arthur at the restaurant, where Zaphod gets drunk. Finally Arthur lands back on Earth in a time-travel warp that places him two million years before its destruction by the Vogons, leaving him a happy man. Although *The Restaurant at the End of the Universe* began as a rewrite of the radio script, at the point where Zaphod, with hangovers in both his heads, picks up Ford and Arthur, the trajectory of the books veers sharply from that of the radio episodes. This is Adams's favorite book, and it is certainly one of his sunniest, with most of the satire aimed at the vagaries of language rather than the sins of man.

The next book, *Life, the Universe, and Everything* (1982) was written while Adams was losing his girlfriend; consequently, the first draft is not as cheerful as the two previous books. In this book, Zaphod and Trillan split up, Slartibartfast takes Ford and Arthur to confront an ancient universal nightmare, and cricket (also spelled Krikkit) is damned as a nasty game. Once he had rewritten the book, however, so that Arthur admits to saving the universe twice in one day, Adams did not feel it was half bad. Critics, even the fans, were less enthusiastic, rating it poor compared to the first two books. Nevertheless, in 1996 it was adapted by John Carnell into a book version for DC Comics to further edify young readers.

What is the meaning of these three books? Adams has defended himself and his work against the many claims by critics and fans who find messages in his work. "If I'd wanted to write a message I'd have written a message. I wrote a book" (Gaiman, 141). Part of the special humor of Adams's parody version of science fiction is the tone of moral seriousness that surrounds his storytelling, especially about environmental and technological issues. Adams's writing takes a personal tone in which individuals use petty excuses—the common sense of the common man focused on the immediate issues of comfort. Some critics, however, have noted a connection between Adams's work and John Bunyan's *Pilgrim's Progress,* the Puritanical, evangelical allegory of the moral progress of an "innocent abroad in a fantastical world," mainly because one of Bunyan's sources is *The Plain Man's Path to Heaven,* coincidentally authored by Arthur Dent, who shares the name of Adams's protagonist. Adams replies that the critical habit of finding parallels is a game that can become rather ridiculous: "You could pick up the Bible and the telephone directory, and you could prove that each has a direct relationship to the other" (Gaiman, 144). Three stage productions were made of *Hitchhiker's Guide:* a sellout at the Institute of Contemporary Arts in London in May 1979 by Ken Campbell's Science Fiction Theatre Company, a successful Welsh production at Theater Clwyd in February 1980, and a disastrous rock version by Ken Campbell at the huge Rainbow Theatre in London in August 1980. Original Records produced a double album of *Hitchhiker's Guide to the Universe* and then a second record, *The Restaurant at the End of the Universe.* Two singles were released by "Marvin the Paranoid Android" Stephen Moore. A TV series of six shows was made with Alan Bell for BBC, despite a great deal of disagreement about how to translate most effectively the preposterous images conjured up by the radio script into suitable costumes and props. Eventually the sight of the main character, Arthur Dent, wearing a dressing gown over pajamas, a comfy contrast to the streamlined gold or silver spacesuits of other sf films, caused consternation among conservative viewers and lively debate among others. Finally a decision was made to discontinue the series.

Beyond the First Hitchhiker Series

During the early 1980s Adams also worked with John Lloyd on two sf episodes with an environmental message for *Dr. Snuggles,* an animated children's show. Dr. Snuggles, concerned about a river too nervous to run into the sea reputed to be disappearing, discovers that aliens have been taking the water from Earth, assuming that humans don't want or really care about anything in which they throw so much trash. In 1982 Adams traveled to California to write *The Meaning of Liff,* also with John Lloyd.

Drinking a lot of beer on the beach of Malibu, they devised new definitions for the "huge wodges of human experience" that are arbitrarily ignored by the Oxford English Dictionary. "Recognizing that warm spot in the chair made by the previous sitter" became *shoeburying* and "standing in the kitchen trying to remember why you are there" is *woking* (Gaiman, 109). The small, thin volume garnered much attention by British readers, some of whom reported a coincidental parallel to the Monty Python film title of the same year written in caps on a marqee as *THE MEANING OF LIFE* but which had lost the bottom bar of the last "e," so that "life" became "liff." Surprisingly, the book is still little known in America, even among Adams fans.

In 1983 Adams attempted to organize the Hitchhiker material into a film, but the project didn't pan out; however, his Los Angeles experiences appear in his next book, *So Long, and Thanks for All the Fish,* published in 1984. The title refers to chapter 23 in *The Hitchhiker's Guide to the Galaxy,* which points out that man has always assumed superior intelligence because of his accomplishments—"the wheel, New York, wars and so on—while all dolphins had ever done was muck about in the water having a good time. But conversely, the dolphins had always believed that they were far more intelligent than man—for precisely the same reasons" (105). Just before the Vogons destroy the Earth, the dolphins send a message encoded in a display of flips and clicks that observers assume is play: "So long, and thanks for all the fish." Then they disappear, but not before leaving at least three people a farewell gift, a bowl that holds a fuller message from the dolphins encapsulating their fears for the Earth as an unavoidable disaster strikes, and then their joy in discovering an Earth that will replace the old one. The destruction of the old Earth and its subsequent replacement minus the dolphins is perceptible only to Arthur Dent, his new girlfriend, Fenchurch, and John Watson, who prefers to be called Wonko the Sane.

Arthur first meets his girlfriend Fenchurch while hitchhiking and meets her again as he tries to make conversation while buying charity tickets from an intrusive saleslady. Wonko may be Ford Prefect in disguise, or just another alien. At any rate, Arthur and Fenchurch travel off Earth to hear God's Final Message to His Creation, which is an apology for all the inconvenience. On the last leg of their journey to hear the message that has eluded Fenchurch so painfully, the couple meet the depressive robot Marvin, whom they assist during his last hours. The message was predicted nearly two thousand years ago by "one man . . . nailed to a tree for saying how great it would be to be nice to people for a change" (Prologue). The message brings them ineffable peace.

While this book mocks traditional religious and philosophical pretensions of grandeur and sentiment, the tone is gentle. Obviously, the author respects the essential core of kindness and love in the Christian message, and he values authentic human relationships. The romantic scenes between the prosaic Arthur Dent and the tentative Fenchurch are charmingly sweet, and Arthur's last meeting with the plaintive robot Marvin is wonderfully kind. Overall, Adams's humor in this work is more loving than in the previous volume; however, in the epilogue to the collection of this series, "Young Zaphod Plays It Safe," he returns to his former caustic defensiveness.

In 1984 Adams indulged his growing fascination with technology by working out a fiendishly addictive computer game with Steve Meretzky, which begins, as do the other versions of the *Hitchhiker's Guide,* "You are Arthur Dent, waking up with a hangover on the morning that your house is demolished." Up to a point, the game is faithful to the book, but soon players are left only with their *Guide,* their towel, their Sub-Etha Sensomatic Thumb, and an unidentified gift from a relative. Successful on both sides of the Atlantic, it introduced yet another slice of the population to the humorous possibilities of science fiction.

Adams's Detective Series

In 1987 Adams published the first book of a second sequence, *Dirk Gently's Holistic Detective Agency,* which was as pessimistic in its view of Earth as his previous works and darker in tone. Dirk Gently, the Anglicized version of an otherwise unpronounceable, impossible-to-spell name, smokes himself into consciousness too late for much of anything each morning in an apartment filthy with the dregs of bills, old food, and foggy memories. Somehow this model of ineptness bumbles toward the solution of just enough cases to keep Gently from losing his apartment. Full of nasty asides directed at almost every aspect of British urban life, the book's success warranted a second volume. *The Long Dark Tea-Time of the Soul* (1988) continues the story in a book that became more popular than the first, though neither was as popular as the Hitchhiker series. This book begins as Kate Schechter tries to buy a ticket to Norway and is delayed by a Norse whose glacial slowness of both manner and mind is slightly less maddening than the cheeriness of the ticket agent. An explosion interrupts all this, and Detective Dirk Gently is summoned to investigate. He finds the head of a former client revolving on a hi-fi turntable, stuck on the lyrics "Don't pick it up, pick it up, pick i—." From there, the case goes downhill. Punched in the nose by a young boy, attacked by a swooping eagle, and verbally pummeled by almost everyone else, Dirk finally ends up in the hospital, having accidentally helped Kate find the perpetrator of the explosion and identify the murderer. The villain is simply divine.

Return to the Hitchhiker Series

Adams returned to the Hitchhiker series in 1992 with *Mostly Harmless,* which refers to a passage of the *Hitchhiker's Guide* written by Ford and quoted in the fifth chapter of *So Long, and Thanks for All the Fish.* After 15 long years of research during which Ford waited impatiently for a ride to come by so he could hitchhike away from Earth, his editors had pared down his work to a simple entry: "Earth: mostly harmless" (490). In this book Ford returns to the editorial offices of the *Hitchhiker's Guide,* and finding them modernized into an ineffable shade of blandness and gray, he "borrows" the new editor's identification card. With this useful form of credit, he sets out on a long journey to save Earth from fragmenting into the myriad futures available in all the dimensions of space and time, as well as to save the *Guide* from becoming useless. Meanwhile, Arthur Dent is mourning the inexplicable disappearance of his girlfriend, Fenchurch. And in another dimension, British TV news star Tricia McMillan is in New York, ruining her one opportunity to become rich and famous in North America and mourning the life she never lived on another planet. However, time folds and space warps. Tricia, as Trillan, the girlfriend of Zaphod Beeblebrox, has arranged to have the daughter she wants, and Arthur is the father. Ford Prefect manages to hear "Love Me Tender" sung by Elvis the King, who, by the way, was not abducted by aliens but left of his own accord. The book is a bitter picture of publishers and television producers, and is none too gentle with New York or the British game of cricket either; but the zany plot, the wacky language, and the deft asides are vintage Adams, and the characters are bid a loving adieu. It is a fitting end to the five-volume Hitchhiker's Guide, advertised on the book jacket as a series that "gives new meaning to the word trilogy."

Except that it is not the end. In 1994, *The Illustrated Hitchhiker's Guide* appeared; in 1996, *The Ultimate Hitchhiker's Guide*; and in 1997, *Starship Titanic: The Official Strategy Guide*. Adams also got involved in a project that involves traveling around the world to publicize the problem of endangered animals, and he began a new life as a husband and father, marrying Janet Belsen in 1991. Their daughter is named Polly Jane Rocker.

Adams invites an industry of commentary as well as Hitchhiker toys, shirts, and other media. One example is Neil Gaiman's *Don't Panic: The Official Hitchhiker's Guide to the Galaxy Companion* (1988), written with a nod to Adams's style as well as the content of his life and works. This "official" guide to Adams focuses more on his writing than on his life, providing valuable commentary on this important humorist whose work is so close to satire. Is Adams writing science fiction? He claims to have read the beginnings of many works of sf, appreciating the ideas explored more than the style in which these books were written. He uses sf as a vehicle for his ideas, but he certainly does not consider himself a missionary for the genre. He is influenced as much by the verbal twists of P. G. Wodehouse as by the satiric bite of Vonnegut. *The Hitchhiker's Guide to the Galaxy* is typical of sf in its pessimistic attitude about finding meaning or purpose in human life. Life just happens, without any ultimate explanation.

The humor comes from the juxtaposition of human earnestness about themselves and their home and the larger view of Earth as a fairly insignificant planet. Ordinary humanity becomes ridiculous because of its self-importance. The writer's attitude toward humanity is what draws the line between satire and humor. Like the TV characters of Mork and the family in *3rd Rock from the Sun,* Arthur Dent and Ford Prefect want to join hands with humanity; they yearn to share in that illogical aspect of humanity called "love," and not just the erotic or sexual aspects. Ultimately the human impulse to care for others and about others is what saves their lives from being wholly meaningless. Satire is cruel when nothing about the object of ridicule is desirable or worth emulating. Humor recognizes the redeemable quality of the humans at the butt of its jokes. While satirists separate themselves from their objects, humorists include themselves in their own jokes.

Chronology: Douglas Adams's Life and Works

1952   Born 11 March in Cambridge, England, to Janet Donovan Adams, a nurse, and Christopher D. Adams, a postgraduate theology student.

1974   Receives bachelor of arts degree from Cambridge University.

1978   BBC radio series begins: *Hitchhiker's Guide to the Galaxy.*

1979   *The Hitchhiker's Guide to the Galaxy* is published in England.

1980   *The Restaurant at the End of the Universe* is published.

1981   *Hitchhiker's Guide to the Galaxy* broadcast in America by National Public Radio and published by Pocket Books.

1982   Writes *The Meaning of Liff* with John Lloyd in California.

   The Restaurant at the End of the Universe becomes a best-seller in America.

   Life, the Universe, and Everything is published.

1984   *So Long, and Thanks for All the Fish* is published.

1987   *Dirk Gently's Holistic Detective Agency* is published.

1988   *The Long Dark Tea-Time of the Soul* is published.

1992   *Mostly Harmless* is published.

1996   Comic book adaptation of *Life, the Universe and Everything* by John Carnell and others for DC Comics.

1997   *Starship Titanic: The Official Strategy Guide* is published.

Other Science Fiction Humorists

Besides Douglas Adams, other humorous writings in the field of sf include Frederic Brown's *What Mad Universe?*, Robert Sheckley's *Dimension of Miracles* and *Mindswap,* and William Tenn's short stories. Terry Pratchett (1948–   ), another humorist from the United Kingdom, worked as a journalist until 1980 and as a publicity officer for the Central Electricity Generating Board until 1987. After his retirement his publications attracted the attention of readers attuned to his humorous edge, particularly the

Discworld series, which re-creates the world as a flat disk borne on the back of a turtle, an image familiar in ancient mythologies. Pratchett's works include *The Colour of Magic* (1983), *Equal Rites* (1987), *Wyrd Sisters* (1988), *Pyramids* (1989), *Guards! Guards!* (1989), *Eric* (1990), *Moving Pictures* (1990), *Witches Abroad* (1991), *Small Gods* (1992), and *Lords and Ladies* (1992). The Books of Nomes trilogy—*Truckers* (1989), *Diggers* (1990), and *Wings* (1990)—is about tiny invisible aliens trying to escape from Earth. *Only You Can Save Mankind* (1992) features a young player of arcade games who "must help the space warriors of an arcade game escape futile combat with human players."

Despite the reputation of science fiction for seriousness of intent, sf writers and their critics are a funny group. Like other tightly knit communities, they drop each other's names to tease their readers. They collaborate, cooperate, and squabble. In his book *The SF Book of Lists* Maxim Jakubowski annotates several books full of in-jokes in which characters from one story pop up as names in another work (71–72). Several authors invite real people into their works, often their fellow sf writers. H. G. Wells appears in Brian Aldiss's "The Saliva Tree" and Christopher Priest's *The Space Machine*. Philip Dick uses himself as a character in *Valis*. Even worse than appearing as a character in someone's else's writing is being the subject of a parody. A few authors of parodies are James Blish, Arthur C. Clarke, and John Sladek. Frequent victims include J. G. Ballard, Isaac Asimov, and H. P. Lovecraft.

Humor in Science Fiction Commentary

Much of the commentary about sf is wittier than critical writing in general. *The Encyclopedia of Science Fiction* (1993) by John Clute and Peter Nicholls is as chock-full of valid information as any other encyclopedia, but the clever turns of phrase and smart quotes make it a joy to read, even for a nonscholar. Some of the humor comes from the wry awareness of aficionados about sf's traditional place on the "outside," at the margins of the literary world, a world that is now trying to embrace it with open arms.

Many members of the sf world take great pride in shunning the literati who formerly raised their patrician noses at science fiction, labeling sf writers mere plebeians among the cultural elite. The type of intelligence that appreciates sf often senses the ridiculous pomposity of self-absorbed humanity that forgets to recognize the vastness of the universe and the wide sweep of time outside our personal and cultural history.

Douglas Adams wrote about humorous writing: "A wit says something funny on the spot. A comedy writer says something very funny two minutes later. Or in my case, two weeks later" (Gaiman, 99). What is funny is noticing how frivolous, whimsical, and inconsequential our lives are in the great realm of space and time. What is funny is often so precisely true that we laugh from the core of our being in surprised recognition. Because it is the purpose of sf writers to think about what is precisely true about the larger population of humanity, the scope of their humor often takes great courage from readers to recognize and to appreciate.

10. Cyberpunk

Bleak and bloody, tawdry and tin-can cheap, cyberpunk captures the vision that many writers and thinkers of the 1980s saw when they imagined the future of young people as depicted in popular media: mesmerized by limitless violence and loveless sex on television, in films, on video, and in games. How will these young people mature with no sense of community, no self-imposed discipline, no ethical restraint? Writers of the literature that would become labeled cyberpunk only saw the young sliding into disenchantment with traditional values. Cyberpunk imagery combines the ennui of information overload with the coldness of robotic mechanism to generate an attitude of tough fatalism about a humanity that seems to care little about itself or others.

Definition

The film *Blade Runner* (1982) set the scene for cyberpunk: bleak, gray, mean-spirited streets, crowded with unindividualized humans and littered with cheaply printed ads for momentary experiences with forgettable people. It's a world motivated completely by profit. In *The Encyclopedia of Science Fiction,* critics Clute and Nicholls describe this view as one where junk and high-tech ingenuity are valued equally. Central to cyberpunk is an emphasis on "bodily metamorphosis, media overload, and destructive sex" (288). Plastic surgery is as common as hair coloring, stimulus comes from everywhere, and the overriding ethic is that any itch should be scratched—immediately.

A postmodernist type of fiction, cyberpunk is a culminating image of the gritty street scenery of many twentieth-century creations. The Ashcan school of fine arts in the first decades and the realist genres of literature produced work meant to shock the audience into noticing everyday life by overstepping former boundaries of good taste or politeness. Increasingly unbridled by sensitivity or censorship, this artistic zeitgeist could end only in images of humanity with no sense of propriety or control. What is called cyberpunk in science fiction, like "splatterpunk horror" and performance arts that verge on pornography and violence, was inevitable.

The term cyberpunk was coined by Bruce Bethke in a short story, published in 1983 in *Amazing Stories*.[1] One critic has summed up this subgenre as fiction that "deals with a junked-up future of virtual realities, console cowboys and bodies held together with implants, bio-engineering and hard drugs"[2] The root word "cybernetics," first used publicly by mathematician Norbert Wiener in 1947, draws from a Greek word meaning pilot or controller. It describes the science of systems—managing the way systems work, how they process information to govern themselves, and the way they can best be designed. Similar to system theory in computer science, cybernetics is a field meant to encompass both biological and mechanical sciences without favoring either.[3]

Cyborg, a contraction of cybernetic organism, refers to the melding of the two. For example, a person who receives a mechanical heart is a type of cyborg because the feedback devices incorporated within the mechanism are cybernetic. The TV series *Six Million Dollar Man* popularized the idea introduced in Martin Caidin's *Cyborg* (1972), though the term "bionic man" was used more commonly by the general public. The concept of humans engineered mechanically began to make sense.

Cyberpunks are individuals motivated by mere survival and pleasure rather than any larger purpose. As Clute and Nicholls point out, "The new world is an environment, not a project" (Clute and Nicholls, 491). There is no missionary zeal for rescuing or fixing, no motivation to work toward any other goal but avoiding pain and achieving comfort and stimulation. Can literature that describes such a self-indulgent and self-abusing lifestyle engage us except to inspire a satiric backlash? As a genre, cyberpunk seems limited in scope. But as columnist Gerald Jones points out, besides being a convenience for booksellers and publishers, genres typically arise "from the collective imagination of writers who find themselves drawn to similar themes and narrative strategies. Not surprisingly, . . . the borders between genres tend to be as permeable as a Balkan truce (fluid, fuzzy, unstable)."[4] Once the boundaries of cyberpunk were established by a few novels and commentators and a few examples were published, writers went on to different formats and labels. About six years after the term cyberpunk began to be noted by critics, the mainstream public became aware of it as a genre with their discovery of William Gibson.

William Gibson

Born in 1948 in Conway, South Carolina, to William Ford Gibson, a contractor, and Otey Williams Ford, Gibson spent most of his youth in a small Appalachian town in southwest Virginia, where he escaped boredom by reading the more radical sf works by J. G. Ballard, Phillip K. Dick, and William S. Burroughs and listening to the music of Lou Reed. After dropping out of high school in 1967, Gibson moved to Toronto, Canada, where he wandered aimlessly for a few years before marrying language teacher Deborah Thompson in 1972. They shifted their home to Vancouver on the western coast of Canada, where he earned a bachelor's degree at the University of British Columbia. While his wife taught, he took care of their two children and began to write sf short stories. In Vancouver he became increasingly aware of the Japanese dominance in technology, a concern that pervades his writing, especially in his Neuromancer works. Some of the stories collected in *Burning Chrome* (1986) portray this growing recognition of Japan's influence on modern culture and the waning preponderance of Western ethics.

Although Gibson did not invent the concept of cyberpunk, his *Neuromancer* (1984) is considered its first definitive example. The title is a three-part pun, combining neuro, referring to the nervous system; necromancer; and new romancer. This novel begins in Chiba, a port city teeming with crime, where the sky is "the color of television, tuned to a dead channel" (3) and the air seems to "have teeth" (15). The world has become completely technologized. Twenty-four-year-old Case has grown up living for the vicarious thrills of virtual reality, "jacked into a custom cyberspace deck that projected his disembodied consciousness into the consensual hallucination that was the matrix" (5). He has been an expert player in this world of high-stakes computerized crime, but he has made the mistake of stealing from his own corporation and been punished in the cruelest way possible. After poisoning his nervous system and stealing his knowledge with it, his enemies have left this young console cowboy of cyberspace imprisoned in his own medically adjusted body. Now as an "artiste of the slightly funny deal" (4), he trades in genetic materials and hormones in the Night City, where the Cheap Hotel rents out coffins to customers strung out on drug cocktails, where "the electronic thunder of the arcades" (10) rumbles constantly and criminals roam who would kill for implanted microprocessors and other gear, easy, quick sex, and other cheap thrills. The "romance" of the title comes from Case's relationship with Linda Lee, an addict whose relentless hungers drive her to rip him off, but whose upper lip reminds him of "the line children draw to represent a bird in flight" (8). At the end of the first chapter, she is slaughtered . . . or so it seems; the magic of virtual reality makes these players of this not-so-distant future uncertain of what is permanent and what is being presented through holograms. Case's particular necromantic talent at manipulating this virtual world is his mastery of ICE—intrusion countermeasures electronics, a computer virus that can break into even the tightest security. The theme of illusive reality weaves throughout this inverted romantic adventure. Case is not even an antihero. His venue is too small and mean. Rather than honor, he is motivated by base fear and greed; he tries to betray his cronies at every corner he comes to. He's a punk, and in this, Gibson is breaking with traditional sf. There is no wonder at technological achievement or possibility. It's all taken for granted. As John Clute notes, "The Neuromancer trilogy, *Neuromancer* (1984), *Count Zero* (1986), and *Mona Lisa Overdrive* (1988), is all about escaping the flesh" (Clute and Nicholls, 491). The protagonist of the first novel, Case, prefers the cheap and unnatural; in the expensive resort Rue Jules Verne he doesn't even recognize the smell of freshly cut grass (124).

Playing too fast and loose, Case is on an obvious track toward suicide, asking to be destroyed by the thugs he cheats, when he is contacted by Molly, a mirror-eyed girl with scalpel blades embedded in her dark red nails, who is as talented at sex as at violence. She rescues Case and brings him to work for the secretive Armitage, who offers to repair the young man's nervous system in return for his services in a mysterious military mission.

The second section finds Case at home in BAMA—the Boston-Atlanta Metropolitan Axis. He and Molly wait for directions from their boss, Armitage, and wonder who—or what—he represents. The mysterious Wintermute, which seems to oversee so much evil, is described as part of a larger artificial intelligence, like a lobe of a brain. Flashbacks that seem more like present experience than past memories further confuse Case. When he is arrested in the luxurious Riviera, he honestly has no idea how to respond. His old friend Finn tries to explain the mind to him: "The holographic paradigm is the closest thing you've worked out to a representation of human memory, . . . but you've never done anything about it. I can access your memory but that's not the same as your mind" (170). Villa Straylight works like a wasp's nest, sending random attacks from a segmented center, turning inward to avoid the "bright void beyond the hull" (173). In contrast to corporate hierarchical power, this is like a clan of like-minded organisms, all coded with the same purpose, like wasps . . . or so he had thought. Now Case realizes that the power may not be as organized as he had imagined, but more a "ragged tangle of fears, the same strange aimlessness" (203).

The figure of Armitage has been built up as a hologram using the designer's memories of the Screaming Fist military special forces as a base, but various assignments and manipulations have

caused him to disintegrate into senselessness. The boss of Wintermute turns out to be unprepossessing, but Case gets to stay alive
in a denouement that peels back layer after layer of image, finally
revealing an even more complex core. Mere immortality and control without purpose are not enough to make living worthwhile.
Personality and purpose matter. Case returns to his home and
resumes a "normal" life. Armitage is cracking, Wintermute is
omnipotent, but Case will not leave Molly. As the pilot of the ship
Garvey puts it, "We mus' move by Jah love, each one" (192). The
ultimate message is as romantic as they come.

Although Gibson incorporates sophisticated terminology in his
writing, his computer systems' degree of self-consciousness seems
virtually impossible . . . but then, this is science *fiction*. Gibson's
slick language and sleek, smooth pace satisfy most technologically
literate readers. His plot moves not so much in logical progression
but as a collection of images that accumulate to indicate a probable story. This reflects recent changes in educators' and psycholo-
gists' ideas about the way young people learn—more by association of immediately visible or aural images than by linear logical
threads; it also suits quick readers who absorb the whole image
sequence at one sitting to comprehend the whole effect rather
than those who read by reflecting on each part during the
process. It's more like dot-matrix media, which is comprehended
instantaneously and as a nonstop continuum, than the traditional
literary experiences of printed books, which are more fragmented
and absorbed over long spans of linear time.

Norman Spinrad in "The Neuromantics" (1986)[5] argues that
cyberpunk joins the romantic elements of fiction with science, a
fusion he welcomes after the split he sees in the 1960s debate
between New Wave and hard sf. In romantic fiction the images of
nature usually are good and beneficial, whereas in cyberpunk the
natural world is spoiled, and natural allusions are usually
unpleasant: "like a water spider crossing the face of some stag-
nant pool" (202). Case accompanies Molly through a computer
program called simstim, where he can literally enter her skin—
feel, see, and hear what she is. "Dreaming real" is a medium
where someone else's image invades the consciousness of others,

as when Case imposes his memory of Molly on all of them (141). This is certainly unlike the tradition of romantic fiction, where naturalism and privacy are highly valued. The focus on individual motivations, at the expense of ignoring social implications and the dynamics of larger groups, certainly is typical of romantic literature, as is the celebration of physical responses and emotional stimulation. So too is the lightning-jagged language that mimics the internal rhythms of the book, the disjointed spontaneity of the plot, and the superficial personas of the characters who speed through time and experience without pondering consequences or weighing connotations. The sound of the language does not so much control the story as reflect the pace and surface that define it. While the stylistic music of cyberpunk is harder driving and less comfortable than the lyric melodies of traditional romantic literature, it is music nonetheless, as mentally and physically effective to its listeners as any other.

In this first novel Gibson's unerring sense of style in portraying the world of the displaced, the poetic precision of his imagery in capturing the telling detail, and his jazzy pace immediately won him a devoted following. *Neuromancer* won the Hugo, the Nebula, and the Philip K. Dick awards, and many of Gibson's numerous readers dubbed the language and the mannerisms of his characters as cool. Critics, however, have lamented that Gibson's vision of the near future offers no hope, no promise. The mean, bleak picture he paints seems to depict that this is all that is possible, like the gritty detective stories so stylish in the 1940s and '50s, which epitomized the postwar breakdown of traditional aspirations toward beauty and grace. Examining Gibson's Mervyn Kihn stories "The Gernsback Continuum" and "Hippie Hat Brain Parasite," the critic Thomas A. Bredehoft concludes that Gibson's dystopic vision connotes the failure of the utopian dreams of science fiction of the past.[6] After writing screenplays in Hollywood, Gibson, collaborating with Bruce Sterling, wrote an even more pessimistic dystopia, *The Difference Engine* (1990). He portrays nineteenth-century Britain as if the early development of Babbage's computer had enabled a utilitarian practicality, the era's favorite ethic of progressive liberals, to be carried to an ultimate extreme. Rather than the messy freewheeling energy of London painted by Dickens or the effete refinement so often portrayed in other depictions of the Victorian era, England is described as grimly neat, organized into a colorless mediocrity with few interesting extremities. The novel is amazingly believable.

Bruce Sterling

Also hailed as an early proponent of cyberpunk is Bruce Sterling (1954-), who edited the first well-known anthology of this subgenre, *Mirrorshades: The Cyberpunk Anthology,* in 1986. His enthusiasm for using information technology and biological engineering for change attracted many readers who were fascinated with the new possibilities of science and industry. The anthology was not only popular, but it received much critical acclaim as well: "Here was a bunch of writers doing what sf authors are supposed to do best, surf-riding on the big breakers of change" (Clute and Nicholls, 289). In Sterling's own writing the characters are young and blasé, the plots hard-edged and full of realistic details. His extensive knowledge of scientific technology and his ability to write understandable technical descriptions earned him recognition as a sf genius of the 1980s. He is credited with defining the cyberpunk subgenre in his fanzine *Cheap Truth* (1984–1986) and in *Mirrorshades,* thus establishing its hard-edged style and "highly detailed realism closely informed by scientific speculation and extrapolation." According to Colin Greenland, "Sterling is one of the most globally minded of North American sf writers, seeing civilization as an intricate and unstable mechanism, and pitting the search for equilibrium against our insatiable demands for knowledge and power" (Clute and Nicholls, 289).

Cyberpunk as Social Commentary

As social commentary, cyberpunk warns against the selfish hedonism of 1980s American culture, the "me generation" that encouraged many individuals to indulge their personal quests for intellectual and emotional stimulation rather than committing energy to resolving social problems. As a genre it portrays the destructive results of individuals obsessing over personal problems, shirking their relation to collective humanity. As such, it is part of the polemic tradition of science fiction written for the young, which has struggled to prevent the kinds of futures its older, more experienced authors fear. In this case, it is cautionary literature written by and about the young, in the hope of shocking contemporaries who hold the reins of power into controlling the effects of their new inventions.

Sterling's *Holy Fire* (1996) explores the implications of extending life beyond the normal span, thus increasing the proportion of the elderly population. Ninety-one years old, medical economist Mia Ziemann participates in a medical rejuvenation experiment that seems to work; she looks and feels twenty. To go along with her new body, Mia adopts a new name—Maya—and new friends. Discarding her former life, she tries to start all over again. Mia, or Maya, is not an attractive character, so the motivation for reading this, and similar literature, does not arise from caring about the protagonist. Rather it is the fascination of tracing out the implications of a technological event that is foreseeably possible, if not probable. Already, the medical world debates the ethical dilemma of extending the lives of infants with severe mental or physical handicaps, including drug addiction or birth trauma. The debate surrounding Dr. Jack Kevorkian's assistance to patients who prefer immediate, painless suicide to an extended life of pain and hardship has publicized the issues of medically extended life. Readers can imagine facing the dilemmas traced in *Holy Fire* in their own lifetimes.

A Cyberpunk Female: Pat Cadigan

In the small group of cyberpunk authors included in Sterling's anthology *Mirrorshades,* Pat Cadigan (1953–) is the only woman. She is often cited as the first woman to write cyberpunk effectively. Her narratives focus less on the technological toys of Gibson and Sterling and more on the cybernetic possibilities for mental control. In *Mindplayers* (1987) a psychologist enters her patients' dreams in order to distinguish between the various personalities there. The theme of psychic fracture continues in her later work *Synners* (1991), which describes a near future when mental imagery and ideas are transmitted like viruses into other people, colonizing within other brains. This idea becomes even more complex in *Fools* (1992), as personality becomes fragmented further into computerlike programs that interact in a confusing melange of characters, personalities, and intelligences.

Cadigan's emphasis on personality, simulated stimulus (simstim), and the passive roles of her female characters raises interesting questions about gender differences in speculative fiction. Does literature still display the stereotypical split between the male-dominated, action-packed tales of high adventure and the more passionate, relational world of personality? Cadigan's work is just as gritty and mean in tone and describes just as bleak an environment as that of Gibson and Sterling, but its setting is more internal and personal. She is as much the princess of cyberpunk as they are the princes. The question now is whether the kingdom still exists.

The Impact of Cyberpunk Literature

Critics continue to explore the impact of cyberpunk on both the field of literature, especially science fiction, and its young readers. Lauraine Leblanc has examined how cyberpunk authors construct different definitions of gender in worlds where technology can replace physical strength and social status as a means to manipulate power relationships among people. Leblanc—in surveying Gibson's *Neuromancer,* Pat Cadigan's *Mindplayers,* and Laura J. Nixon's *Glass Houses*—finds similarities in how the violent petty criminals called "razor girls" use technology to undermine traditional male roles of power.[7] Other critics use the Internet and other appropriate media to review the recent surge of feminist cyberpunk where women protagonists succeed in the traditionally male domain of high tech.[8]

Christine Kenyon Jones, in her study of the "sf and romantic biofictions" of Brian Aldiss, William Gibson, and Bruce Sterling, has noted similarities between those authors' portrayal of cyborg personalities and the Frankenstein myth.[9] However, in the twentieth-century world of computerized electronics, the fabricated creature is both more real and more unreal than Mary Wollstonecraft Shelley ever imagined. More normal than monstrous, a cyborg is made up of mechanical parts embedded in a human, whereas Shelley's creation is more like a true human, with its own self-conscious soul. The most independent cybernetic creations lay a bridge toward imagining humans whose reality is completely engineered, whose lives are more "virtually perceived" than actually experienced.

Is cyberpunk dead in the 1990s? Though the term is no longer applied to new fiction, the effects of this movement continue in the energetic pace of much writing and in the proliferation of media themes. A growing number of writers outside science fiction, from poets to novelists, have begun to use flashy and extensive technological metaphors in their writing. One subgenre, the techno-thriller, fast-paced and suspenseful, depends on both the fear and the fascination of its readers for its plots. While bothersome to traditionalists who expect literature and science to treat separate realms of thought, this melding of ideas has proved stimulating to many writers. They find its imagery deeply appropriate to explain the bizarre reality of a Nintendo generation—a reality increasingly complicated by the steady stream of detailed information from every corner of the world and by the ever-changing technology available to almost anyone. Cyberpunk has forced us to evaluate the implications of an increasingly technological environment. Although the cyberpunk trend seems to have played itself out, its impact is still visible.

Chronology: Cyberpunk

1982   The film *Blade Runner* presents a world dominated by punks who exploit, and are exploited by, high technology.

1983   Bruce Bethke's "Cyborg" appears in *Amazing Stories.*

1984   William Gibson's *Neuromancer* is published; wins the Hugo, Nebula, and Philip K. Dick awards.

1984–1986   Bruce Sterling's fanzine *Cheap Truth* defines and publishes cyberpunk fiction.

1986   Bruce Sterling edits *Mirrorshades: The Cyberpunk Anthology.*

1987   Pat Cadigan's *Mindplayers* is published.

1990   *The Difference Engine* by Gibson and Sterling is published.

1991   Cadigan's *Synners* is published.

1992   Cadigan's *Fools* is published.

11. Science Fiction on Film: *Star Trek*

As John Clute points out in his discussion of sf film, "Up to the moment when the first moving picture began to flicker on screens in front of awed (even frightened) audiences, cinema itself was SF" (Clute, 252). Cinema demonstrated the magic of science, and many of the first films freely mixed fantastic imagery with technological inventions, amazing their audiences with elaborate sets and special effects as well as with the medium itself. Thus the partnership between science fiction and film dates from the inception of cinema as entertainment. In fact, French filmmaker Georges Méliès's 21-minute film version of Jules Verne's *Le Voyage dans le Lune* in 1902 was the first movie lasting more than a few minutes. Méliès had used sf images in his previous fantasies of under five minutes, such as a mechanical man in *Gugusse et l'Automate* (1897), but the collection of special effects in this film was phenomenal for the time, using double exposure and elaborate models to astound the viewers. In 1907 Méliès produced an 18-minute version of Verne's *Deux Cent Milles Lieues sous les Mers* (*20,000 Leagues Under the Sea,* 1890). The first sf movie made in the United States was J. Searle Dawley's *Frankenstein* in 1910. While these first films often contained silly plots and characters, the inventiveness of their producers rewarded viewers with an increased sense of wonder, the same motivation that drew many readers to sf. *Metropolis* (1926) is a classic, still effective in its portrayal of machines and an urban setting conveying the overwhelming power of technology, beginning a theme that culminates with the cyberpunk imagery of the 1980s.

Science Fiction Films Gain Popularity

During the 1930s, film remakes of classic sf stories were popular: another version of Shelley's *Frankenstein* (1931), Robert Louis Stevenson's *Dr. Jekyll and Mr. Hyde* (1932), *The Invisible Man* (1933), and Hilton's *Lost Horizon* (1936). Special effects became more sophisticated, especially the stop-motion photography of *King Kong* (1933), which is still impressive today. This archetypal beauty and the beast monster film is still part of our popular language. During this decade, *Flash Gordon* (1936) and *Buck Rogers* (1939), film series based on comic book successes, established science fiction films as a market for young people. *Flash Gordon,* with its dramatic space opera plot, pitted the souped-up everyman Flash against Ming the Merciless from the planet Mongo, establishing a stereotype that continues today. The comic strip regenerated into a popular radio serial, the film series, several novels, and a film parody, *Flesh Gordon* (1974). *Buck Rogers* was the first sf comic strip in the United States to attract a long-running readership of adults and older children. The film copied the comic strip format by releasing 12 episodes played at Saturday matinees throughout the 1940s and it was imitated by a TV serial (ABC) in 1950–1951.

The 1940s saw little else in science fiction cinema except slapstick send-ups of *Frankenstein* and *Invisible Man* (1933) with comedians Bud Abbott and Lou Costello. The field exploded, however, after World War II and the detonation of the atomic bomb. In the 1950s viewers watched films about space exploration and alien monsters landing on Earth, illustrating a conservative nervousness about allowing scientific experimentation and exploitation to continue unmonitored. A typical example is *Invasion of the Body Snatchers* (1956), a paranoid film about aliens invading not just Earth but its people. The film was remade in the seventies.

An early import from Japan was the popular film *Godzilla* (1954), a conventional monster movie. With a name that combined the English word gorilla and the Japanese word for whale (kujira), the film spawned a series of sequels.

Science Fiction Cinema Succeeds

Clute and Nicholls cite 1968 as a key date in the history of science fiction cinema (Clute, 222), just as it is often cited as the beginning of young adult literature as a self-conscious genre. For the first time sf films were successful commercially, indicating public acceptance of the genre as a respectable form of adult entertainment. *Barbarella,* a light satire on the sexy doll-toy vision of women in sf, signaled the public's awareness of science fiction clichés. The star of *Charly,* Cliff Robertson, won the first Oscar for best actor awarded to someone playing in a science fiction film. *Planet of the Apes* was commercially successful on a large scale; an exemplar of excellent special effects and makeup technology, it is one of the first films that attracted the general public to consider science fiction themes. *2001: A Space Odyssey,* also widely popular, inspired audiences with its classical-music theme and its thought-provoking speculation about the future.

Star Wars and Other Commercial Successes

The next boom year was 1977, when *Close Encounters of the Third Kind,* using wonderful special effects and a philosophically complex story, evoked a sense of wonder and awe rare in recent sf films. The huge popularity of *Star Wars,* which grossed over a million dollars and garnered seven Academy Awards, finally proved that sf films could be profitable and reflected a cultural nostalgia for the simplistic competition of good against bad. Two years later, in 1979, the success of *Star Trek: The Motion Picture* cemented this pattern. In *Star Wars* Luke Skywalker, a young hero played by Mark Hamill, embarks on a mission to rescue a fair maiden, Leia, played by Carrie Fisher, from the evil Galactic Empire. Evil is represented by the dragon-breathed Darth Vader (James Earl Jones), cloaked in the traditional black garb of threat and evil. An older mentor, Obi-Wan Kenobi (played by Alec Guinness), whose spirit power is depicted as awareness of the supernatural, is contrasted to the competent but feckless recklessness of the mercenary adventurer at war, Han Solo, played by Harrison Ford. The musical score is inspiring and the special effects are dazzling. Like many sf films before it, *Star Wars* captures the familiar victory of good over evil in a colorful, fast-paced story that satisfied a huge audience by reiterating a familiar cultural pattern in new and glamorous garb. Two sequels repeated the feat: *The Empire Strikes Back* (1980) and *The Return of the Jedi* (1983) illustrate the theme of victory through strength, both moral and physical, without rubbing its viewers' noses in any messy goriness or blood. The violence and destruction are safely antiseptic and distant, made possible through the development of technology. *Star Wars'* success as a cultural icon continues in the late 1990s as toy companies wage a multimillion-dollar war over rights to capitalize on the continuing popularity of action figure toys portraying its characters.

The most commercially successful film ever made is *E.T.: The Extraterrestrial* (1983), a sentimental movie suitable for children but also attractive to adults who harken back to the time when doing the right thing was simple. The 1980s produced a spate of sf films meant to entertain more than to preach, prophesy, or speculate. *Honey, I Shrunk the Kids* (1989) replays the conventional theme of the eccentric inventor who makes a mistake; its special effects and fast-paced humor attracted a sizable mainstream audience. In *Bill & Ted's Excellent Adventure* (1988) an innocent pair of Southern California boys travel back and forth in time, escaping pain and peril by following their simplistic motto: "Party on, dudes." This light-hearted, light-witted adventure is pure entertainment, harmlessly funny and mindless.

Cyberpunk and Cynicism

The decade of the eighties also produced *Blade Runner* (1982), universally acknowledged as the precursor to the cyberpunk phenomenon in sf. This film's cynicism—wet, gray, and steamy— pours off the screen. Based on Philip K. Dick's work, the film's setting and mood are repeated in the work of William Gibson and Bruce Sterling, as well as in other films that follow. *Akira* (1990) exemplifies both the growing influence of Japanese culture and artistic talent on sf productions and the transfer of comic-book graphics to film. It also shows the influence of cyberpunk cynicism on human culture and its densely violent environments. The dismal, disjointed portrayal of Gotham City in the popular *Batman* films and comics also reflects the cyberpunk aesthetic, but a persistent heroic-savior impulse keeps the character of Batman from falling completely under the spell of this genre.

Alien[3] (1992) shows the feminist influence on serious films. The heroine, Ripley, lands on a misogynist planet, unwittingly bringing along a parasite to which she finally must sacrifice herself to save humanity. Bloody and fierce, with unrelenting violence and horror, this film focuses on the superior survival strengths of its female hero in the face of a macho all-male society. The heroic adventure film returns to the forefront in the nineties with *Independence Day* (1996) and yet another version of *Star Trek*. Sf films are now advertised like others, as part of the mainstream. In the nineties, old stories are retold and the real stars are the increasingly sophisticated and splendiferous special effects. People still like to be amazed.

Science fiction has become so respectable that it appears on television; potentially, it can enter every living room in the United States and most middle-class homes in the world. In his article "The Third Generation of Genre SF," Brian Stableford notes that the format of sf most people see is changing now that it is popularized more by TV and movie series than by the magazine short stories and paperback novels of its previous two "generations."[1] The medium of television demands a format that can be viewed within an hour, necessitating a plot predictable enough to be comprehended by the viewing public in this time slot yet stimulating enough to hold interest. Stableford identifies three types of formula used in TV science fiction:

1. In law-enforcement shows such as *Mission Impossible* and *The Six-Million Dollar Man,* the hero and the hero's partners represent a benevolent organization that guards the innocent public from some outside threat. The mission and the identity of these agents must be kept secret, necessitating complications that increase suspense. As in other law-enforcement shows, the hero is usually stronger in a special way, like the technologically enhanced hero of *The Six-Million Dollar Man.*

2. A "special secret agent" or "wandering vigilante" moves from setting to setting fighting for justice, but not for a particular agency. Examples include *Doctor Who* and *Quantum Leap,* where the main characters move not only from place to place, but also in time, recreating the notable events, personalities, and technologies of other historical cultures.

3. The "running man" formula adds even more suspense because the protagonist not only spends his or her life working toward a larger purpose but must also escape some enemy, often vaguely defined. Prime examples are *The Invaders, The Fugitive,* and *Planet of the Apes,* in which apes with humanlike intelligence and motives tyrannously subjugate the few remaining humans on the planet. Heroes are also victims in these shows (324).

Stableford notes that the overriding theme of each formula depends on paranoia. Science fiction elements make the world different, but they don't necessarily make the world better. In a recent series, *The X-Files,* the sense of impending catastrophe grows as the sense of trust in science as savior is undermined.

According to Stableford, even the relationship between characters is mistrustful in these science fictions. To save expenses, screenwriters must tell the story from a relatively limited background, such as the bridgehead and the space station on *Star Trek*. In this fixed setting, conversation is often the vehicle to move the plot along, so there must be more than one character on stage; the protagonist must have a sidekick or partner who is similar enough to share a viewpoint but also of a different gender, racial, or ethnic background, or with different values, to guarantee some interesting tension. In *Star Trek* the logical Spock is countered with Kirk's emotional approach to adventures. In *The X-Files* Mulder and sidekick Scully avoid romance in an oddly neurotic relationship. Stableford theorizes that if these TV series continue, characters will become more eccentric and self-absorbed, which runs counter to the ethical stance of American public education, which increasingly encourages cooperation, tolerance of differences, and global thinking (324).

No other televised science fiction series has been more popular than *Star Trek*. "There is something compelling about it that triumphs over costumes and logic. It attracts; it involves; and finally, it affects. It can grab hold and not let go,"[2] writes Nicholas Meyer, a writer and director of the series, who cannot fully explain the incredible attraction of the series over more than 30 years: "At its best, *Star Trek* appears to function as pop allegory/ pop metaphor, taking current events and issues—ecology, war and racism, for example—and objectifying them for us to contemplate in a science fiction setting. The world it presents may make no sense as either science or fiction, but is well and truly sufficient for laying out human questions" (Meyer, 49). Perhaps the very simplicity and conventionality of this eternal series explains its longevity to such a huge number of viewers. Hundreds of journal and magazine articles and scores of books have tried to delineate its history and analyze its appeal.

Gene Roddenberry: Creator of *Star Trek*

By the time he became the executive producer of the first episode of *Star Trek* at age 45, Gene Roddenberry (1921–1991) had already lived many adventures. He began as an asthmatic and rather gawky boy, born in Texas and reared in Los Angeles, who preferred books to friends, imbibing tales by Zane Grey, the legends of Hawkeye, and the alien characters of the sf magazine *Astounding Stories.* He grew into a tall, bear-shaped man with large ideas and great personal presence, whose charm was rooted in the values of freedom and justice he learned from westerns and sf adventures. An adventurer in his own right, he flew 89 combat and reconnaissance missions during World War II in Guadalcanal before the age of 25. In 1947 he was awarded a Civil Aeronautics Commendation for heroic behavior when he emerged alive from crash-landing a Pan-Am jet in the Syrian desert, maintaining control so others would survive. During the 1950s he served in the Los Angeles police force, learning firsthand about the narcotics trade, skid row, and other dangers, which he translated into successful scripts for TV shows including *Dragnet, Have Gun Will Travel,* and *The Naked City.* He married Majel Barrett, with whom he enjoyed a long-term intellectual and emotional partnership. It is fitting that his ashes were scattered from the space shuttle *Enterprise* after his death in 1991.

Many of Roddenberry's ideas are preserved in letters to his best friend, Charles Muses. Both felt that the trend during the second half of the twentieth century to deconstruct traditional definitions of reality, breaking down illusions and even hope about the fate of humanity, was a necessary catharsis before a better future could be built. *Star Trek* was based on Jeffersonian principles that education would lead society to recognize the mistakes of the past and fashion a much-improved future by avoiding those errors.

In keeping with this urge to learn, Roddenberry also opposed the kinds of censorship that prevent young viewers from knowing the whole truth. In a congressional statement about the effects of TV viewing on the morality of youth, Roddenberry claimed that what is wrong with the violence on TV is that it is dishonest. He wants people to see "that if a grown man hits another man in the face with his fist, knuckles break, and bones shatter, and that it is a messy, harmful, stupid thing to do."[3] Roddenberry was a passionate believer in telling the truth about life as he perceived it, even masked and dressed in the images and metaphors of a fictional future, and this was his main motive in proposing the first *Star Trek* stories. He wanted to make a difference.

Star Trek: **The Beginning**

The *Star Trek* TV series, which has procreated films, books, articles, and a huge subculture, premiered on 8 September 1966 and ran for three years until it was discontinued because of low ratings and general disinterest, despite outraged protest by a passionate core group of loyal fans. Basically a space adventure following the traditional patterns of heroic romance, *Star Trek* introduced some aspects new to TV science fiction. Unlike the previous anthologies of unrelated sf stories, *Star Trek* was a series with a setting and characters who developed together over time. This important difference allowed the writers to explore the characters' interactions not only with each other but also with the alien worlds they encountered. More than a showcase for technological inventions or ideas that could be described in less than an hour, *Star Trek* could and did address complicated social and political issues. Setting the series in the twenty-third century diluted the potentially controversial nature of many of its themes: the horrors of war; prejudice against racial, gender, and ethnic differences; ecological dangers; the nature of intelligence and of humankind; and the use and misuse of technology. Perhaps because the series addressed and influenced so many issues relevant to society in the late 1960s, some of the viewpoints expressed seem dated now. At that time, however, many aspects of the series were considered fairly liberal and, in some circles, daring. Not only did the series feature a black female character as a military officer, but it also starred a green-blooded alien with pointy ears, an odd hairline, and eyebrows that did not conform to conventional standards of attractiveness. In the mid-sixties the major TV networks, concerned about advertising money, struggled to attract and keep viewers' attention without offending anyone. In fact, in an early NBC brochure advertising the series, photos of Spock were retouched to remove the tips of his ears and the slant of his eyebrows.[4] The first pilot show, titled

"The Cage," was rejected by NBC because the screening audience, including women, found the female officer, named Number One, too "pushy" and "annoying," and Mr. Spock revolting and childish (Shatner, 65). Fortunately, the second pilot, "Where No Man Has Gone Before," so thrilled the network executives with its special effects and fast-paced action that they ignored the fact that the characters remained the same; Mr. Spock and Number One survived.

The action takes place aboard a giant spaceship, the U.S.S. *Enterprise,* and the various worlds it visits. Designed by Walter M. Jeffries, the ship is dish-shaped with the engine separated from the main hull and colored a neutral gray to more easily reflect various light effects from the different parts of space. The ship, with its crew of several hundred, is an emissary of the United Federation of Planets of the twenty-third century, sent to explore new worlds and to uphold the ideals of truth and justice. Typically the ship meets an aggressive alien or lands on a planet where aliens of one sort seem to be invading or destroying the property of weaker aliens. Often the aliens first seem as omnipotent and wise as gods, but soon reveal a flawed side that causes them to be dangerous. A common trait of the aliens is the ability to communicate telepathically. No matter how threatening or evil the enemy appears at first, the ultimate message of all the *Star Trek* episodes, in books and films, is that human Earthlings will survive and prevail—but only after learning that the urge to exclude and triumph over those who are different brings unnecessary pain to both sides. The eventual theme song, "The Future Is Ours," takes on a broader, even contrary meaning: "us" includes "them."

An early episode, "The Menagerie," adapted from the pilot of the series, won a Hugo for best dramatic presentation in 1967. Another Hugo went to Harlan Ellison's "City on the Edge of Forever" in 1968, an episode often considered the best of the lot, later reprinted in *Six Science Fiction Plays* (1976).

Star Trek Characters
Piloting the U.S.S. *Enterprise* was Captain James Tiberius Kirk, played by William Shatner, a protagonist depicted as impetuous,

bold, and earnest like traditional adventure heroes. Though he has been compared to C. S. Forrester's swashbuckling mariner, Horatio Hornblower, Roddenberry conceived him as a more complex character: "Captain Kirk was Hamlet, the flawed hero ... who knows what he has to do, but agonizes over it" (Fern, 67), looking braver and more confident than he feels. Down deep, like many real-life people, he doesn't believe he is strong enough to be the leader he needs to be, but he persists in trying. He's basically a good man who sometimes has to bend the rules a bit to achieve what he sees as the greater good, an energetic enthusiast who is impatient with caution, fear, and ignorance.

Second in command is science officer Lieutenant Spock, an alien from the planet Vulcan, who has joined the crew of the *Enterprise.* His is the voice of logic, uncolored by the emotional baggage most humans insist on carrying. Often his rationality is contrasted to Kirk's human passion: Kirk is heart, Spock is mind. But, like Kirk, Spock has more than one dimension. Roddenberry explains, "Spock is, to me, the essence of evolution ... he's a profound thinker. His logic is nearly perfect. . . . but if the problem is emotional, he is not so capable" (Fern, 69). Vulcans are humanoids whose ancestors were a passionate and violent people, traits that almost caused their extinction. In reaction they developed a philosophy of self-control, suppressing emotion and focusing on logic. Spock is half Vulcan, but he is also human on his mother's side. With twice the emotions and half the inherent control, he finds it difficult enough to act as a true Vulcan. But as the only Vulcan in a predominantly Earthling crew, he is continually tempted by their emotions, humor, and warmth and thus develops a careful, conscious control. Roddenberry felt that Spock should appear often on the screen in order to remind viewers that the action was taking place in the twenty-third century. Leonard Nimoy, who portrayed Spock for almost 30 years, actually became so involved in the character that it affected his personality off the screen; onlookers often perceived him as distant and unemotional even outside the studio. Nimoy invented the four-fingered split salute, which is actually a Jewish rabbinical blessing; the neck pinch to stun any luckless victim into submission with a limited amount of messy violence; and the complex relationship between him and his first in command. In real life, he has remained close to Shatner, who played Kirk for the same number of years.

Argumentative, quibbling, and frustrating but also a loyal friend, Dr. Leonard "Bones" McCoy, played by Deforest Kelley, was third in command, a foil to Captain Kirk's young, impetuous adventurousness and the calm, controlled Mr. Spock. Dr. "Bones" was a cranky and querulous, perennially anxious, little-minded man reminding the larger-than-life characters of their links to humanity. Crewman Mr. Sulu was enthusiastically played by George Takei, whose Oriental features had previously limited his roles to stereotypical characters. Takei brought his flashy swordplay to the role, adding drama to the plot and fear to the lives of the other actors.

Montgomery "Scotty" Scott, played by James Doohan, is the dour engineer who "beams up" Kirk when he wants to travel without moving a muscle. In novels of sea adventures, the chief engineer is traditionally a Scot who saves the ship with his Scottish ingenuity and persistence when the engines fail—as they often do.[5]

The character who originally created much controversy among the network executives was Lieutenant Uhura, a black woman with authority almost equal to that of Kirk. Played by actress Nichelle Nichols, the character was of the Bantu nation of the United States of Africa. For most of the first TV series she was pretty much a passive onlooker, a normal role for women characters at that time. In later episodes and films her role expanded along with the nation's quickly growing awareness of the limitations of gender and ethnic stereotyping.

The Principle and Practice of Diversity
Critics have complained that this inclusive casting was merely a superficial desire to excite an audience without offending anyone: "The defect in this liberal internationalism was that all these characters behaved in a traditional White Anglo-Saxon Protestant manner: only Spock was a truly original creation." But famed sf writer Arthur C. Clarke, a friend of Roddenberry for

more than 20 years, felt that the inclusion of these token characters had an important impact on viewers: "At a dark time in
human history, *Star Trek* promoted the then unpopular ideals of
tolerance for differing cultures, and respect for all life forms—
without preaching and always with a saving sense of humor"
(Fern, xi). Roddenberry's dream was a world where people
respect each other's differences. His inclusion of a female black
officer brought praise from Dr. Martin Luther King as well as
from other admirers who felt he was breaking important boundaries.

A central principle of the *Star Trek* universe is the motto "Infinite Diversity in Infinite Combinations," abbreviated as IDIC and
symbolized by a Vulcan ornament that Spock wears, first seen in
the episode "Is There in Truth No Beauty?" The IDIC ornament
has been copied into jewelry by fans as "a tribute to the ideal of
universal tolerance for all life forms" (Fern, 223). Yet Roddenberry didn't believe that simple diversity is necessarily a virtue:
"It's one thing to celebrate it because it exists. It's another thing
to mourn its passing if it no longer works. That's like saying people shouldn't marry other races because we have to preserve
racial purity—that we have to stay distinct, diverse. The opposite
of taking delight in diversity isn't to condemn it—it's just to allow
it to change naturally. We may become diverse in a way we don't
know about yet" (Fern, 20).

Star Trek: The Next Generation

After years of encouragement from fans, Roddenberry wrote a
pilot for a new series, which began in 1987 and lasted for seven
seasons until 1994. Roddenberry's influence waned as he became
increasingly ill up until his death in 1991. After a slow start, the
series ultimately was well received by critics and viewers alike.
Set 80 years after the original *Star Trek,* the themes reflected the
ambiguous moral confidence of the 1980s as compared to the earlier righteousness of the sixties. New characters were added.
Commander Data, played by Brent Spiner, is a robot programmed

with perfect logic whose greatest concern is to experience human emotion, like the Tin Man in Frank Baum's *Wizard of Oz.* Captain Jean-Luc Picard, played by Patrick Stewart, is a stately captain of the *Enterprise* and Security Chief Worf, played by Michael Dorn, displays courtesy and intelligence that belie his glowering Klingon appearance. Well-known guest stars have included Whoopi Goldberg as a straight-talking bartender and John DeLancie as Q, dangerously intelligent and insincerely charming with no compassion for human sentimentalism.

Individual Independence or Collective Cooperation?

A main focus of *Star Trek: The Next Generation* is the struggle between individual independence and concern for the safety and welfare of humanity. Roddenberry felt that people were basically good, but as a whole acted immaturely, needing moral leadership to grow beyond the preadolescent stage of the late twentieth century. *Star Trek* depicts a future where the domestic problems of hunger and homelessness have been solved and the human race is ready to devote its time and energy to learning and exploring space. Have the problems of how to survive as a race been solved collectively as humans learn to cooperate as one, or was protection of individual rights the answer? Although Roddenberry was fascinated by the idea of collective consciousness as a way to function globally, his writing indicates a preference for independent individualism of humans. Two of the worst enemies in late vintage *Star Trek* were the Borg and Q. Collective cooperation is rational. The effectiveness of the Borg lies in their ability to act logically, like a swarm of insects, dangerous because of that inexplicable collective mentality that focuses the efforts of the group on one target. Q as represented by the single character is "charming, insincere, manipulative, callous. . . . Q has little or no compassion for the human race he loves to taunt, but that doesn't matter. It is the questions that matter, and how the human race will answer some of these questions that matter" (Fern, 30). In an interview just before his death, Roddenberry explained that the tension between individual rights and the necessity for humanity to act cooperatively may even result in a new strand of humanity, a socio-organism "in which the individual units no longer function in any capacity as individuals. They may specialize, but not without the knowledge and cooperation of the whole group. It's a kind of interdependence in which the whole is greater than the sum of its parts" (Fern, 16). In a 1985 letter to his friend Charles Muse, Roddenberry theorized how this necessity might result in a new kind of human diversity: "Or is it possible the human creature is dividing (as some species in the past have done) and becoming two human types, individuals and sorg [socio-organism]?" (quoted in Fern, 21).

The Impact of *Star Trek*

Hard-core followers, who call themselves "Trekkers" in contrast to the outsider term "Trekkies," have preserved the *Star Trek* vocabulary, which can be understood all over the world. "Beam me up, Scotty" is a popular greeting; "Live long and prosper" is a friendly benediction; and "to boldly go where no man has gone before" is a promise, recognizable as Trek-speak because of its split infinitive and the utter seriousness of its tone. The four-finger wedged greeting helps fellow Trekkers identify each other at the numerous conventions that still continue 30 years after *Star Trek*'s conception. The pointed ears and slanted eyebrows of Nimoy's Mr. Spock are still recognizable to children at costume parties. The original U.S.S. *Enterprise* hangs in the Smithsonian museum in Washington, D.C., next to the Wright Brothers' *Kitty Hawk* In 1996, on the 30th anniversary of *Star Trek*'s first TV appearance, Mattel offered a gift set of its Barbie and Ken dolls dressed as crew members of the Starship *Enterprise,* thus combining two American iconographic images of the second half of the twentieth century. Barbie, costumed as an engineering officer, wears a short red dress and black boots and carries a miniature communicator and tricorder. Ken is a commanding officer with the standard gold jersey, black pants, and boots and is armed with a phaser. *Star Trek* still lives.

Star Trek in Print and on Film

In 1979 *Star Trek: The Motion Picture* was released by Paramount, produced by Gene Roddenberry and directed by Robert Wise, based on a story by Alan Dean Foster and a screenplay by Harold Livingston, and using most of the original characters from the TV series. The focus on Mr. Spock's struggle to void himself of human emotion to become more like his Vulcan antecedents was unusual for sf films, which tend to be more action oriented. In *Star Trek II: The Wrath of Khan* (1982), directed by Nicholas Meyer with a screenplay by J. B. Sowards, Captain Kirk is called upon to rescue an old lover and the head of a terraforming project, Dr. Carol Marcus, and meets his own son. In this dark film about loss, Mr. Spock dies. The enemy Khan is played by Ricardo Montalban, and Kirstie Alley appears as an alien student pilot. In *Star Trek III: The Search for Spock* (1984), written by Harve Bennett and directed by Leonard Nimoy, Spock returns to life, but Kirk loses his son and his ship, the *Enterprise.* In *Star Trek IV: The Voyage Home* (1986), based on a story by Leonard Nimoy and Harve Bennett and directed by Leonard Nimoy, the crew travels back through time to capture a whale from San Francisco Bay. *Star Trek V: The Final Frontier* (1989), directed by William Shatner and using a story by William Shatner, Harve Bennett, and David Loughery, begins on Earth where Captain Kirk defies gravity in Yosemite National Park and is rescued by McCoy and Spock. *Star Trek VI: The Undiscovered Country* (1991), directed by Nicholas Meyer, celebrated the 25th anniversary of *Star Trek* by establishing a new peaceful relationship between humans and their former enemies the Klingons. As with the end of the Cold War between the USSR and the United States, peace is not automatic or easy to guarantee. Recent films are *Star Trek: Generations* (1994), *Star Trek: First Contact* (1996), and *Star Trek: The Final Frontier* (1997). The next one—perhaps the last, perhaps not—is *Star Trek: Insurrection* (1998).

In a reversal of the trend of making movies based on books, the current mode is to publish novelized versions of popular films. The Star Trek movies are a prime example. A virtual library of books and articles retells the stories originally written for the TV and movie screens, describing the technical aspects of making these films, recording the history of how *Star Trek* came to be, and reporting the gossip as told by various participants, fans, and hangers-on. There are also the T-shirts, buttons, plastic ears, phasers, and other toys that reflect the popular interest in this nonthreatening version of sf.

The financial success of these films and spin-off industries is one indication of the extent to which science fiction has moved from the margins of adolescent culture to acceptance by the mainstream. Science fiction has become an acceptable metaphor to use in depicting, analyzing, and discussing social, political, and cultural changes. Indeed, it has become normal to think of sf as part of the future reality most of us will live to see rather than a fantasy none of us expects.

What does the popular acceptance of science fiction as a conventional genre imply about what motivates us as a culture to continue to live as we do? What do we expect to see in the foreseeable future? How shall we live our lives? An overview of new themes and trends in science fiction may point to some answers.

12. New Themes and Trends

"The Golden Age of Science Fiction Is Twelve," writes David G. Hartwell, borrowing a phrase from Peter Graham for the title of his essay in *Age of Wonders:* "Science fiction is preeminently the literature of the bright child, the kid who is brighter perhaps than her teachers."[1] He describes how Robert A. Heinlein, in a speech at the Third Annual World Science Fiction Convention in Denver in 1941, claimed superiority for sf readers who think "in terms of racial magnitude—not even centuries but thousands of years" (Hartwell, 91).

The main motivation behind science fiction, and the source of its power and appeal, is escape from the strictures of everyday thinking, allowing the imagination to see beyond what we have been taught is real and possible. The young, and people with youthful, curious minds, are more apt to tolerate this kind of speculation.

Perhaps the dawn of technology and industry spurred the imagination to visualize with scientific imagery in the same way the Renaissance keyed on images of travel and discovery. Science fiction flourished in North America in the early decades of the twentieth century, when science and technology were considered the salvation of humanity from poverty, crime, dirt, and disease. Especially in the 1950s when Sputnik orbited the Earth, and soon afterward when humans landed on the moon, the frontier for human exploration no longer was bound by geography; topology, physics, and astronomy became the central areas of scientific interest. Now, at the dawn of the twenty-first century, are our

199

minds still 12 years old? Is our collective mind still awed by the possibility of scientific research and technological invention? In a Piagetian sense, 12-year-olds are just recognizing the difference between literal facts and abstract or metaphorical thought. It is evident in their choice of humor that celebrates puns and other quirks of language. For intelligent readers with young minds, science fiction, drawing heavily on the literal machinery of science and technology to explore the complexity of ideas, is an exciting venue. Their discovery of this kind of literature is often the beginning of a long career of reflective thinking and delight in intellectual pursuits. While many adult readers have been traumatized by the escalating, dizzying rate of technological change since World War II into a permanent state of what Alvin Toffler has termed future shock,[2] young minds, despite the whirligig of modern time, retain their enthusiasm for the new and different. Many adults have lost their sense of "Oh, wow!" about technological progress because they are legitimately tired of being forced to learn new habits, or they have lived long enough to recognize the complex implications of rapid change. Much of the sf written for adults is conservative, reflecting a pessimism about the use of future technology and a yearning for an idealized vision of the rural past.

Literature for young people, including science fiction written for youth, has traditionally ended hopefully, positing an optimistic belief in new beginnings. Heroes made wise at a young age, such as Douglas Hill's Cord McKiy, Orson Scott Card's Ender Wiggin, and Octavia Butler's Lauren Olamina, will avoid the mistakes of their elders and begin a new way of life. Young readers, inspired by their first understandings of the ironical viewpoint, still believe in their own abilities to change the world by proclaiming their newly discovered principles. They are on the cusp of abstract thinking; they believe that their own sense of logic is universal, that all humans are motivated as they are.

Science fiction for 12-year-olds—including the universal 12-year-old in each of us—began with Jules Verne's *Journey to the Centre of the Earth* in 1863, which celebrated the possibility of not-yet-invented technology to explore previously unimaginable frontiers. Mary Shelley's work was deeper, probing more into the central dilemmas of science, but was more sophisticated and less hopeful, recognizing the human foibles that could dirty and complicate the clean sweep of progress promised by theoretical science. Although the story of Dr. Frankenstein's monster is beloved by adolescents, hers is an adult novel with levels of complexity young readers may not fully comprehend. In 1910 Victor Appleton wrote the first science fiction novel specifically marketed for children, *Tom Swift and His Airship,* part of a popular series about a young hero whose virtue and hard work always paid off in success. In the early decades of the century, young readers followed the adventures of comic-strip heroes Buck Rogers and Flash Gordon in the newspapers; read the stories by some of the best writers in the field in the sf magazine *Amazing Stories,* which began in 1926; and enjoyed the pulp fiction space operas of the middle decades of the twentieth century—all exciting but all merely precursors to the rich harvest yet to come. In the 1960s Madeleine L'Engle's *A Wrinkle in Time* (1962) was recognized as a classic, an excellent book by any literary standards. Not only science fiction, this work features parents who are scientists and who share their enthusiasm and knowledge with their children. Both the plot and character development center around sophisticated physics, the concept of tessellation. Many readers of children's literature meet science fiction for the first time through this novel.

Since then, sf novels, films, and short stories have joined the mainstream of popular culture as media events worthy of consideration. A growing number of recent writers use science fiction as a pulpit from which to urgently preach their views about ethics, politics, and ecology or to teach a lay audience about physics and space. Science fiction is becoming an acceptable method of teaching, of speculating about the future impact of government policies, our cultural habits of consumption and community, and our attitudes toward the material world.

Part of sf's growing appeal is that modern science is bringing to life the strange ideas and imaginings that once were fiction. So much that seemed wildly fanciful in the past is now possible, though perhaps not probable. Technology has moved the frontiers of exploration from Earth to the moon, Mars, and beyond. The considerable power unleashed by scientific knowledge and its technological instruments is, in science fiction, a source of wishful excitement and vicarious desire, attaining secret insights, skills, machinery, and weaponry that seem to promise instant heroism and the illusion of greatness. To some people, however, science's mastery-urge is a source of profound anxiety, especially its occasional use of cheap thrills to titillate nerves and senses, activating the shallowest impulses of human nature though sometimes playing a part in fiction of a wider scope: "The last few years have seen the rise of a publishing category known as the techno-thriller, essentially a fast-paced action-suspense genre that exploits our fascination with (and fear of) technology. The overlap between this new genre and science fiction, while perplexing to booksellers, has proved stimulating to many writers" (Jakubowski, 75). Science fiction has always appealed to both the philosophical mind that wants to speculate about the future in order to plan, and the part of our minds that wants to play with novelty and stimulation. In a world so ruled by science and technology, science fiction is increasingly the most relevant arena for both tendencies.

And increasingly, young readers and consumers of science fiction are demanding more-sophisticated media. Virtual-reality devices and computerized games provide constant, instantaneous novelty and stimulus, at a pace and with an immediacy that no book can provide. But they are passive media, requiring a kind of focused awareness different from the thought processes of reading, which translates printed symbols into new images formulated from memory and invented from associations remembered from the past. Reading is an actively creative process; virtual-reality games are reactive. There is room for both kinds of science fiction entertainment, especially among intelligent consumers who delight in the intellectual stimulation of speculative fiction. While films, games, and other technologies astound their viewers with increasingly complex special effects, science fiction readers will still enjoy the printed versions of space adventures. They will also enjoy the increasing use of science fiction for satiric social commentary that ridicules ethnocentric thinking and competitive consumerism. When fictional alien characters from other civilizations react with the logic of the truly naive to some of the self-destructive habits of humans on Earth, intelligent readers can laugh or grimace in agreement. The increasing complexity and intensity of more-serious science fiction demand an equally sophisticated intellectual response, and this challenge is gratifying to readers, both faithful fans of science fiction and the growing number of new readers.

Critic and scholar James Gunn summarizes a current definition of today's science fiction by contrasting it with mainstream fiction's focus on characters' reactions to the repeated patterns of life: "Science fiction . . . exists in a world of change and the focus is on external events."[3] While this may be an accurate differentiation, it is interesting to note recent trends of sf that focus on the effects of future technology on individual lives. New directions for extrapolation seem to be pointing inward.

For many writers, the new frontiers are mental. "Mindspeech," telepathy, empathy, travel through time and space, even using mental powers to colonize other minds—these are increasingly common themes in the more recent works of Pamela Service, Piers Anthony, Octavia Butler, and Pat Cadigan. The question of how individuals communicate and relate to each other is a central focus, an increasingly relevant issue as Earth's inhabitants outside of fiction interact more frequently and personally.

As individuals become more aware of each other's motivations and ideas, questions about coping with new people and foreign cultures arise. Traditionally, in our competitive Western culture, the strongest force won the right to make choices for and about the territory and the people in its power. Newer science fiction illustrates a trend toward cooperation as a mode of sharing scarce resources. Douglas Hill's space adventures end with individuals from disparate ethnic backgrounds overcoming their former prejudices and creating new communities. Works by H. M. Hoover and Orson Scott Card tout the necessity for tolerating differences to preserve traditional family values. Now, the message of most speculative media for the young is that war and competitive destruction are too dangerous for humans. Individualism must give way to communities that work together to survive. What motivates individuals to form a community? Many science fiction works paint futures so desolate that individuals are driven to cooperate in order to survive, adapting to conditions that resemble the past before the evolution of sophisticated technology. Others posit communities held together by the power of technology to impose control over the knowledge of a whole society.

A powerful example is Lois Lowry's *The Giver* (1993). This kind of story frustrates and fascinates readers both young and old who are willing to grapple with the profound questions the author poses so dramatically. The novel takes place in a perfectly controlled community, the kind of place designed by thinkers who have heeded the warnings against overpopulation with its concomitant hunger, crime, and unemployment. Lowry's world is orderly, calm, and secure, offering comfort to every citizen, insuring a career path carefully selected to fit each individual, a world so logical as to exclude color, caring, and passion—the messiness that distinguishes humans from robots. It is a reasonable world made possible by technology and logic, a rational plan intended to provide the greatest good for the greatest number. It is one of those successful socialist utopias, a world given much lip service by many liberal Democrats who tend to be teachers, librarians, and readers of young adult literature.

Twelve-year-old Jonas is approaching the age when the life-work chosen for him is revealed to him. When he discovers he will be the next Receiver of Memory, he is apprenticed to the Giver, who transmits to him the color, the emotions, the pain, the joy, love, and death—the story of his people, who can remain sane and comfortable because he will bear their suffering. In the process of receiving the truth about his cultural history, Jonas learns the cost of comfort. Overpopulation is controlled by killing newborns who do not conform to standards of physical or mental health. Crime is controlled by expelling people who threaten social order, or by destroying any impulses that disturb the calm. People and events are perfectly controlled for the good of the average. When

Jason rebels, he is forced to submit wholly to the law of this society, or to leave. The open-ended finale hands to the reader the responsibility for deciding the appropriate ending. Lowry's book is emblematic of the best science fiction now being written. Simple answers are no longer acceptable. Wooden characters and boring, predictable plots will not entertain; nowadays there is too much competition for readers' attention to tolerate unskillful writing and sloppy thinking. Recent science fiction writers like Greg Bear, Pat Cadigan, Octavia Butler, Orson Scott Card, and Samuel Delany write complex, thought-provoking, difficult fiction. Others like Douglas Hill, H. M. Hoover, Pamela Sargent, Piers Anthony, William Gibson, and Bruce Sterling dramatically illustrate the problems of current cultural habits. All share a pessimistic fear about the impact of our decisions about science and technology on human society on Earth. But they also share a hope that humans will survive by working together.

This is an old vision. David Langford, in his "Twelve Favorite SF Clichés," encapsulates a traditional sf ending: "And I shall call you Eve! says the last man to the last woman after the holocaust, in a favourite version of the 'shaggy God story.' " God either is revived or is actually an alien or some other surprising twist in the traditional format. At any rate, the human story turns out to be recursive.

More-recent endings tend to be variations on the threat of radical differences, keying on a survivalist theme: "Invaders from Space! . . . an invading fleet battles its way through the planetary defences and despite enormous losses touches down at last on the target area—whereupon great fiery letters appear in the sky, saying GAME OVER—PLEASE INSERT COIN."[4] Both scenarios offer a hopeful solution to our worst fears, the ultimate end of humanity.

In her introduction to *The Norton Book of Science Fiction* (1992), coeditor Ursula K. Le Guin summarizes the categories of literature as delineated by one of sf's most respected scholars, Samuel R. Delany: "Reporting and history . . . deal with what happened; realistic fiction, with what could have happened; fantastic fiction, with what could not have happened. And science fiction deals with what has not happened."[5] At least, not yet. For Delany, science fiction is predictive or extrapolative, describing what might happen. The cautionary tale "deals with what hasn't happened—yet. And the tale of parallel or alternate worlds deals with what might have happened, but didn't" (Delany, 27) In a sense, the imaginative, projective, enhanced worlds of science fiction offer a fuller vision of reality than realistic literature, yet a reality whose seductive or terrifying exaggerations remind the reader that it is *not yet* reality, still only the art of the possible.

For the young person, full of energy, enthusiasm, and ideas, science fiction continues to offer hopeful wisdom about the reality we are just learning. The field of science fiction is a most appropriate arena for any reader as wise and as hopeful as 12-year-olds in their intimations of innocence and their first bloom of knowledge about the world and the people in it, and about its endless speculative possibilities for re-vision.

Notes and References

1. Introduction and History

1. Chris Baldick, *The Concise Oxford Dictionary of Literary Terms* (New York: Oxford University Press, 1990), 200.

2. William Rotsler, ed., *Science Fictionisms* (Salt Lake City: Gibbs Smith, 1995), 111; hereafter cited in text.

3. Maxim Jakubowski, *The SF Book of Lists* (New York: Berkley, 1983), 257; hereafter cited in text.

4. Harry Shaw, *Dictionary of Literary Terms* (New York: McGraw-Hill, 1972), 335.

5. Dick Allen, *Science Fiction: The Future* (New York: Harcourt Brace Jovanovich, 1983); hereafter cited in text.

6. James Gunn, "On the Road to Science Fiction: From Heinlein to Here," in *Science Fiction: The Future.*

7. John Clute and Peter Nicholls, eds., *The Encyclopedia of Science Fiction* (New York: St. Martin's, 1995), 124; hereafter cited in text.

8. E. F. Bleiler, ed., *Science Fiction Writers: Critical Studies of the Major Authors from the Early Nineteenth Century to the Present Day* (New York: Scribner's, 1982), 5.

9. Baird Searles et al., *Reader's Guide to Science Fiction* (New York: Avon, 1979), 266.

2. The Classical Masters

1. John Clute, *Science Fiction: The Illustrated Encyclopedia* (New York: Dorling Kindersley, 1995), 134; hereafter cited in text.

3. A New Master: Orson Scott Card

1. Richard E. Geis, review of *Ender's Game* and *Speaker for the Dead,* by Orson Scott Card, *Science Fiction Review* 15.1 (February 1986): 14–15.

2. Michael R. Collings, "Adventure and Allegory," *Fantasy Review* 9.4 (April 1986): 20.

3. Elaine Radford, "Ender and Hitler: Sympathy for the Superman," *Fantasy Review* 10.5 (June 1987): 11; hereafter cited in text.

4. Orson Scott Card, "Response," *Fantasy Review* 10.5 (June 1987): 13–14, 49–52.

5. Wendy Morris, review of *Children of the Mind,* by Orson Scott Card, *Roanoke Times,* January 12, 1997.

6. Both stories published by Hatrack River Publications.

4. Science Fiction Adventure: Douglas Hill

1. "Douglas Hill," in *Contemporary Authors New Review,* vol. 4, ed. Ann Evory (Detroit: Gale Research, 1989), 300; hereafter cited in text.

2. Janice Antczak, *Science Fiction: The Mythos of a New Romance* (New York: Neal-Schuman, 1985).

5. Other Visions, Other Worlds: H. M. Hoover

1. H. M. Hoover, "SF—Out of This World," *Language Arts* 57.4 (April 1980): 426; hereafter cited in text.

6. Feminism and Science Fiction: Pamela Sargent

1. Pamela Sargent, ed., *Women of Wonder: Science Fiction Stories by Women about Women* (New York: Vintage, 1975), xiv; hereafter cited in text.

2. Ursula K. Le Guin and Brian Attebery, ed., *The Norton Book of Science Fiction: North American Science Fiction, 1960–1990* (New York: Norton, 1993), 17; hereafter cited in text.

3. Jeffrey M. Elliot, *The Work of Pamela Sargent: An Annotated Bibliography and Guide* (San Bernardino, Calif.: Borgo, 1990), 5; hereafter cited in text.

4. Jill Engel, "Letters from Upstate New York: A Correspondence with Pam Sargent." Netscape, November 1990. (http://www.owt.com/users/gcox/sargent/intrview.htm); hereafter cited in text.

5. Sarah Lefanu, *In the Chinks of the World Machine: Feminism and Science Fiction* (Bloomington: Indiana University Press, 1988), 19.

6. Pamela Sargent, "A Case for Fantasy," *The ALAN Review* 19. 3 (Spring 1992): 20; hereafter cited in text.

7. Beyond Gender and Racism: Octavia Butler

1. Stephen Potts, " 'We Keep Playing the Same Record': A Conversation with Octavia E. Butler," *Science-Fiction Studies* 3 (November 1996): 333; hereafter cited in text.

2. Joanna Russ, review of *Kindred,* by Octavia Butler, *Magazine of Fantasy and Science Fiction* 58.2 (February 1980): 96.

8. Science Fantasy: Pamela Service and Piers Anthony

1. Pamela F. Service, "On Writing Sci Fi and Fantasy for Kids," *The ALAN Review* 19.3 (Spring 1992): 17–18; hereafter cited in text.

2. "Pamela Service," in *Contemporary Authors New Review,* vol. 47 (Detroit: Gale Research, 1996), 391.

3. Piers Anthony, *Bio of an Ogre* (New York: Ace, 1988); hereafter cited in text.

9. Humor in Science Fiction: Douglas Adams

1. Neil Gaiman, *Don't Panic: The Official Hitchhiker's Guide to the Galaxy Companion* (New York: Pocket, 1988), 23; hereafter cited in text.

10. Cyberpunk

1. Bruce Bethke, "Cyborg," in *Amazing Stories* (1983).

2. Brace, Marianne, "Cyberpunk," *The Guardian* (London), March 16, 1994, 42.

3. Norbert Wiener, *Cybernetics* (New York: Dutton, 1947).

4. Gerald Jones, "Science Fiction," in *New York Times Book Review,* March 10, 1996, 19.

5. Norman Spinrad, "The Neuromantics," in *Science Fiction in the Real World* (Carbondale: Southern Illinois University Press, 1990).

6. Thomas A. Bredehoft, "The Gibson Continuum: Cyberspace and Gibson's Mervyn Kihn Stories," *Science-Fiction Studies* 22.66 (July 1995): 252.

7. Lauraine Leblanc, "Razor Girls: Genre and Gender in Cyberpunk Fiction," *Women and Language* 20.1 (Spring 1997): 71.

8. See alt.cyberpunk FAQ list; gopher: Cyberpunk (Anachron Library); search Cyberpunk and Feminist on other sites.

9. Christine Kenyon Jones, "SF and Romantic Biofictions: Aldiss, Gibson, Sterling, Powers," *Science-Fiction Studies* 24.1 (March 1997): 47.

11. Science Fiction on Film: Star Trek

1. Brian Stableford, "The Third Generation of Genre SF," *Science-Fiction Studies* 3 (November 1996): 321–30.

2. Nicholas Meyer, "Star Trek: The Director's Chair," *Omni* 14:3 (December 1991): 49.

3. Yvonne Fern, *Gene Roddenberry: The Last Conversation* (Berkeley: University of California Press, 1994), 33.

4.   William Shatner, with Chris Kreski, *Star Trek Memories* (New York: HarperCollins, 1993), 56.

5.   Patty Campbell, personal correspondence, December 13, 1997.

12. New Themes and Trends

1.   David G. Hartwell, *Age of Wonders: Exploring the World of Science Fiction* (New York: TOR, 1996), 91.

2.   Alvin Toffler, *Future Shock* (New York: Random House, 1970).

3.   James Gunn, "The Worldview of Science Fiction," in *Extrapolation* 36.2 (Summer 1995): 91.

4.   David Langford, "Twelve Favorite SF Clichés," in Jakubowski, *The SF Book of Lists* (New York: Berkley, 1983), 75.

5.   Samuel R. Delany, "About 5750 Words," in *The Jewel-Hinged Jaw: Notes on the Language of Science Fiction* (New York: Berkley, 1977), cited in Ursula Le Guin and Brian Attebery, *The Norton Book of Science-Fiction,* (New York: Norton, 1993), 27.

Selected Bibliography and Filmography

1. Introduction and History

Primary Sources

NOVELS

Shelley, Mary Wollstonecraft. *Frankenstein*. London, 1818; New York: Scholastic, 1997.

Verne, Jules. *Journey to the Centre of the Earth*. Paris, 1863; (in English) London, 1870; New York: HarperCollins, 1996.

———. *Twenty Thousand Leagues Under the Sea*. Paris, 1872; (in English) London, 1873; New York: Viking, 1995.

Wells, H. G. *The Time Machine*. London, 1895; New York: Scholastic, 1997.

———. *The Island of Doctor Moreau*. London, 1896.

———. *The Invisible Man*. London, 1897, New York, Playmore, 1995.

———. *The War of the Worlds*. London, 1898, Boston, Charles Tuttle, 1993.

SF PERIODICALS

Aboriginal Science Fiction. Woburn, Mass.: Second Renaissance Foundation. Ed. Charles Ryan.

Amazing Stories. [1926–]. New York: TSR Hoblies. Ed. Kim Mohan.

Analog Science Fiction/Science Fact. New York: Dell. Ed. Stanley Schmidt.

Asimov's Science Fiction. New York: Dell. Ed. Gardner Dozois.

The Magazine of Fantasy and Science Fiction. West Cornwall, Conn.: Mercury Press. Ed. Edward Ferman.

Locus: The Newspaper of the Science Fiction Field. Oakland, Calif.: Locus Publications. Ed. Charles N. Brown.

New York Review of Science Fiction. Pleasantville, N.Y.: Dragon Press. Publ. David Hartwell.

Science Fiction Age. Herndon, Va.: Sovereign Media Co. Ed. Scott Edelman.
Science Fiction Chronicle: The Monthly SF and Fantasy Newsmagazine.
Brooklyn, N.Y.. Ed. Andrew Porter.
VOYA (Voice of Youth Advocates). Lanham, Md.: Scarecrow Press. Ed.
Cathi Dunn MacRae.

INTERNET RESOURCES

Genreflecting: mancon.com/genre
Internet Speculative Fiction Data Base: cu:online.com/~avonruff/
sfdbase.html
Science Fiction Resource Guide file: sflovers.rutgers.edu/pub/sf-lovers/
Web/sfresource.guide.html
Tardy SF Reviews: cs.latrobe.edu.au/~agapow/Postviews/titleindex.html
Web's Rev of SF and Fan: cyberus.ca/~ddrt/
Yahoo—Arts: literature: Science Fiction: Authors: yahoo.com/Arts/
Literature/ GeneralScience_Fiction_Fantasy_Horror/Authors/

Secondary Sources

Allen, Dick. *Science Fiction: The Future.* New York: Harcourt Brace
Jovanovich, 1983.
Antczak, Janice. *Science Fiction: The Mythos of a New Romance.* New
York: Neal-Schuman, 1985.
Baldick, Chris. *The Concise Oxford Dictionary of Literary Terms.* New
York: Oxford University Press, 1990.
Barron, Neil, ed. *Anatomy of Wonder: A Critical Guide to Science Fiction.*
4th ed. New Providence, N.J.: R. R. Bowker, 1995.
Blieler, E. F., ed. *Science Fiction Writers: Critical Studies of the Major
Authors from the Early Nineteenth Century to the Present Day.* New
York: Scribner's, 1982.
Clute, John, and Peter Nicholls, eds. *The Encyclopedia of Science Fiction.*
New York: St. Martin's, 1995.
Clute, John. *Science Fiction: The Illustrated Encyclopedia.* New York:
Dorling Kindersley, 1995.
Delany, Samuel R. *The Jewel-Hinged Jaw: Notes on the Language of Science Fiction.* New York: Berkley, 1977.
del Rey, Lester. *The World of Science Fiction, 1926–1976.* New York: Ballantine, 1980.
Gunn, James. "On the Road to Science Fiction: From Heinlein to Here."
In *Science Fiction: The Future.* Ed. Dick Allen. New York: Harcourt
Brace Jovanovich, 1983.
Hartwell, David G. *Age of Wonders: Exploring the World of Science Fiction.* New York: TOR, 1996.
Herald, Diana Tixier. *Teen Genreflecting.* Englewood, Colo.: Libraries
Unlimited, 1997.

Jakubowski, Maxim. *The SF Book of Lists*. New York: Berkley, 1983.

Jonas, Gerald. "Science Fiction." *New York Times Book Review,* March 10, 1996, 19.

Le Guin, Ursula K., and Brian Attebery, eds. *The Norton Book of Science Fiction: North American Science Fiction, 1960–1990*. New York: Norton, 1993.

Pringle, David. *The Ultimate Guide to Science Fiction*. New York: Pharos, 1990.

Rogow, Roberta. *Futurespeak: A Fan's Guide to the Language of Science Fiction*. St. Paul, Minn.: Paragon House, 1991.

Rosenberg, Betty, and Diana Tixier Herald. *Genreflecting: A Guide to Reading Interests in Genre Fiction*. 3d ed. Englewood, Colo.: Libraries Unlimited, 1991.

Rotsler, William, ed. *Science Fictionisms*. Salt Lake City: Gibbs Smith, 1995.

Searles, Baird, Martin Last, Beth Meacham, and Michael Franklin. *Reader's Guide to Science Fiction*. New York: Avon, 1979.

Shaw, Harry. *Dictionary of Literary Terms*. New York: McGraw-Hill, 1972.

Stableford, Brian. "The Third Generation of Genre Science Fiction." *Science-Fiction Studies* 3 (November 1996): 321–30.

Suvin, Darko. *Metamorphoses of Science Fiction*. New Haven, Conn.: Yale University Press, 1979.

3. A New Master: Orson Scott Card

Primary Sources

"ENDER" SERIES
Ender's Game. New York: Tor, 1985.
Speaker for the Dead. New York: Tor, 1986.
Xenocide. New York: Tor, 1991.
Children of the Mind. New York: Tor, 1996.

"ALVIN MAKER" SERIES
Seventh Son. New York: Tor, 1987.
Red Prophet. New York: Tor, 1988.
Prentice Alvin. New York: Tor 1989.
Alvin Journeyman. New York: Tor, 1995.
The Crystal City. (in press: available on the Web at http://www.hatrack.com)

"WORTHING SAGA"
The Worthing Chronicles. New York: Tor, 1989.

"HOMECOMING" SERIES
The Memory of Earth. New York: Tor, 1992.

The Call of Earth. New York: Tor, 1992.
The Ships of Earth. New York: Tor, 1994.
Earthfall. New York: Tor, 1995.
Earthborn. New York: Tor, 1995.

"MAYFLOWER" SERIES
Lovelock, with Kathryn H. Kidd. New York: Tor, 1991.
Pastwatch: The Redemption of Christopher Columbus. New York: Tor, 1998.

INDIVIDUAL SF NOVELS
Capitol. New York: Baronet/Ace, 1978; revised as *The Worthing Saga.*
Hot Sleep. New York: Baronet/Ace, 1978; replaced by *Worthing Chronicle.*
Songmaster. New York: Dial/Dell, 1979/1980; New York: Tor, 1987.
A Planet Called Treason. New York: St. Martin's, 1979.
Wyrms. New York: Tor, 1987.
Treason. New York: St. Martin's, 1988.
The Abyss, with Jim Cameron. New York: Pocket, 1989.

OTHER NOVELS
Hart's Hope. New York: Berkley, 1983; New York: Tor, 1988.
Woman of Destiny. New York: Berkley, 1984; revised as *Saints.* New York: Tor, 1988.
Lost Boys. New York: HarperCollins, 1992.
Treasure Box. New York: HarperCollins, 1996.

SHORT FICTION
"Unaccompanied Sonata" and Other Stories. New York: Dial, 1980.
Maps in a Mirror: The Short Fiction of Orson Scott Card. 4 vols. New York: Tor, 1990.

Secondary Sources

Collings, Michael R. *The Work of Orson Scott Card: An Annotated Bibliography and Guide.* Bibliographies of Modern Authors Series, no. 19. San Bernardino, Calif.: Borgo, 1996.
———. *In the Image of God: Theme, Characterization and Landscape in the Fiction of Orson Scott Card.* Westport, Conn.: Greenwood, 1990.
———. "Adventure and Allegory." *Fantasy Review* 9.4 (April 1986): 20.
Easton, Tom. Review of *Speaker for the Dead,* by Orson Scott Card. *Analog Science Fiction/Science Fact* 106.6 (June 1986): 183–84.
Geis, Richard E. Review of *Ender's Game* and *Speaker for the Dead,* by Orson Scott Card. *Science Fiction Review* 15.1 (February 1986): 14–15.
"Orson Scott Card." *Contemporary Authors New Review.* Vol. 47. Detroit: Gale Research, 1995.
"Orson Scott Card." *Contemporary Literary Critics.* Vol. 50. Detroit: Gale Research, 1987.

Radford, Elaine. "Ender and Hitler: Sympathy for the Superman." *Fantasy Review* 10.5 (June 1987): 11–12, 48–49. See also Orson Scott Card, "Response," *Fantasy Review* 10.5 (June 1987): 13–14, 49–52.

4. Science Fiction Adventure: Douglas Hill

Primary Sources

"LEGIONARY" SERIES
Galactic Warlord. New York: Atheneum, 1980.
Deathwing Over Veynaa. New York: Atheneum, 1981.
Day of the Starwind. New York: Atheneum, 1981.
Planet of the Warlord. New York: Atheneum, 1982.
Young Legionary: The Earlier Adventures of Keill Randor. New York: Atheneum, 1983.

"HUNTSMAN" SERIES
The Huntsman. New York: Atheneum, 1982.
Warriors of the Wasteland. New York: Atheneum, 1983.
Alien Citadel. New York: Atheneum, 1984.

"COLSEC" SERIES
Exiles of ColSec. New York: Atheneum, 1984.
The Caves of Klydor. New York: Atheneum, 1985.
ColSec Rebellion. New York: Atheneum, 1985.

SCIENCE FANTASY
Blade of the Poisoner. New York: Atheneum, 1987.
Master of Fiends. New York: Atheneum, 1987.

EDITOR
Alien Worlds. London: Heinemann, 1981.
Planetfall. New York: Oxford University Press, 1986.

Secondary Sources

Antczak, Janice. *Science Fiction: The Mythos of a New Romance.* New York: Neal-Schuman, 1985.
"Douglas Hill." *Contemporary Authors New Review.* Vol. 4. Detroit: Gale Research, 1989.

5. Other Visions, Other Worlds: H. M. Hoover

Primary Sources

NOVELS
Another Heaven, Another Earth. New York: Viking, 1981.

Away Is a Strange Place to Be. New York: Dutton, 1990.
The Bell Tree. New York: Viking, 1982.
Children of Morrow. New York: Four Winds, 1973.
The Delikon. New York: Viking, 1977.
The Lost Star. New York: Viking, 1979.
Only Child. New York: Dutton, 1992.
Orvis. New York: Viking Press, 1987.
The Rains of Eridan. New York: Viking Press, 1977.
Return to Earth. New York: Viking Press, 1980.
The Shepherd Moon. New York: Viking Press, 1984.
This Time of Darkness. New York: Viking Press, 1980.
Treasures of Morrow. New York: Four Winds, 1976.
The Winds of Mars. New York: Dutton, 1995.

SHORT FICTION

"The Mushroom." *The Big Book for Our Planet.* New York: Dutton, 1993.

AUTOBIOGRAPHY

Autobiography Series: Something about the Author. Vol. 8. Chicago: Gale Research, 1989.

"Details, Details." *The Horn Book* (September/October 1988): 590–92.

"H. M. Hoover." *Speaking for Ourselves.* Ed. Don Gallo. Urbana, Ill.: NCTE Press, 1990.

Secondary Sources

Antczak, Janice. *Science Fiction: The Mythos of a New Romance.* New York: Neal-Schuman Publishers, 1985.

———. "The Visions of H. M. Hoover." *Children's Literature Association Quarterly* (Summer 1985), 163–65.

Barron, Neil, ed. *Anatomy of Wonder: A Critical Guide to Science Fiction.* New York: Bowker, 1987.

"H. M. Hoover." *Contemporary Authors New Review.* Vol. 22. Detroit: Gale Research, 1993.

Greenlaw, M. Jean. "Science Fiction: Images of the Future, Shadows of the Past." *Top of the News,* Fall 1982, 465–66.

Harrison, Barbara G., and Gregory Maguire. *Innocence and Experience: Essays and Conversations on Children's Literature.* New York: Lothrop, Lee & Shephard, 1987.

Hoover, H. M. "SF—Out of This World." *Language Arts* 57:4 (April 1980): 425–28.

"H. M. Hoover." *Something about the Author.* Vol. 44. Chicago: Gale Research, 1986, 1994.

20th Century Children's Writers. London: St. James, 1989–1995.

6. Feminism and Science Fiction: Pamela Sargent

Primary Sources

NOVELS
Beneath the Red Star. San Bernardino, Calif.: Borgo, 1996.
The Best of Pamela Sargent. New York: Bantam, 1987.
Cloned Lives. Greenwich, Conn.: Fawcett, 1976.
A Fury Scorned. New York: Pocket Books, 1996.
The Golden Space. New York: Timescape Books, 1982.
The Mountain Cage. London: Cheap Street, 1983. (chapbook)
Ruler of the Sky. New York: Crown, 1993. (feminist historical fiction)
The Shore of Women. New York: Crown, 1986.
Starshadows and Blue Roses. New York: Ace, 1977.
The Sudden Star. New York: Fawcett, 1979.
Watchstar Trilogy. Clarkston, Ga.: White Wolf, 1996.

"ALIEN" SERIES
The Alien Upstairs. Garden City, N.Y.: Doubleday, 1983.
Alien Child. New York: Harper, 1988.

"EARTHMINDS" SERIES
Watchstar. New York: Pocket, 1980.
Earthseed: A Novel. New York: Harper, 1983.
Eye of the Comet. New York: Harper, 1984.
Homesmind. New York: Harper, 1985.

"VENUS" SERIES
Venus of Dreams. New York: Bantam, 1986.
Venus of Shadows. Garden City, N.Y.: Doubleday, 1988.
Child of Venus. Garden City, N.Y.: Doubleday, 1994?.

SHORT FICTION
"Aunt Elvira's Zoo." *"Night of the Sphinx" and Other Stories.* Ed. Roger
    Elwood. New York: Lerner, 1974.
The Best of Pamela Sargent. With a foreword by Michael Bishop. Ed.
    Martin H. Greenberg. Chicago: Academy Chicago, 1987.
"A Friend from the Stars." *"The Missing World" and Other Stories.* Ed.
    Roger Elwood. New York: Lerner, 1974.
"The Invisible Girl." *"The Killer Plants" and Other Stories.* Ed. Roger
    Elwood. New York: Lerner, 1974.
Starshadows: Ten Stories. New York: Vintage Books, 1977.
Ten Tomorrows. Ed. Roger Elwood. New York: Fawcett, 1973.
Two Views of Wonder. Ed. Thomas N. Scortia and Chelsea Quinn Yarbro.
    New York: Ballantine, 1973.
Wandering Stars. Ed. Jack Dann. New York: Harper, 1972.

EDITOR

Bio-Futures: Science Fiction Stories about Biological Metamorphosis.
New York: Vintage, 1976.

*More Women of Wonder: Science Fiction Novellettes by Women about
Women.* New York: Vintage, 1976.

*The New Women of Wonder: Recent Science Fiction Stories by Women
about Women.* New York: Vintage, 1978.

Afterlives: Stories about Life after Death. With Ian Watson. New York:
Vintage, 1986.

Women of Wonder: Science Fiction Stories by Women about Women. New
York: Vintage, 1975.

Secondary Sources

Elliot, Jeffrey M. *The Work of Pamela Sargent: An Annotated Bibliography and Guide.* San Bernardino, Calif.: Borgo, 1990.

Engel, Jill. "Letters from Upstate New York: A Correspondence with
Pam Sargent." Netscape, 1990.

Lefanu, Sarah. *In the Chinks of the World Machine: Feminism and Science Fiction.* Bloomington: Indiana University Press, 1988.

Rubens, Philip. "Pamela Sargent." In *Dictionary of Literary Biography.*
Vol. 8. Detroit: Gale Research, 1997.

7. Beyond Gender and Racism: Octavia Butler

Primary Sources

NOVELS

Clay's Ark. New York: St. Martin's, 1984.

Kindred. New York: Doubleday, 1979. 2d ed. New York: Beacon Press,
1998.

Parable of the Sower. New York: Four Walls Eight Windows, 1994.

Wild Seed. New York: Doubleday, 1980.

"PATTERNMASTER" SERIES

Patternmaster. New York: Doubleday, 1976.

Mind of My Mind. New York: Doubleday, 1977.

Survivor. New York: Doubleday, 1978.

"XENOGENESIS" SERIES

Dawn: Xenogenesis. New York: Warner Books, 1987.

Adulthood Rites. New York: Warner Books, 1988.

Imago. New York: Warner Books, 1989.

SHORT FICTION

"Bloodchild" and Other Stories. New York: Four Walls Eight Windows,
1995.

Secondary Sources

Potts, Stephen. " 'We Keep Playing the Same Record': A Conversation with Octavia E. Butler." *Science-Fiction Studies* 3 (November 1996): 331–38.
Russ, Joanna. Review of *Kindred,* by Octavia Butler. *Magazine of Fantasy and Science Fiction* 58.2 (February 1980): 96–97.

8. Science Fantasy: Pamela Service

Primary Sources

NOVELS
Winter of Magic's Return. New York: Fawcett, 1985.
The Reluctant God. New York: Fawcett, 1988.
Vision Quest. New York: Fawcett, 1989.
Under Alien Stars. New York: Fawcett, 1990.
Being of Two Minds. New York: Fawcett, 1991.
All's Faire. New York: Fawcett, 1993.
Stinker from Space. New York: Fawcett, 1993.

Secondary Sources

Service, Pamela F. "On Writing Sci Fi and Fantasy for Kids." *The ALAN Review* 19.3 (Spring 1992): 17–18.

8. Science Fantasy: Piers Anthony

Primary Sources

NOVELS
But What of Earth? With Robert Coulson. Toronto: Laser, 1976.
Chthon. New York: Ballantine, 1967. Reprinted, New York: Berkley, 1982.
The ESP Worm. New York: Tor, 1992.
Fractal Mode. New York: Ace, 1992.
Ghost. New York: Tor, 1986.
Isle of Woman. New York: Tor, 1994.
Macroscope. New York: Avon, 1969.
Mute. New York: Avon, 1981.
Phthor (sequel to *Chthon*). New York: Berkley, 1975.
The Pretender. With Frances Hall. San Bernardino, Calif.: Borgo, 1979.
Prostho Plus. London: Gollancz, 1971; New York: Bantam, 1973.
Rings of Ice. New York: Avon, 1974.
Steppe. New York: Tor Books, 1985.
Virtual Mode. New York: Ace, 1991.

"APPRENTICE ADEPT" SERIES (SCIENCE FICTION/FANTASY)
Split Infinity. New York: Ballantine, 1980.

Blue Adept. New York: Ballantine, 1981.
Juxtaposition. New York: Ballantine, 1982.
Out of Phaze. New York: Ace Books, 1987.
Robot Adept. New York: Ace Books, 1988.
Unicorn Point. New York: Ace Books, 1989.
Phase Doubt. New York: Ace Books, 1990.

"BATTLE CIRCLE" SERIES
Battle Circle (omnibus volume). New York: Avon, 1978.

"BIO OF A SPACE TYRANT" SERIES
Refugee. New York: Avon, 1983.
Mercenary. New York: Avon, 1984
Politician. New York: Avon, 1985.
Executive. New York: Avon, 1985.
Statesman. New York: Avon, 1986.

"CLUSTER" SERIES (SCIENCE FANTASY)
Cluster. New York: Avon, 1977.
Chaining the Lady. New York: Avon, 1978.
Kirlian Quest. New York: Avon, 1978.
Thousandstar. New York: Avon, 1980.
Viscous Circle. New York: Avon, 1982.

"OMNIVORE" SERIES
Omnivore. New York: Ballantine, 1968.
Orn. New York: Avon, 1971.
Ox. New York: Avon, 1976.

SHORT FICTION: CONTRIBUTOR
Cheetham, Anthony, ed. *Science against Man.* New York: Avon, 1970.
Harrison, Harry, ed. *Nova One: An Anthology of Original Science Fiction.* Delacorte, 1970.
Ellison, Harlan, ed. *Again, Dangerous Visions.* Garden City, N.Y.: Doubleday, 1972.
Gerrold, David, ed. *Generation.* Dell, 1972.
Schochet, Victoria, and John Silbersack, eds. *The Berkley Showcase.* New York: Berkley, 1981.

AUTOBIOGRAPHY
Bio of an Ogre. New York: Ace Books, 1988.

9. Humor in Science Fiction: Douglas Adams

Primary Sources

RADIO SERIES
Hitchhiker's Guide to the Galaxy. British Broadcasting Company (beginning 1978).

Hitchhiker's Guide to the Galaxy. National Public Radio (beginning 1981).

NOVELS

The Hitchhiker's Guide to the Galaxy. New York: Ballantine, 1979.
The Restaurant at the End of the Universe. New York: Ballantine, 1980.
Hitchhiker's Guide to the Galaxy. New York: Pocket, 1981.
The Meaning of Liff. New York: Crown, 1982.
The Deeper Meaning of Liff. New York: Crown, 1993.
Life, the Universe, and Everything. New York: Ballantine, 1982.
So Long, and Thanks for All the Fish. New York: Pocket, 1984.
Dirk Gently's Holistic Detective Agency. New York: Pocket, 1987.
The Long Dark Tea-Time of the Soul. New York: Pocket, 1988.
Mostly Harmless. New York: Ballantine, 1992.
Starship Titanic: The Official Strategy Guide. New York: Crown, 1997.

Secondary Sources

Adams, Douglas. *Douglas Adams.* New York: Ballantine, 1995.
Gaiman, Neil. *Don't Panic: The Official Hitchhiker's Guide to the Galaxy Companion.* New York: Pocket, 1988.

10. Cyberpunk

Primary Sources

NOVELS

Cadigan, Pat. *Mindplayers.* New York: Bantam, 1987.
———. *Synners.* San Francisco: Wired Books, 1991.
———. *Fools.* New York: Bantam, 1992.
Gibson, William Ford. *Neuromancer.* New York: Ace, 1984.
———. *Count Zero.* New York: Arbor House, 1986.
———. *Mona Lisa Overdrive.* New York: Bantam, 1988.
———. *Idoru.* New York: Putnam, 1996.
Sterling, Bruce. *The Artificial Kid.* New York: HarperCollins, 1980.
———. *Schmistrix Plus.* New York: Arbor House, 1985.
———. *Holy Fire.* New York: HarperCollins, 1996.

SHORT FICTION

Bethke, Bruce. "Cyborg," in *Amazing Stories.* 1983.
Gibson, W. F., John Shirley, Bruce Sterling, and Michael Swanwick. *Burning Chrome.* New York: Arbor House, 1986.
Sterling, Bruce, ed. *Mirrorshades: The Cyberpunk Anthology.* New York: Arbor House, 1986.

Secondary Sources

Bredehoft, Thomas A. "The Gibson Continuum: Cyberspace and Gibson's Mervyn Kihn Stories." *Science-Fiction Studies* 22.66 (July 1995): 252.

Clute, John, and Peter Nicholls, eds. *The Encyclopedia of Science Fiction.* New York: St. Martin's, 1993.

Jones, Christine Kenyon. "SF and Romantic Biofictions: Aldiss, Gibson, Sterling, Powers." *Science-Fiction Studies* 24.1 (March 1997): 47.

Jones, Gerald. "Science Fiction." *New York Times Book Review,* March 10, 1996, 19.

Leblanc, Lauraine. "Razor Girls: Genre and Gender in Cyberpunk Fiction." *Women and Language* 20.1 (Spring 1997): 71.

Spinrad, Norman. "The Neuromantics." (1986). Reprinted in *Science Fiction in the Real World.* Carbondale: Southern Illinois University Press, 1990.

11. Science Fiction on Film: *Star Trek*

Filmography

1902 *Le Voyage dans la Lune.* Star of France Studio. Produced and directed by Georges Méliès, who played the inventor. 21 min. Tinted. First medium-length film.

1910 First film version of Mary Shelley's *Frankenstein.* Made by J. Searl Dawley of the Edison Company.

1916 Debut of underwater photography in Stuart Paton's adaptations of two Jules Verne novels, *Vingt mille lieues sous les mers* (1870) and *L'ile mysterieuse* (1875). Universal Studios.

1926 *Metropolis.* Paramount Studio. Written and directed by Fritz Lang, with his wife and collaborator, Thea von Harbou, who appeared in the film. Starring Brigitte Helm and Alfred Abel. 182 min. Tinted version came out in 1927. U.K. release print, also by Paramount, in 1927. Reconstructed and adapted by Giorgio Moroder in black and white.

1931 *Frankenstein.* Universal. Directed by James Whale. Starring Boris Karloff, Colin Clive, Mae Clarke, Edward van Sloan, and Dwight Frye. Screenplay by Garrett Fort, Robert Florey, and Francis Edward Faragoh. Based on an adaptation by Florey and John L. Balderston of the play by Peggy Webling; based in turn on *Frankenstein, or The Modern Prometheus* (1818) by Mary Shelley. 71 min. B/w.

1932 *Dr. Jekyll and Mr. Hyde.* Paramount. Produced and directed by Rouben Mamoulian. Starring Frederic March, Miriam Hopkins, and Rose Hobart. Screenplay by Samuel Hoffenstein and Percy Heath. Based on *The Strange Case of Dr. Jekyll and Mr. Hyde* (1886) by Robert Louis Stevenson. 98 min. cut to 81 min. B/w.

1933 *King Kong.* RKO. Directed by Merian C. Cooper and Ernest B. Schoedsack. Starring Fay Wray, Robert Armstrong, and Bruce Cabot. Screenplay by James A. Creelman and Ruth Rose. From a story by Cooper (codirector), with credit also to Edgar Wallace. Special effects designed and supervised by Willis H. O'Brien. 100 min. B/w.

1933   *The Invisible Man.* Universal. Directed by James Whale. Starring Claude Rains, Gloria Stuart, Henry Travers, William Harrigan, and Una O'Connor. Screenplay by R. C. Sherriff and Philip Wylie. Based on *The Invisible Man* (1897) by H. G. Wells. 71 min. cut to 56 min. B/w.

1935   *The Bride of Frankenstein.* Universal. Directed by James Whale. Starring Boris Karloff, Colin Clive, Elsa Lancaster, and Ernest Thesiger. Screenplay by John Balderston and William Hurlbut. 80 min. B/w.

1936   *Lost Horizon.* Columbia. Directed by Frank Capra. Starring Ronald Coleman, Jane Wyatt, Sam Jaffe, Edward Everett Horton, and H. B. Warner. Screenplay by Robert Riskin. Based on *Lost Horizon* (1933) by James Hilton. 133 min. cut to 109 min. B/w.

1936–1940   *Flash Gordon.* Thirteen 2-reel episodes in 1936, 1938, and 1940. Universal. Directed by Frederick Stephani. Starring Buster Crabbe, Jean Rogers, Charles Middleton, Frank Shannon, and Priscilla Lawson. Screenplay by Frederick Stephani, George Plympton, Basil Dickey, and Ella O'Neill. Based on the comic strip. B/w.

1939   *Buck Rogers.* Serial film. Universal. Directed by Ford Beebe and Saul A. Goodkind. Starring Larry (Buster) Crabbe, Constance Moore, C. Montague Shaw, Jack Moran, and Anthony Ward. Screenplay by Norman S. Hall and Ray Trampe. Based on the comic strip. B/w.

1954   *20,000 Leagues Under the Sea.* Walt Disney. Directed by Richard Fleische. Starring James Mason, Kirk Douglas, Paul Lukas, and Peter Lorre. Screenplay by Earl Felton. Based on Jules Verne's *Vingt mille lieues sous les mers* (1870; translated in the U.K. as *Twenty Thousand Leagues under the Sea* in 1872). 127 min. Color.

1954   *Gojira,* translated as *Godzilla, King of the Monsters.* Japan; expanded with new footage in the 1956 U.S. version. Toho/Embassy. Directed by Inoshiro Honda. Starring Takashi Shimura, Akira Takarada, and Akihiko Hirata (and Raymond Burr in the U.S. version). Screenplay by Takeo Murata and Honda. Based on a story by Shigeru Kayama. 98 min. cut to 81 min. for U.S. release. B/w.

1956   *Invasion of the Body Snatchers.* Allied Artists. Produced by Walter Wanger. Directed by Don Siegel. Starring Kevin McCarthy, Dana Wynter, Carolyn Jones, and King Donovan. Screenplay by Daniel Mainwaring and Sam Peckinpah (uncredited). Based on *The Body Snatchers* (1955) by Jack Finney. 80 min. B/w.

1959   *Journey to the Center of the Earth.* 20th Century-Fox. Produced by Charles Brackett. Directed by Harry Levin. Starring Pat Boone,

James Mason, Arlene Dahl, Thayer David, Peter Ronson, and Diane Baker. Screenplay by Walter Reisch and Leigh Brackett. Based on *Voyage au centre de la terre* (1864) by Jules Verne. 132 min. Color.

1963   *The Nutty Professor*. Paramount. Produced and directed by Jerry Lewis. Starring Lewis, Stella Stevens, Dell Moore, Kathleen Freeman, and Howard Morris. Screenplay by Jerry Lewis and Bill Richmond. 107 min. Color. Remake of the Jekyll and Hyde theme; one of Lewis's best films.

1966   *Fahrenheit 451*. Anglo-Enterprise and Vineyard/Universal. Directed by François Truffaut. Starring Julie Christie, Oscar Werner, Cyril Cusack, and Anton Diffring. Screenplay by François Truffaut and Jean-Louis Richard. Based on *Fahrenheit 451* (1953) by Ray Bradbury. 112 min. Color.

1968   *Barbarella*. De Laurentiis-Marianne/Paramount. Directed by Roger Vadim. Starring Jane Fonda, John Phillip Law, Milo O'Shea, David Hemmings, and Anita Pallenberg. Screenplay by Tery Southern, Jean-Claude Forest, Roger Vadim, Vittorio Bonicelli, Brian Degas, Claude Brule, Tudor Gates, and Clement Biddle Wood. Based on the comic strip by Claude Forest. 98 min. Color.

1968   *Charly*. Selmur and Robertson Associates. Directed by Ralph Nelson. Starring Cliff Robertson, Claire Bloom, Lilia Skala, and Dick van Patten. Screenplay by Stirling Silliphant. Based on *Flowers for Algernon* (1959, expanded in 1966) by Daniel Keye. 105 min. Color.

1968   *Night of the Living Dead*. Image 10 Productions/Walter Reade-Continental. Directed by George A. Romero. Starring Duane Jones, Judith O'Dea, Karl Hardman, and Keith Wayne. Screenplay by John Russo. 96 min. cut to 90 min. B/w.

1968   *Planet of the Apes*. Apjac/20th Century-Fox. Directed by Franklin J. Schaffner. Starring Charlton Heston, Roddy McDowall, Kim Hunter, Maurice Evans, and James Whitmore. Screenplay by Michael Wilson and Rod Serling. Based on *La Planete des singes* (translated in the U.S. as *Planet of the Apes*) (1963) by Pierre Boulle. 112 min. Color.

1968   *2001: A Space Odyssey*. Produced and directed by Stanley Kubrick. Starring Keir Dullea and Gary Lockwood. Screenplay by Stanley Kubrick and Arthur C. Clarke. Based loosely on "The Sentinel" (1951) by Arthur C. Clarke. 160 min. cut to 141 min. Color. Originally in Cinerama.

1977   *Star Wars*. 20th Century-Fox. Directed by George Lucas. Starring Mark Hamill, Harrison Ford, Carrie Fisher, Alec Guinness, and Peter Cushing. Screenplay by George Lucas. 121 min. Color.

1977   *Close Encounters of the Third Kind.* Columbia. Directed by
       Steven Spielberg. Starring Richard Dreyfuss, François Truffaut,
       Teri Garr, Melinda Dillon, Gary Cuffey, and Bob Balaban.
       Screenplay by Steven Spielberg. 135 min. Color.
1978   *Superman.* Dovemead/International Film Production. Directed by
       Richard Donne. Starring Christopher Reeve, Margot Kidder,
       Gene Hackman, Valerie Perrine, Ned Beatty, Jackie Cooper, and
       Marlon Brando. Screenplay by Mario Puzo, David Newman,
       Leslie Newman, Robert Benton, with Tom Mankiewicz as creative
       consultant. Based on a story by Mario Puzo. 143 min. Color.
1979   *Star Trek: The Motion Picture.* Paramount. Produced by Gene
       Roddenberry. Directed by Robert Wise. Starring the lead players
       from the *Star Trek* TV series, along with Periss Khambatta and
       Stephen Collins. Screenplay by Harold Livingstone. From a story
       by Alan Dean Foster. 132 min. Color.
1979   *Alien.* Brandywine/20th Century-Fox. Produced by Gordon Car-
       roll, David Giler, and Walter Hill. Directed by Ridley Scott. Star-
       ring Sigourney Weaver, John Hurt, Tom Skerritt, Veronica
       Cartwright, Harry Dean Stanton, Ian Holm, and Yaphet Kotto.
       Screenplay by Dan O'Brannon. Based on a story by Dan O'Bran-
       non and Ronald Shusett. 116 min. Color.
1980   *The Empire Strikes Back.* Lucasfilm/20th Century-Fox. Executive
       producer George Lucas. Directed by Irvin Kershner. Starring
       Mark Hamill, Harrison Ford, Carrie Fisher, Billy Dee Williams,
       and Frank Oz. Screenplay by Leigh Brackett and Lawrence Kas-
       dan. Based on a story by George Lucas. 124 min. Color.
1982   *E.T.: The Extraterrestrial.* Universal. Directed and coproduced by
       Steven Spielberg. Starring Dee Wallace, Henry Thomas, Peter
       Coyote, Roberta McNaughton, and Drew Barrymore. Screenplay
       by Melissa Mathison. 115 min. Color.
1982   *Blade Runner.* Blade Runner Partnership-Ladd Co.-Sir Run Run
       Shaw/Warner. Directed by Ridley Scott. Starring Harrison Ford,
       Rutger Hauer, Sean Young, Daryl Hannah, and William Sander-
       son. Screenplay by Hampton Fancher and David Peoples. Based
       on *Do Androids Dream of Electric Sheep?* (1968) by Philip K.
       Dick. 117 min. Color.
1983   *Return of the Jedi.* Lucasfilm/20th Century-Fox. Executive pro-
       ducer George Lucas. Directed by Richard Marquand. Starring
       Mark Hamill, Harrison Ford, Carrie Fisher, Ian McDiarmid, and
       David Prowse. Screenplay Lawrence Kasdan and George Lucas.
       Based on a story by George Lucas. 132 min. Color.
1988   *Bill and Ted's Excellent Adventure.* Interscope Communication/
       Soisson-Murphey/De Laurentiis. Directed by Stephen Herek. Star

ring Keanu Reeves, Alex Winter, and George Carlin. Screenplay by Chris Matheson and Ed Solomon. 89 min. Color.

1989   *Honey, I Shrunk the Kids.* Walt Disney. Directed by Joe Johnston. Starring Rick Moranis, Mat Frewer, Thomas Brown, Amy O'Neill, and Robert Oliveri. Screenplay by Ed Naha and Tom Schulman. From a story by Stuart Gordon, Brian Yuzna, and Ed Naha. 93 min. Color.

1990   *Akira* (an animated film). Akira Comittee. Directed by Katsuhiro Otomo. From a screenplay by Katsuhiro Otomo and Izo Hashimoto. Based on the graphic epic *Akira* (begun 1982) by Katsuhiro Otomo. Animation studio: Asahi. Chief animator: Takashi Nakamura. 124 min. Color.

1996   *Independence Day.* Centropolis/20th Century-Fox. Directed by Roland Emmerich and Dean Devlin. Starring Will Smith, Harry Connick Jr., Bill Pullman, Jeff Goldblum, Mary McConnell, Judd Hirsch, Margaret Colin, Robert Loggia, Harvey Fierstein, Brent Spiner, and Vivica Fox. Screenplay by Emmerich and Devlin. 119 min. Color.

Secondary Sources

Asherman, Allan. *The Star Trek Compendium.* New York: Pocket Books, 1989.

Fern, Yvonne. *Gene Roddenberry: The Last Conversation.* Berkeley: University of California Press, 1994.

Meyer, Nicholas. "Star Trek: The Director's Chair." *Omni* 14.3 (December 1991): 48–51.

Shatner, William, with Chris Kreski. *Star Trek Memories.* New York: HarperCollins, 1993.

12. New Themes and Trends

Gunn, James. "The Worldview of Science Fiction." *Extrapolation* 36.2 (Summer 1995): 91.

Hartwell, David G. *Age of Wonders: Exploring the World of Science Fiction.* New York: Tor, 1996.

Minyard, Applewhite, ed. *Decades of Science Fiction.* Lincolnwood, Ill.: NTC, 1998.

Toffler, Alvin. *Future Shock.* New York: Random House, 1970.

Index

The Author

Suzanne Elizabeth Reid is an assistant professor at Emory and Henry College where she teaches courses in Education, English, Literature for Children and Young Adults, and directs an annual Summer Intensive English Language Institute. She has published articles about teaching and young adult literature in journals including *The ALAN Review*, *Virginia English Bulletin,* and *Signal.* She is also the author of two other books in Twayne's United States Authors Series, *Presenting Cynthia Voigt* and *Presenting Ursula K. Le Guin.* When she is not teaching, reading, and writing, she likes to bike with her husband, garden, and visit with friends, including her two grown children, Jenny and Tristan.

The Editor

Patricia J. Campbell is an author and critic specializing in books for young adults. She has taught adolescent literature at UCLA and is the former Assistant Coordinator of Young Adult Services for the Los Angeles Public Library. Her literary criticism has been published in the *New York Times Book Review* and many other journals. From 1978 to 1988 her column "The YA Perplex," a monthly review of young adult books, appeared in the Wilson Library Bulletin.

She now writes a column on controversial issues in adolescent literature for *Horn Book* magazine, "The Sand in the Oyster." Recently she has been traveling the country to lead her "YA Biblioramas," intensive workshops on young adult fiction for teachers and librarians.

Campbell is the author of five books, among them *Presenting Robert Cormier,* the first volume in the Twayne Young Adult Author Series. In 1989 she was the recipient of the American Library Association Grolier Award for distinguished achievement with young people and books. A native of Los Angeles, Campbell now lives on an avocado ranch near San Diego, where she and her husband, David Shore, write and publish books on overseas motorhome travel.